GENEALOGICAL ABSTRACTS

OF

PRINCESS ANNE COUNTY, VA. COURT RECORDS

FROM **DEED BOOKS 6 & 7**
AND **MINUTE BOOKS 6 & 7**

1740–1762

BY

ALICE GRANBERY WALTER

CLEARFIELD

Reprinted for
Clearfield Company, Inc., by
Genealogical Publishing Co., Inc.
Baltimore, Maryland
1996, 2006

International Standard Book Number: 0-8063-4626-4

Made in the United States of America

FOREWORD

"On the motion of Thurmer Hoggard its ordered that the Clerk deliver to him his wifes part of her fathers estate sold at outcry and lodged in the office". This one item was the principal reason for abstracting these records.

After a thirty-five year search for the maiden name of Thurmer's wife it seemed plausible to think that a complete abstraction of all the genealogical data, the deaths and outcrys for several years would certainly contain the name of her father. This book no doubt does give his name, however it is going to take a thorough compilation of a lot of material to try and prove which man it is.

The above, perhaps, will clarify my reasons for doing this manuscript in the first place. I originally intended it to be my last resort for an answer before giving up the search as a hopeless task. There was no intention to publish as I had only planned one copy for my own personal use.

However, some "nuggets of pure gold" in genealogical tidbits have turned up in unexpected items making this work too valuable to keep to myself. It is offered simply to benefit others who have failed to find some of their answers.

All genealogical facts, the wills, marriages, deaths and much of the information in the deeds about land holdings and showing neighbors are included, Estates sold at outcry and deaths have been fully noted for the years 1748-1750. Audits, Appraisements and Inventories have been given briefly, and any genealogical information contained therein is given. The totals are given where legible to indicate the size of the estate. The Deeds consist of a lease and release following a day or so later and sometimes cover as many as four or more pages of the original records. Some bounds are given, however, the abstracts always state whether or not the original record contains the bounds. The Minutes contain many items which only state "referred to the next Court". Unless noteworthy they are not given.

Brevity became a necessary evil in abstracting the records of over two thousand six hundred pages. The page numbers in the original record books are given to facilitate documentation and also in obtaining copies of the original records. It is possible to request copies from the Virginia State Library in Richmond, Virginia and the Book and Page Numbers should be given.

It should be noted that the Eastern Shore referred to in many of these records does not always mean the same place. In earlier records Eastern Shore always meant the Eastern side of the Lynnhaven River. In this book the Eastern Shore of Lynhaven Parish can and sometimes does refer to the Back Bay section as does the Upper Precinct of Lynhaven Parish. There was also an Eastern Shore of Linkhorn Bay. Do not jump to any conclusions without first examining the records.

My old reliable typewriter expired during work on this. It had given fifteen years of faithful service, With this new one I really look forward to cleaner, clearer manuscripts in the future.

TABLE OF CONTENTS

Foreword

++
ABBREVIATIONS

wd = will dated   Nco = Norfolk County

wp = will proved or probated   PAc = Princess Anne County

DB = Deed Book   Adm: = Administrator

MB = Minute Book   Exor:= Executor

VM = Vestryman   Exix:= Executrix

th:= thence   Appr:= Appraiser or Appraisal

nw or Nun-w. = nun-cupative will   Wit: = Witness

(x) or an initial (A) = the mark made by a person instead of a signature

12 Apr 1739 - Recd: from JOHN NICHOLAS who intermarried with YATES
6 DB 1 PAc   admistratrix of JOHN BOLITHO decd. full paymt of all
                that was due on account of the personal estate of JOHN
BOLITHO decd., my uncle.........THO: BOLITHO
Wit: JAMES KEMPE & WILLIAM NIMMO   (No date of recordation given.)

 7 Apr 1730 - Recd: of my brother JOHN MOSELEY full satisfaction
6 DB 1 PAc   signed: EDW: MOSELEY
               Wit: CHAS: SAYER & ANTHO: MOSELEY
The above Discharge recorded at the request of MAJ: ffRA: MOSELEY
10 Feb 1741/2.

8 Mar 1713/14- MARK POWELL of PAc to MAXIMILLIAN BOUSH.....a mulatto
6 DB 1 PAc   slave girl called Rose....This is not recorded.

21 Jan 1744/5- Rec'd. of MR. SAMUEL TENANT full satisfaction of all
                debts &c.........of MARY ANNE THOROWGOOD's Estate, the
wife of JOHN THOROWGOOD.   signed: JOHN THOROWGOOD

(NOTE: All of the above is on the left hand page before page one of
this book. All of the dates are out of order and the above are not
in error. This must have been the only blank paper available when
these items were recorded. AGW)
                Page 1 which is so numbered follows:

12 Dec 1740 - Rec. 12 Feb 1740/1 - ROGER (X) WILLIAMSON of PAc.,
6 DB 1 PAc   Eldest son & heir of RICHARD WILLIAMSON decd., to
                COL: ANTHONY WALKE. GENT:.. ..RICHARD in his last will
dated 1 Sep 1721 gave unto his son JOHN WMSON: land which said RICHARD
bought of CAPT: WILLIAM CRAFORD joining to the land whereon said JOHN
then lived...60 acres.......land only good to said JOHN for life 9 because of a mistake in writing the will) JOHN by lease & release dated
1 & 2 Jun 1732 sold to said COL: ANTHONY WALKE.....Nly in an Antient
line that parted said land from WALKS land thence Ely bounding on the
MAIN ROAD that leads to NORTH RIVER th Sly with JAMES KEMPS Land & along
KEMPS Land to the ASHEN SWAMP, along Swamp bounding Wly on the land
called PORTENS RIDGE to the first station ....

4 Feb 1740/1 - Inventory of the Estate of JOHN JAMES decd.
6 DB 4 PAc   Total ₤ 67.2.10

8 Mar 1740/1 - Inventory of RICHARD POOLE decd. THOMAS HAYNES adm. of
6 DB 5 PAc   said Estate. Cash in his house at time of his death
                was ₤ 10.6.10   Sum total ₤ 249.9.4
(A long list of Princess Anne County names is given)

7 Jan 1740/1 - Audit of the estate of MR. JOHN WISHARD administered by
6 DB 6 PAc   WILLIAM ROBINSON, GENT: administrator of MR. WISHARD decd.
                A long list of Princess Anne County names.
Amt: of the sales of personal estate ₤ 124.7.3 - Total ₤ 188.11.9½
Recorded 5 Mar 17 1740/1.

1

2 Mar 1740/1 -   Rec. 4 Mar 1740/1 - JAMES KEMPE GENT:, Sheriff of PAc.
6 DB 7 PAc   of the one part & JOHN HOLT of the same place of the
                  other part........MR. WILLIS WILSON JUNR: lately in our
County hath recovered a debt of 88 1 tob agst: HENRY CAPPS for debt.....
(This is about land and is very hard to read)

4 Mar 1740/1 - WILLIAM ROBINSON of PAc
6 DB 9 PAc   wd ?   wp 4 Mar 1740/41
                Trustees: ALEX: CAMPBELL, MR. EDWARD HACK MOSELEY, JOHN
NICHOLAS & WM: NIMMO.
unto son - TULLY ROBINSON the Manner Plantation houses with improvements
whereon I nowe live with all lands adjoining.....in the case of lack of
male heirs said land & Plantation to son WILLIAM ROBINSON & if he is
without male heirs to daughters of son TULLY if he leave any..........
to TULLY....200 acres of Marsh at or near the TABLE OF PINES in PAc &
called LITTLE ISLAND.....unto sons TULLY & WILLIAM 200 acres called
PORTERS RIDGE.... ..to son WILLIAM the Plantation on the EASTERN SHORE
which I bought of JOHN HANCOCK . ..200 acres.... ..WILLIAM underage....
to WILLIAM my lott of land in Norfolk BOROUGH , 370 acres at LONG ISLAND
bought of HENRY MOORE.....Ł 400 money. Residue to sons TULLY & WILLIAM.
If sons die reversion to sisters SARAH SMITH, MARY ROBINSON & ANNE HANCOCK.
(NOTE: This will is full of conditions.

11 Oct 1740 - Codicile to WILLIAM ROBINSON's will pvd. 4 Mar 1740/1
6 DB 11 PAc   .... have purchased of REODOLPHUS MALBONE & JOB GASKING
                250 acres in PAco joyning on LONDON BRIDGE RIVER........
unto son WILLIAM ROBINSON........

4 Mar 1740/1 - Rec. 5 Mar 1740/1 - RICHARD GARDNER & ELIZABETH his wife
6 DB 12 PAc   to WILLIAM CONSAUL of the same place....50 acres in the
                EASTERN SHORE SWAMP...... Signature is: RICHARD GARNER

5 Mar 1740/1 - RICHARD GARNER & ELIZABETH his wife release to WILLIAM
6 DB 12 PAc   CONSAUL of the above land. Recorded the same day.

1 Jan 1740/1 - Rec. 5 Mar 1741/2 - 1738 is in the margin.
6 DB 14 PAc   Audit of the Estate of RICHARD POOLE decd. Total Ł 307.0.11½

1 Apr 1741   - CHARLES MALBONE of PAc.
6 DB 15 PAc   wd 6 Dec 1740 wp 1 Apr 1741
                Exor: wife MARGARET MALBONE
sons: JAMES MALBONE my plantation ....he is underage..... ...
     WILL: MALBONE underage, CHARLES MALBONE.
Residue to wife MARGARET for her natural life........................

1 Apr 1741   - JOHN SHIPP of PAc.
6 DB 15 PAc   wd ?   wp 1 Apr 1741 Exor: wife & son WILLIAM
                son WILL^m: SHIPP the Plantation that he lives on.
son FRANCIS SHIPP.......Daus KATHERINE EDWARDS & MARY ALLEN?
wife ANNE SHIPP the residue of estate..... (this will is faded)

1 Apr **1741**   - FRANCIS THOROWGOOD
6 DB 16 PAc   wd 13 Feb **1740/1** wp 1 Apr **1741**
               wife AMY...... "hers and mine children"
Eldest son JOHN THOROWGOOD.... ... other children not named.

1 Apr **1741**   - CASON BUSKEY & MARY his wife, said MARY was only dau-
  6 DB **17** PAc   ghter of JOHN CANNON & ELIZABETH his wife who was one of
the two sisters & co-heirs of EDWARD LAND JUNR: decd. to COL: ANTHONY
WALKE 1/2 of all that tract of land in the WESTERN SHORE whereon EDWARD
LAND grandfather of said MARY formerly lived containing 670 acres......
Dated .... 1 Mar **1740/1.**

1 Apr **1741**   - JOHN WOODHOUSE decd. Audit of his Estate
6 DB 18 PAc   Total ₤ 61.8.8   Dated 10 Mar **1740/1**

1 Apr **1741**   - BENJAMIN DAUGE of the County of CURRITUCK, NORTH CAROLINA
6 DB 19 PAc   selling to JOHN FENTRIS in County of Princess Anne a
               parcel of land in Princess Anne County....130 acres
being the same land that JAMES DAUGE gave in his last will to his son
RICH^d: DAUGE........ beginning on the CYPRESS SWAMP.........bounding
on CORNELIUS HENLYS...... ..& JAMES LAMOUNT.......& JOHN DAUGES line....
. ..... WILLM: DAUGE............ on 6 DB 21 is the release............
The above land 130 acres JAMES DAUGE gave in his last will to his son
RICH^d: DAUGE and by lease & release........BENJA: DAUGE to save & keep
harmless the said JOHN FENTRIS ....
(NOTE: the Lease is dated 20 Mar 1700, however the release is dated
21 Mar 1740. It looks like the clerk forgot to include the forty in the
lease.)

29 Sep 1740 Rec 1 Apr **1741** - GEORGE MOSELEY to CAPT: THO: QUAY of Norfolk
6 DB 22 PAc   County....a Plantation of 50 acres of land in Princess
               Anne County.........which MR: TULLY EMPEROR purchased of
JOHN EDMUNDS JUNR: in the year 1697 & by said JOHN EDMUNDS decd. to the
said TULLY EMPEROR..

30 Mar 1740/1 Rec 1 Apr **1741** - JAMES (‡) ALBRITTON & ELIZA: his wife
6 DB 24 PAc   to WILLM: WEBLIN......130 acres in Princess Anne County
               known by the name of KENDALS ISLAND (or HENDALS?) which
said JAMES bought of ROBT: DEARMAN by lease & release dated the 4 & 5
October 1736......................

1 Apr **1741** Rec the same day - CHARLES SMYTH of PAc to RICHARD DUDLEY,
6 DB 26 PAc   Planter........190 acres on the WESTERN SHORE of PAc.
               on a Creek called BENNETS CREEK purchased by the said
CHARLES SMYTH as follows: 140 acres of this land purchased of BANNISTER
LISTER? & MARG: his wife by deeds dated 5 & 6 Mar 1733 & 50 acres purchased
of JOHN HARPER by deeds dated 28 & 29 Jul 1739.

1 Apr **1741**   - An Inventory of the Estate of JAMES LAMOUNT decd. 1740
6 DB 28 PAc.   Signed by THOMAS LAMOUNT & MARY (X) JONES.

5 May 1741 - FRANCIS SPRATT of PAc, Planter - Rec. 7 May 1741
6 DB 28 PAc   to JAMES MOORE.... 650 acres whereon FRANCIS SPRATT
               now lives ....

5 May 1741 - Rec 6 May 1741 - WILL^m: NIMMO. Atty at Law to FRANCIS
6 DB 32 PAc   SPRATT, Planter......250 acres whereon said FRANCIS
               SPRATT now lives.

20 Oct 1741 - Rec 7 May 1741 - ANTHO: WALKE JUNR son & heir of COLL:
6 DB 35 PAc   THO^s: WALKE decd. to THO^s: WALKE JUNR, GENT............
               300 acres in Parish of Lynhaven & is bounded as set forth
in a Deed by ARTHUR MOSELEY of Norfolk County unto said COLL: THO^s:
WALKE father to both of the parties to these presents dated 16 Mar 1691/2.

5 May 1741 - Rec 6 May 1741 - JAMES WISHART to THO^s: WISHART 260 acres
6 DB 37 PAc   in Princess Anne County at a place called LITTLE CREEK
               whereon the said THO^s: now lives & also 80 acres near the
HEAD of the EASTERN BRANCH of ELIZABETH RIVER and is the remainder of 180
acres given by JAMES KEMP unto THO^s: WISHART & MARY his wife, father and
mother of the said JAMES by Deed of Gift 7 Sep 1698...the other 100 acres
thereof being sold by said JAMES WISHART unto ARTHUR BAXTER............

30 Jun 1741 - Whereas CAPT: JAMES WISHART of ACCOMAC COUNTY by his ind-
6 DB 39 PAc   enture of Bargain and Sale dated 5 May 1741 has conveyed
               unto me. THO^s: WISHART of Princess Anne County the fee
simple estate .... 340 acres........ & whereas it appears that HANNAH wife
of said JAMES WISHART is sickly & impotent....... she was privily examined
in ACCOMAC COUNTY & relinquished her dower...........................

7 Nov 1740 - Rec 6 May 1741 - WILLIAM MOSELEY to JAMES LANGLEY.........
6 DB 40 PAc   One lott or 1/2 acre in NEWTOWN adjoyning upon a lot of
               MR. M^cKEMLER .... beginning on the Westermost Street
running WNW 20 poles to COL: MOSELEYS CREEK............................

xx May 1741 - EDITH the wife of WILL^m: MOSELEY relinquished her right of
6 DB 42 PAc   dower to a previous deed................................

28 Apr 1741 - Rec 7 May 1741 - RICH^d: DUDLEY... for the love and affection
6 DB 42 PAc   I bear unto my sons RICH^d: DUDLEY & JOHN DUDLEY & towards
their future support &c......... 190 acres in WESTERN SHORE of LINHAVEN on
BENNETS CREEK & lately purchased by me of CHARLES SMITH .... to
son RICH^d: 140 acres which was purchased by said CHARLES SMITH of BANNIS-
TER LESTER & MARY his wife by Deeds of 5 & 6 Mar 1733/4.........unto son
JOHN DUDLEY 50 acres of the aforesaid tract which was purchased by CHARLES
of JOHN HARPER by deeds 28 & 29 Jul 1739.

15 Apr 1740 - Rec 6 May 1741 - KATHERINE LILBURN of PAc Spinster & daugh-
6 DB 44 PAc   ter of WILL^m: LILBURN decd have oblxxxx an order of Court
               dated 1 Oct 1735 aget JNO: CONNYER who marryed with the
widdow of the Decedent to pay to me the said ORPHAN......my proper part
of my said fathers estate according to Audit 1 Sep 1736.................

9 May 1741 - JOHN SHIPP's Inventory.... (it is a short one)
6 DB 45 PAc

6 May 1741 - JOHN SMYTH
6 DB 45 PAc   wd 10 Jan 1740/1 wp 6 May 1741 by THO: LANGLEY &
               Exor: wife MARY &   MARTHA (M) BOND
                  SIMON WHITEHURST & son JAM$: SMYTH
son JAMES SMYTH .... my plantation 127 acres & 50 acres at CREDY? NECK
son WILL^m: .... the other half of my land at Lynhaven with reversion to
son JOHN.................... "all my children"......................
wife MARY reversion during natural life.

20 Feb 1740/1 - Rec 6 May 1741 - THO: BRINSON's Decd. Inventory
6 DB 46 PAc   Total ℔ 18.11.09

1 Apr 1741 - 6 May 1741 - JOHN LOVETT JUNR. decd...... Audit of his
6 DB 46 PAc   Estate. To ISABEL LOVETT a proportionable part of her
               father's estate ℔ 21.3.9¼ . To WILL^m: LOVETT D^o ℔21.3.9¼
To WILL^m: LOVETT's legacy ℔ 6.00.00.. To LANCASTER LOVETT for funeral
Expenses ℔ 2.17.2. (William Lovett's total came to ℔ 27.3.9¼.) There are
many more Princess Anne County names. The TOTAL was ℔ 158.19.6

10 Sep 1738 - No date given for Return - Audit of THOMAS NICHOLSON Decd
6 DB 47 PAc   Amount of Appraisal ℔ 67.10.2
              Balance due to Orphans (not named) ℔ 15.17.6
The Audit was taken at the house of MRS. NICHOLSON wife of THOMAS.

2 Jun 1741 - Rec 3 Jun 1741 - HENRY DAULEY & MARY his wife to JOHN CAPPS
6 DB 47 PAc   100 acres on the South side of the said JN^o: CAPPS his land
              whereon he now lives.... at a gum in the said CAPPS line &
along a line of marked trees to JOHN CANNONS line & down said CANNONS line
.... in the UPPER PRECINCT of the EASTERN SHORE.

(NOTE:: The UPPER PRECINCT of the EASTERN SHORE usually means the BACK BAY
area and not the EASTERN SHORE of LYNNHAVEN RIVER. In so many of these
records South is called UP and North is called DOWN, in Norfolk County
as well as Princess Anne County. AGW)

3 Jun 1741 - JACOB LANGLEY of Princess Anne County
6 DB 49 PAc   wd 27 Aug 1740 wp 3 Jun 1741 by MATTHEW ELLEGOOD & JOEL
              Other wit: CHARLES MALBONE   CORNICK
Exor: JEREMIAH LANGLEY
Bro: WILL^m: LANGLEY one shilling
bro: NATHAN LANGLEY ℔ 5.& my best bed & furniture & my great copper kettle.
bro: JAMES LANGLEY my silver tankard & silver hafted sword & silver headed
cane & ℔ 5. Bro: ABRAHAM LANGLEY one shilling....... to MR. GEORGE IVY who
intermarried with my sister ELIBETH LANGLEY one shilling..... to my sister
MARGARET JOHNSON ℔ 5..... to MR. JOHN WISHARDwho intermarried with my sis-.
ter JOYCE one shilling........ to my cousin WILL IVY one gold ring.........
to my cousin JACOB LANGLEY son of my brother WILL^m: my negro man named
George with reversion to the next younger brother............ to my cousin
JOSEPH LANGLEY the choice of my mares at the marshes.... to my loving bro:

JEREMIAH LANGLEY my now dwelling house & plantation..... 250 acres & 50
acres of Swamp land I bought of JNO: CONSOLVO... 2 negroes Robin & Dinah
& their increase & residue of my Estate..... he paying all my debts &c...

15 Oct 1739 - Rec 9 Jun 1741 - COCKROFT OULDS, Planter to AMBROSE BUR-
6 DB 50 PAc   FOOT, Planter..... a parcel of woodland in Princess Anne
               County.... 50 acres near land called HANNAHS..... and a
line that parts JAMES HARRISON & said OULDS........ to a CYPRESS SWAMP

30 Jun 1741 - Rec 1 Jul 1741 - ERASMUS HAYNES & DINAH his wife of 1st part
6 DB51 PAc   ANTHO: LEGGETT son & heir of AMY LEGGETT decd wife of
               ALEXANDER LEGETT of the 2od part to COLL: ANTHONY WALKE
of the 3rd part....... 68 acres beginning at a pine in the line of LAN-
CASTER LOVETTS .... down to BROCKS SWAMP that divides this land and
that land JOHN WOODHOUSES to JOHN LOVETT to EDWᵈ: ATWOODS line along
ATWOODS line to a mkd oak thence along the line that divides this land
and that land JOHN WOODHOUSE sold to WILLᵐ: ATWOOD to the first station
being part of a tract which LEWIS PEROINE? sold to JNO: FULCHER 1 Mar 1698
(The name PEROINE may be PURVINE)

10 May 1741 - Rec 1 Jul 1741 - GRIFFIN FLOYD of North Carolina to THOˢ:
6 DB 54 PAc   MORGAN of Princess Anne County.... 100 acres in the UPER
               PRECINCT of the EASTERN SHORE.... running along JOHN
DAULYS line ...... a Northerly course to a gum ...... thence NE on JOHN
SMYTHS line thence (-can't read may be latitude) GRACE SHERWOODS line....

3 Jun 1741 - Rec 3 Jul 1741 - JACOB LANGLEYS Inventory
6 DB 56 PAc   Total ⌁ 130.12.10

11 Mar 1740 - Rec 5 Aug 1741 - JOHN (+) McNEIL & ELIZABETH his wife,
6 DB 57 PAc   said ELIZABETH is one of the two daughters & co-heirs of
               JOHN SALMON late of Princess Anne County who was grandson
& heir at law of JOHN SALMON the ELDER formerly of the County of LOwer
Norfolk........ to .... RICH: CORBETT ..... Whereas JOHN SALMON the
ELDER by his will dated 22 Mar 1678/9 duly recorded in Lower Norfolk....
gave unto his son JOHN, grandfather of said ELIZABETH 1/2 of the land
being the Eastward side whereon he lived and also gave unto his son
WILLᵐ: the other half & appointed that neither of his said sons should
have power to sell their land..... but it should fall to the next heir.
..... 250 acres in Parish of Lynhaven .... ELIZABETH privily examined.

3 Aug 1741 - Rec 5 Aug 1741 - THOˢ: LOVE & SARAH his wife, which SARAH
6 DB 58 PAc   is one of the two daughters & coheirs of JNO: SALMON &c..
... (see previous deed) selling the other part of land...... 250 acres
to RICH: CORBETT........ SARAH is privily examined................. ..

30 Jul 1741 - Rec 5 Aug 1741 - JNO: ASHBY & AMY his wife to MORRICE HILL
6 DB 61 PAc   70 acres on the North side of MUDDY CREEK in Princess Anne
               County being part of a Dividend whereon JOHN ASHBY liveth
.... on JOHN HILLS line .... BONNEYS RUN .... to JNO:
RAYNEYS line ...... along said RAINEYS line.............................

4 Jun 1741 - Rec 5 Aug 1741 - THOROWGOOD SPRATT to JAMES NIMMO ......
6 DB 64 PAc   200 acres at NANNEYS CREEK adjoining upon the Plantation
                the said NIMMO bought of MAJ: SPRATT Decd likeways his
right the said MAJ: SPRATT sold said JAMES for a priviledge & the marsh
adjoining the said land down to MOORES ISLAND as far as the 200 acres of
land reaches.

13 Apr 1741 - Rec 5 Aug 1741 - GEORGE MOSELEY to MR: JEREMIAH LANGLEY
6 DB 66 PAc   of Norfolk County...... 260 acres of land in Princess
                Anne County & is the land whereon said GEORGE MOSELEY
now liveth together with one negro man called Robin.....Bounds are not
given.

5 Aug 1741 - Inventory of JOHN SMYTH decd. A short Inventory.
6 DB 67 PAc

5 Aug 1741 - NATH¹: NEWTONs bond of ⊢ 1000. to the King as having been
6 DB 67 PAc   appointed Sheriff of Princess Anne County.

6 Aug 1741 - Rec 2 Sep 1741 - MESSRS: ALEXANDER CAMPBELL & SPROWELL
6 DB 68 PAc   of the Burrough of Norfolk to ROBT: TODD of Princess
                Anne County.....one acre or 2 lotts of TOWN LAND which
ALEXANDER CAMPBELL & SPROWELL purchased of JNO: FITZ in NEWTOWN in PAc
bounded on East by MR. SAM: SMYTH. on the West by EDWARD DENBY, on the
South by the River & on the North by the Street.

20 Jan 1741 - Rec 2 Sep 1741 - CAPT: WILLIAM COX & ANNE his wife to
6 DB 70 PAc   CAPT: WILLIAM KEELING.... 50 acres bounded on the land of
                EDMUND ABSALOM on the North, on the land of READ: MALBONE
on the West, on the land of CAPT: COX where HORATIO WOODHOUSE lives on
the South and on the ROAD and ADAM KEELINGS land on the East & is the
same land that was given by HENRY HARRISON to his wife FRANCES.........

8 Aug 1741 - Rec 3 Sep 1741 - WILL^m: COX & ANN (x) his wife to ADAM
6 DB 73 PAc   KEELING ...... 100 acres on the EASTERN SHORE (this would
                be the Eastern Shore of Lynhaven River) Bounded on the
land of aforesd ADAM KEELING on North side, on land of LEM¹::CORNICK. on
the South, on land of COLL: MAX¹: BOUSH, on the West & is the same land
whereon HORATIO WOODHOUSE SENR: now lives ....

2 May 1741 - Rec 5 Sep 1741 - FRANCES SPRATT, Planter to JAMES MOORE
6 DB 75 PAc   of the Burrough of Norfolk, Mariner ... negroes: Old
                Mingo, Old Tom Indian, Cowley, Old Mary, Bab & her 2
children, Kate and Phillis, a girl named Rose,young Tom Indian and Dick.

2 Sep 1741 - I, RICHARD CORBETT....... Whereas JOHN SALMON late of
6 DB 77 PAc   Lower Norfolk County by his Deed of Sale dated 6 Oct 1686
                .... sold unto THO: SOLLEY, Cooper 300 acres formerly
patented by WILL^m: EDWARDS bounded in the said deed & whereas by a con-
dition on the back of the deed signed by JNO: SOLLEY it doth appear that
the land aforesd conveyed to the said THO: SOLLEY who conveyed as a security to warrant the title of two parcels of land therein mentioned to be
conveyed by WILL^m: EDWARDS & ELIZA: his wife unto the sd THO^s: SOLLEY is

by a Deed granted for the same by them dated 19 Mar 1693/4 duly recorded
& whereas 1/2 of the Land conveyed as a Security to warrant the Title...
is now in the possession of WILL^m: SALMON of Princess Anne County & conveyed to said THO: by the said WILL^m: EDWARDS & ELIZ: is now in the possession of said RICH^d: CORBETT and whereas THO^s: LOVE and SARAH his wife
 (one of the 2 daughters & coheirs of JNO: SALMON son of JOHN SALMON) by
the deed dated with these presents....... (This release is from RICH^d:
CORBETT to WILL^m: SALMON. (See pp 57 & 58 about this same property -
McNEIL & LOVE to CORBETT.)

24 Jul 1741 -   Rec 2 Sep 1741 - Audit of Estate of JNO: GISBORN Decd.
6 DB 78 PAc   .... the widows third part given her in her husbands
                will which she sold to (PRETTY?) & CHARLES SWENY as per
contra....... EDWARD GISBORN & JOHN GISBORN are both named but no
relationship given........ ELIZA: & JNO: GISBORN Exix: & Exor of JOHN
GISBORN decd. Dated 22 Jun 1741 returned 24 Jul 1741.

31 Aug 1741 -   Rec 2 Sep 1741 - An Additional Audit of the Estate of
6 DB 79 PAc   RICH^d: POOLE decd.... To sundry goods.......signed by
                the Auditors of this Date which belongs to the Estate of
HENRY BUTT Decd the use whereof was given to ANN his wife, lately wife
of RICH^d: POOLE during life and part whereof where? appraised in said
POOLES Estate and the rest sold by said POOLE in his lifetime the use
whereof belongs to CAPT: THO^s: HAYNES and the said ANN in the right of
said ANN his wife Amounting in all to the sum of ₤ 69.5.8.
To balance due to MR: POOLES Estate ₤ 33.3.0 By Bale in a former Audit
dated 1 Jan 1740/1 ₤ 109.0.4. Balance due to THO^s: HAYNES in right of
his wife ANN late widdow of said RICH^d: POOLE to be ₤ 22.2.0

27 Jul 1741 -   Rec 7 Oct 1741 - THO^s: (C) CREED to JAMES COTTON .. 150
6 DB 79 PAc   acres in the NORTH WOODS in Princess Anne County. No
                bounds given.

20 Sep 1741 -   Rec 2 Oct 1741 - BENJ: CUMINGS & ELIZ: (+) his wife of
6 DB 82 PAc   Norfolk County to GILES RANDOLPH of Norfolk County 200
                acres, a Plantation in BLACK WATER in PAc bounded on one
side by JNO: GISBORN and on the other side by the MILL DAM.

28 Mar 1740/1- Rec 7 Oct 1741 - HENRY (H) SOUTHERNE of BLACK WATER
6 DB 84 PAc   PRECINCT, Planter to JOHN CORPREW of the same place ...
                50 acres in BLACKWATER PRECINCT being part of a pattent
of 400 acres granted to HENRY SMITHERS decd in 1686......the bounds are
very sketchy.

5 Aug 1741   - JAMES TENANT, Mariner
6 DB 86 PAc   wd 19 Jul 1741 wp 5 Aug 1741 by EDW: DENBY & CHARLES
                EXORS: SMYTH.
                Friends: JAMES NIMMO & WILL: NIMMO
unto my godson JN^o: THOROWGOOD JUNR: 2 years schooling to be given to
him as soon as he is able to receive it.
unto my grandmother ANN TREVETHAN ₤ 22., unto my cousin MARY ANN
THOROWGOOD soon as she comes to age or is married....... continued

8

unto my brother in law RODERICK CONNER Ŀ 25 at age of 21 years.........
unto my loving brother SAM[1]: TENANT Ŀ 150 at the age of 21 years.......
unto my loving sister ELIZ: TENANT Ŀ 100 at age of 21 or is married....
with reversion to her brother SAM[1]: TENANT. Residue to brother SAM[1]:
TENANT............

3 Sep 1741 - Rec 13 Sep 1741 - Inventory of the Estate of CAPT: JAMES
6 DB 87 PAc   TENANT decd.............a very short one ....
               Total Ŀ 11.14.1

3 Nov 1741 - Rec 4 Nov 1741 - THO[s]: HILL SENR: to THO[s]: Hill JUNR
6 DB 88 PAc   50 acres of land called the HORSE NECK & Bindeth on the
               SAND BANK & FRESH WATER CREEK...(all the bounds given)

11 Nov 1741 - EZRA BROOKE of Lynhaven Parish
6 DB 89 PAc   wd 14 Oct 1741 wp 11 Nov 1741 by WILL: SMYTH & MARTHA
                                                    CONNYER.
               Exors: REV: MR: HENRY BARLOW , MR: PAT BROOKE & ANTHO:
MOSELEY.   My will and desire is that my estate shall be sold.........
residue to my loving wife SARAH BROOKE both in LONDON.................
(His wife is the only person named in this will)

10 Nov 1741 - The Estate of MR: JNO: THOROWGOOD decd.
6 DB 90 PAc   Audit by sale of his estate totaled Ŀ 98. 6.8.

 1 Dec 1741 - Rec 2 Dec 1741 - STEPHEN (S) MUNDEN to THO[s]: HENLY......
6 DB 90 PAc   50 acres on the East side of said THO[s]: HENLYS Land where-
               on he now lives and bindeth...... at a BEAVER DAM at a
mkd tree in the sd HENLYS line............ being the land that was given
by THO[s]: BROCK to his son SAM[1]: BROCK and sold to said STEPHEN MUNDEN by
the son & heir of the said SAM[1]: BROCK decd........................

4 Nov 1741 - Rec 3 Dec 1741 - CAPT: ANTHONY MOSELEY, Mariner to JOHN
6 DB 92 PAc   HARPER....... 200 acres near the REEDY SWAMP...........
               wit: JAMES NIMMO, JAMES THELABALL & JAMES THELABALL

24 Nov 1741 - Rec 3 Dec 1741 - CAPT: ANTHO: MOSELEY, Mariner to JOHN
6 DB 94 PAc   HARPER.... 300 acres binding upon Lynhaven RIVER ....
               and is the same land whereon said JOHN HARPER now liveth
               (no bounds are given)

17 Aug 1741 - 3 Dec 1741 - MOSES (M) FENTRISS SENR: & AARON FENTRISS (A)
6 DB 96 PAc   to GEORGE FENTRISS 15 acres in Princess Anne County on the
               South side of the EASTERN BRANCH commonly called by the
name of WILLIS begin at a pine near the ROAD..... Northly to an oak tree
of JAMES FENTRISS...

28 Nov 1741 - Rec 3 Dec 1741 - JOHN JAMESON, Planter - Deed of Gift to
6 DB 98 PAc   his well beloved son HENRY JAMESON.... unto him all &
               singular my lands whereon I now live... with all my marshes
in the Parish of Lynhaven... known by the name of COWS ENTRY by the RAGGED
ISLAND.... a foal to his sister MARY....Deed to have no effect until after
my decease.

5 Dec 1741   -   THO[s]: NORRIS
6 DB 99 PAc   wd 8 Nov 1741   wp 5 Dec 1741
            Exors: WM: CARTWRIGHT & JAMES CARRAWAY
to son JOHN NORRIS........to dau SARAH NORRIS...........................
to son CHARLES NORRICE ....dau ANN NORRIS....................
son GEORGE NORRIS........... residue to wife ANN NORRIS towards bringing
up my four youngest children.

8 Oct? 1741   -   Rec 6 Jan 1741/2 - ARTICLES OF AGREEMENT: between THOROW-
6 DB 100 PAc   GOOD SPRATT to JAMES MOORE of Norfolk County.............
            100 acres of Pasture Marsh adjoyning the land & now the
property of said THOROWGOOD lying in NANNYS CREEK bounded Nly by aforesd
land & Ely on the line dividing that and CAPT: JAMES NIMMOS land & marsh
& Sly on a Creek dividing the sd 100 acres of Marsh from an ISLAND called
OLD WOMANS ISLAND & Wly on the marsh belonging to sd JAMES MOORE As pur-
chasing from ADAM SPRATT by means a virtue of the DR: wife thereof to
the sd ADAM SPRATT by the will of HENRY SPRATT his father decd & is
herebysaid to belong to sd JAMES MOORE.................................

6 Jan 1741/2 - HENRY JAMES (H)
6 DB 101 PAc   wd no date wp 6 Jan 1741/2 by MATTHEW BRINSON & JOHN
            Exix: wife BRIDGET   DEARMON
son HENRY JAMES the East End of the plantation whereon I now live.
son ROBT: the West End of the said ISLAND to be equally divided between
my two sons with reversion to each other. wife BRIDGET to acknowledge
50 acres of land to my brother MATTHEW JAMES which my brother JOHN JAMES
gave unto me........ wife to have residue during her natural life & if
she has a child within eight months after my decease said child to have
an equal share of my moveable estate.

3 Feb 1741/2 - JAMES THELABALL
6 DB 101 PAc   wd 31 Dec 1741   wp 3 Feb 1741/2 by ELIZA: NICHOLSON & SARAH
                                                         JONES.
Exors: father in law ANTHO: MOSELEY & brother THOS: THELABALL.
Mother ABIGAIL MOSELEY my negro Lewis with reversion to
my brother LEWIS THELABALL
Brother NATH: THELABALL my negro wench Pleasant
Brother THO[s]: THELABALL. .... residue to be divided between my four
brothers THOS: THELABALL, LEM[l]: THELABALL, LEWIS THELABALL & NATHAN[l]: THEL-
ABALL....... My father in law ANTHO: MOSELEY & my brother THOS THELABALL be
my whole and sole exors...

3 Feb 1741/2 - Rec 3 Feb 1741/2 - BRIDGET (X) JAMES exix of HENRY JAMES
6 DB 102 PAc   decd ... selling to ... MATTHEW JAMES 50 acres in the UPPER
            PRECINCT of the EASTERN SHORE.

6 May 1741   - Rec 3 Feb 1741/2 - HENRY JAMES decd - the Inventory of his
6 DB 104 PAc Estate totaled   ₤ 22.9.3

2 Dec 1741   -   Taken 18 Jan 1741/2 Rec 3 Feb 1741/2 - Audit of the Estate
6 DB 105 PAc   of JOHN JAMES decd.   Total ₤ 74.5.2

3 Mar 1741/2 - ELIZABETH WOODHOUSE (E)
6 DB 105 PAc   wd 26 Feb 1741/2 wp 3 Mar 1741/3 by WM: KEELING SENR & JUNR
                Exor: son in law PETER SPARROW
my son WILL^m: WHITE a horse & canoe
daughters ELIZ: KEY & MARY SPARROW one shilling apiece
daughter KEZIA WHITE... pot & pothooks &c...........................
son JAMES WHITE.............. daughter SARAH WHITE.....................
To my three children KEZIA, SARAH & JAMES WHITE the remainder of my estate
when they come of age.

2 Mar 1741/2 - Rec 3 Mar 1741/2 - MARY (W) BERRY to GEORGE WILLIAMSON
6 DB 106 PAc   JUNR: 100 acres .....(bounds are given)......... being
                the same land RICHARD WILLIAMSON gave in his last will
to his daughter MARY BERRY.

2 Mar 1741/2 - Rec 3 Mar 1741/2 - JOHN DYER (‡) & SARAH (S) his wife
6 DB 108 PAc   to JOHN AIRS (HARRIS?) 50 acres ..... part of the same
                land which PETER CRASHLEY gave to his daughter ANN in his
last will........ the wife of MICHAEL EATON..... No bounds given.

2 Mar 1741/2 - Rec 3 Mar 1741/2 - JAMES (‡) MOORE to JOHN DYER........
6 DB 110 PAc   30 acres in the UPPER PRECINCT of the EASTERN SHORE.
                (No bounds given)

1 Mar 1741/2 - Rec 3 Mar 1741/2 - JOHN DYER to RICHARD LISTER.........
6 DB 111 PAc   170 acres......... being the dividend whereon the sd
                JOHN DYER formerly lived and is part of a greater tract
of land granted to one HENRY WOODHOUSE by patent dated 9 Oct 1675 said
patent was given & bequeathed unto JOHN WOODHOUSE by the last will of
the said HENRY WOODHOUSE AND THE said JOHN WOODHOUSE sold the said tract
of land to WILLIAM DYER by a deed recorded in Princess Anne County 6 Nov
1705 & said 170 acres of land was divided out of said pattent & given to
said JOHN DYER by said WILLIAM DYER by Deed of Gift...................

6 Oct 1739   - Rec 7 Apr 1742 - JAMES WHITEHURST & MARGT: (his wife)
6 DB 114 PAc   to ANTHONY WHITEHURST....... 100 acres on the EASTERN
                SHORE lying in CHOLCHESTER NECK...(no bounds given)....
near the SEASIDE lying in COLCHESTER NECK beginning at ASHBYS BRIDGE
binding on the KINGS ROAD thence on the CREEK &c......................

8 Dec 1739   - Rec 7 Apr 1742 - JAMES WHITEHURST to THOMAS WHITEHURST
6 DB 116 PAc   100 acres on the EASTERN SHORE lying in COLCHESTER NECK
                (Some bounds are given in the release.) MARGARET acknow-
ledged the release.

7 Apr 1742 - Rec 7 Apr 1742 - JOHN SHIP to his "well beloved kinsman
6 DB 117 PAc   WILL^m: SHIP & FRANCIS" 100 acres of SWAMPLAND to them
                joining to their high ground. (There is no release and
no further bounds are given)

11

7 Apr 1742   -   JOHN GRIFFEN
6 DB 118 PAc   wd 16 Dec 1741   wp 7 Apr 1742 by JAMES NIMMO & THO[s]: BANKS
                  Exix: wife SARAH
Residue to be divided between my wife and 3 children GEORGE, JAMES and
JOHN GRIFFEN.

4 Apr 1742   -   MARY (X) ROBINSON
6 DB 119 PAc   wd 9 Jan 1741/2 wp 4 Apr 1742
                  Exor: nephew TULLY ROBINSON
daughter ELIZ: McCLENNAHAN at the age of 21 years or day of marriage.
reversion to my two nephews TULLY ROBINSON & WILL[m]: ROBINSON ....
tuition & custody of my said daughter during her infancy unto MRS: ELIZA:
McCLENAHAN SENR:................

7 Apr 1742   -   JAMES WHITEHURST
6 DB 119 PAc   wd 6 Oct 1741   wp 7 Apr 1742 by ANTHO: WHITEHURST &
                  Exor; bro: SOLOMON WHITEHURST   THO[s]: (I) WHITEHURST
daughter MARY WHITEHURST   100 acres
daughter MARXX   100 acres   (this will is faded)
Wife and children MARGRETT WHITEHEAD, MARY and JAMES (MARY & JAMES are
underage) ..... my two brothers ....

3 Mar 1741/2 -   Rec 7 Apr 1742 - Inventory of ELIZ: WOODHOUSE taken at
6 DB 120 PAc   the house of ELIZ: WOODHOUSE decd 16 Mar 1741/2 by
                  HENRY WOODHOUSE, WILL[m]: KEELING & WILL[m]: COX.

7 Apr 1742   -   JOHN (X) PEED
6 DB 120 PAc   wd 20 Jan 1741/2 wp 7 Apr 1742 by HENRY GRIFFIN
                  Exix: wife MARY
wife MARY my house & plantation her lifetime with reversion to my
son WILL[m]: PEED........... sons JNO: PEED & JAMES PEED ....

4 May 1742   -   Rec 5 May 1742 - OWEN JONES to RICHARD CORBETT 100 acres
6 DB 121 PAc   in a place called BLACKWATER........ at a CYPRESS BR.
                  .... along CORBETTS line .... to a corner tree
dividing the land of said CORBETT and THO[s] CORNISH butting Sly along
said CORNISH to the head of a branch called WHITE OAK BRANCH..........

4 May 1742   -   Rec 5 May 1742 - GEORGE STIRRING to HENRY CORNICK 100
6 DB 122 PAc   acres in the EASTERN SHORE......... THO: CANNONS line
                  to South end of CHINKAPINE RIDGE to and along JOHN BUR-
FOOTS line to LOVETTS Land near the BRIDGES called THUNDERBALL PINE BRIDGE
to land that was formerly CASON MOORES bounding on same to the first begin.

5 May 1742   -   Rec same day - JOHN BURFOOT to HENRY CORNICK 200 acres
6 DB 124 PAc   on the EASTERN SHORE begin: at a corner tree of JOHN
                  MUNDAYS to LANCASTER LOVETTS in OLDES SWAMP to a corner
white oak of GEORGE STIRINGS & LANCASTER LOVETTS Westerly to a corner
tree of AMBROSE BURFOOT.........................

7 Apr 1742 - taken 1 May 1742 Returned 5 May 1742 & recorded - Inventory
6 DB 128 PAc   of JAMES WHITEHURST decd. A short Inventory Total ₤44.10.9

12

7 Apr 1742   - Rec 5 May 1742 - An Inventory of the Appraisal of
6 DB 128 PAc   MOSES HENLY Decd........ taken at the dwelling house of
                 CHARLES HENLY......... Amounts to Ł 10.2.8. Items are
not listed.

5 May 1742   - Inventory of the Estate of JAMES THELABALL decd
6 DB 128 PAc   This is only 7 lines long... contains negro wench & child
                ...... beds & furniture .... it is badly faded.

28 May 1742 - Rec 2 Jun 1742 - THOROWGOOD SPRATT to THOMAS MORGAN
6 DB 129 PAc   100 acres lying in the Boarders (borders?) of NANNYS
                CREEK & is part of a greater tract of land formerly be-
longing to MAJ: HENRY SPRATT decd and which sd HENRY SPRATT did give
unto THOROWGOOD SPRATT by his last will ...... a Red oak of HENRY
WHITES line thence Wly to a Holly th N to a gum th E to a gum upon DAULEYS
& HENRY WOODHOUSES line th S to the first station.

1 Jun 1742   - Rec 2 Jun 1742 - JAMES MOORE , Mariner of Norfolk County
6 DB 131 PAc   to WILLIAM DAULEY of Princess Anne County .... 100 acres
                in Princess Anne County running a South course from a gum
in DAULEYS line to a holly in HENRY WHITES line th Wly to an oak th to a
gum in DAULEYS line lying on the W side of DAULEYS line where he now
lives formerly belonging to MAJ: HENRY SPRATT decd.

5 May 1742 - taken 20 May 1742 - Rec 1 Jun 1742 - Audit of the Estate of
6 DB 132 PAc   ALEX: HARVEY decd to (GEORGE?) & WILLIAM WEBLIN orphant
                of WILL^m: WEBLIN decd.   Total Ł 19.11.10 ....
(This is like trying to read words written on a blotter. The name George
may not be right, but looks more like George than anything else .)
.... We have audited & adjusted the estate of ALEX^r: HARVEY decd as
it relates to the orphans of WILLIAM WEBLIN decd & do find that there is
due the said orphans of the said WEBLIN out of said Estate the abovesd
sum of Ł 11.6.7.   Signed: JAMES NIMMO, ANTHO: MOSELEY & THO^s: HUNTER.

2 Jun 1742   -- FRANCIS LAND
6 DB 133 PAc   wd 27 Jan 1741/2 wp 2 Jun 1742 by EDW: FRIZZLE & ROBT:
                 EXors: wife ANN & JOHN WHITEHURST LAND
son JOHN LAND my plantation whereon I now live & 50 acres of Swamp &c .
son FRANCIS LAND 51½ acres of Marsh lying over CORATUCK INLET &c......
dau MARY LAND, sons EDWARD LAND, RICHARD LAND, CORNELIUS LAND
residue to wife ANN.................

2 Jun 1742 - Taken 2 Jul 1742 - Rec 7 Jul 1742 - Inventory of MRS: MARY
6 DB 133 PAc   ROBINSON decd...... not contained in the Deed of Gift
                by her to her daughter ELIZ^a: McCLENEHAN ROBINSON.....
Total Ł 91.6.7 (Her name is given as ELIZ^a: McCLENEHAN without the
ROBINSON in her Mothers will in Jan 1741/2 and she is underage. See
p 119)

2 Jul 1741   - Rec 7 Jul 1742 - Audit of the Estate of HENRY COLLINS d
6 DB 134 PAc   decd. .... to trouble in writing the will, selling the
                Estate &c ..... taken at the house of SAMUEL BOUSH 9
Jul 1741 (1742?) by JOHN THOROWGOOD SENR & JUNR & JOHN HUNTER.

7 Jul 1742   -   Inventory of Sundry Goods given by MRS. MARY ROBINSON
6 DB 135 PAc   to her daughter ELIZABETH McCLENAHAN by Deed of Gift...
                  in the hands of TULLY ROBINSON Exor of the last will
of MARY ROBINSON......... (a list follows the above)

2 Jun 1742 Taken 6 Jul 1742 - Rec 7 Jul 1742 - Inventory & Appraisal of
6 DB 135 PAc   the Estate of JOSHUA HANCOCK.......... Total ₤ 38 15.

5 May 1742   -   JOHN GALLEY
6 DB 135 PAc   wd 20 Aug 1741/2 wp 5 May 1742 Exix: wife BLANDINAH
                  To wife BLANDINAH my whole estate......................

3 Aug 1742   -   Rec 6 Aug 1742 - ROBERT RICHMOND to WILLIAM DALE & PAUL
6 DB 136 PAc   DALE ..... 100 acres of MARSH & sand adjoining to the
                  Marsh of WILLIAM BENSONS running from the BAY to LONG
CREEK given by ROBERT RICHMOND decd to his son said ROBT: RICHMOND
situated in Princess Anne County on the EASTERN SHORE..................

4 Aug 1742   -   Rec 15 Aug 1742 - An addition to the Inventory of JOHN
6 DB 137 PAc   LOVET.... one suit of wearing apparel & 2 old coats,
                  two pair shoes & one half worn hatt.

3 Aug 1742   -   Rec 4 Aug 1742 - WILLIAM (W) RUTLAND to JOHN CANN......
6 DB 138 PAc   beginning at an oak on the edge of GREENLAND SWAMP on the
                  South side of the Swamp in a line of MR: WILLIAM CORNICKS
decd in XXXX for POPLAR RIDGE divd: of land.......... GREENLAND RIDGE.....

6 Jul 1742   -   Rec 4 Aug 1742 - RUTH SOMMERSALL & SUSANNAH PATTON of the
6 DB 140 PAc   ISLAND OF BERMUDOS to CAPT: JOHN HUTCHINGS of the Parish
                  of ELIZ: & County of Norfolk... 3½ lotts in NEWTOWN in
the Northermost corner of NATHANIEL McCLENAHAN dec his lott upon the
MAIN STREET......... to a point binding upon the Eastermost Branch of
ELIZABETH RIVER.......it is the same 3½ lotts which FRANCIS LANDY purchased of COL: EDWARD MOSELEY decd 7 Nov 1713.... 4 Aug 1742 CAPT: THOS:
NEWTON atty of the within named RUTH SOMMERSALL & SUSANNAH PATTON acknowledged in Court the within deed.................

6 & 7 XXX 1742- Rec 4 Aug 1742 - Power of Attorney to CAPT: THOMAS NEWTON
6 DB 142 PAc   of Norfolk County from RUTH SUMMERSALL & SUSANAH PATTON
                  of the ISLAND of BERMUDOS.

3 Aug 1742   -   Rec 1 Sep 1742 - JOHN MALBONE to SOLO: WATERMAN........
6 DB 143 PAc   50 acres in UPER PRECINCT of the EASTERN SHORE.........
                  on MUDDY CREEK ROAD on the one part & SOLO: WATERMANS
other land on the other part & is part of the tract of land whereon
JOHN MALBONE now lives. (No further bounds given)

1 Sep 1742   -   Rec 1 Sep 1742 - SAMUEL SMITH of NORFOLK BURROUGH to
6 DB 145 PAc   ROBERT TODD of Princess Anne County...................
                  all that Lott or ½ acre in NEWTOWN in the street called
the WHARF STREET xxxxxx .... (Both Lease & Release are blurred)

14

30 Aug 1742   -   Rec 1 Sep 1742 - ROBERT BARBER? (BARTEE? OR BAXTER?)
6 DB 146 PAc   & ELIZABETH his wife which said ELIZ: is one of the
                daughters & co-heirs of THOMAS COCKROFT decd to THOMAS
TAYLOR all that 5th part of a Plantation where THOMAS COCKROFT decd
lived........ 138 acres of land . No bounds are given.

16 Aug 1742   -   Rec 1 Sep 1742 - THOMAS WISHART to TULLY WILLIAMSON...
6 DB 148 PAc   80 acres in Princess Anne County on the HEAD of the
                EASTERN BRANCH of ELIZA: RIVER & is the remainder of
180 acres given by JAMES KEMPE unto THOS: WISHART & MARY his wife
father and mother of said THOMAS WISHART party hereunto by Deed of
Gift 7 Sep 1698 duly recorded & by JAMES WISHART the ELDER brother of
the said THOMAS conveyed to him 100 acres part of aforesaid tract being
formerly sold by the said JAMES WISHART unto ARTHUR BACKER? ....

13 Aug 1742   -   Rec 1 Sep 1742 - MR. HENRY WHITE of KNOTS ISLAND in
6 DB 150 PAc   NORTH CAROLINA & THOROWGOOD SPRATT of Princess Anne
                County to JAMES NIMMO of Princess Anne County.........
100 acres of land in NANNEYS CREEK....... 100 acres of which being formerly held by said HENRY WHITE binding Easterly on that 100 acres that
NIMMO bought of MAJ: HENRY SPRATT decd (Bounds are given)

6 Aug 1742   -   Rec 1 Sep 1742 - Inventory of the estate of JOHN BROCK
6 DB 152 PAc   JUNR: decd.   Total £ 12.18.0

4 Oct 1742   -   Rec 4 Oct 1742 - EDWARD DENBY to JOHN HARFORD & ALIFF his
6 DB 152 PAc   wife... .. .one lott or ½ acre in NEWTOWN where JOHN HAR-
                FORD & ALIFF his wife now live formerly belonging to
JAMES XXXXXXXXX ....

6 Oct 1742   -   DAVID SCOTT
6 DB 153 PAc   wd 21 Feb 1741/2 wp 6 Oct 1742
                Exors: Brothers JOHN SCOTT & WALTER SCOTT
Brother JOHN SCOTT...... all my lands..... .. brother WALTER SCOTT under
age of 21............. sister MARY SCOTT.

22 Sep 1742   -   Rec 6 Oct 1742 - Audit of the Estate of CAPT: FRANCIS LAND
6 DB 153 PAc   decd.   Total £ 174.4.8½

4 Feb 1741/2 -   Rec 3 Nov 1742 - MR: JOHN WILSON to MRS: ANNE FENTRIS as
6 DB 153 PAc   Guardian of MRS: MARY ANNE THOROWGOOD..................
                100 acres where the said JOHN WILSON now lives in the
EASTERN SHORE in BACK BAY which said WILSON purchased of GEORGE WISHART
& JAMES KEMPE & was purchased by him from WILLIAM ROBINSON............

1 May 1742   -   Rec 3 Nov 1742 - MOSES FENTRISS JUNR to COL: ANTHONY WALKE
6 DB 155 PAc   350 acres the said MOSES FENTRISS now lives on which was
                purchased by said MOSES FENTRISS of MR. EDWARD HACK
MOSELEY with all houses &c............ bounds are not given.

2 Nov 1742   -   Rec 9 Nov 1742 - JOHN BURFOOT to WILLIAM BROCK..... 177
6 DB 156 PAc   acres lying on East side of LINKHORN BAY..... AMBROSE BUR-
                FOOTS line... to a corner tree of THOMAS BRINSON ... Wly
to a point in LINCOLN BAY............

2 Nov 1742   - JAMES FENTRISS son of JOHN FENTRISS in the North Woods of
6 DB 157 PAc   Princess Anne County to MR: EDWARD HACK MOSELEY, Merchant
                One acre lying on the fork of the Road leading to North
Landing.

25 Sep 1742   - ANDREW NICHOLAS, Marriner & MARY his wife to ROBERT TODD
6 DB 159 PAc   Merchant........ One acre the two NE lotts in NEWTOWN on
                the West side of the Street going down to the KETCH LANDING.

2 Nov 1742 -   THOMAS GARDNER (or GARNOR spelled both ways) to THOMAS
6 DB 161 PAc   WALKE..... 100 acres commonly called LOVETTS OLD PLANTATION
                on the WESTERN SHORE where JOHN LOVETT formerly lived was
exchanged by said LOVETT with ROBERT BOND as by deeds to BOND 2 Jan 1715
No bounds were given.

9 Aug 1742 - Rec 3 Nov 1742 - RICHARD CORBETT to COL⁰: ANTHONY WALKE.....
6 DB 163 PAc   240 acres in Princess Anne County bounded Nly on the land
               of COL⁰: ANTHONY WALKE, Ely on the land of FRANCIS ACKISS,
Sly on land of GEORGE SHIRLEY & GEORGE WILLIAMSON, Wly on land of MRS:
ELIZABETH McCLENAHAN, JOHN WHITEHURST & said COL⁰: WALKE..............

3 Nov 1742   - INVENTORY of FRANCES LAND....... Very short - no figures
6 DB 165 PAc   are given.

18 May 1742   - Rec 1 Dec 1742 - FRANCIS SPRATT, GENT: to JAMES MOORE
6 DB 166 PAc   FRANCIS SPRATT by virtue of the will of his decd. father
                MAJ: HENRY SPRATT decd. being seized of the Manner House
and 250 acres of alnd........ conveyed the said land & appurtenances to
JAMES MOORE...... by deeds dated 5 & 6 May 1741....... (this is a discharge
to MOORE as having paid in full his obligation to SPRATT).

30 Nov 1742   - Rec. 1 Dec 1742 - THOMAS TAYLOR, Ship Carpenter & MARY
6 DB 167 PAc   his wife to PETER DALE, Ship Carpenter of the BURROUGH
                OF NORFOLK........ 99 acres in Princess Anne County
beginning at the Eastermost corner tree of a pattent of 200 acres granted
ARTHUR MOSELEY 18 Mar 1662 then SW 72⁰ by a line of marked trees to a
holly at the CREEK SIDE th bounding on the said Creek to a marked pine
standing near the mouth of BROAD CREEK thence E by a line of marked trees
by BRAYS LAND to the corner tree joyning upon COL: MOSELEY th N 100 pole
to the first station .... the said 90 acres being part of the said
200 acres granted in the said pattent to ARTHUR MOSELEY & conveyed by him
to one WILLIAM MARTIN upon whose decease said land descended to ANNE his
sole daughter who intermarried with JAMES BROUGHTON & they said JAMES &
ANNE by deeds Recorded in Princess Anne County 7 Apr 1736 conveyed the
said land unto the said THOMAS TAYLOR with the priviledges of a SHIPYARD
upon any part of the said land contained in the said pattent & not thereby
sold under the restrictions therein limited as by the said deeds may appear which said 99 acres with the priviledges of the said SHIPYARD ..&c..
(Nugent gives this 200 acres to ARTHUR MOSELEY 5 PB 248 Beginning on a
poynt in the BROAD CREEK Granted to EDWARD WILDER 6 Mar 1662, sold to
NICH: FREEMAN who assigned to said MOSELEY.. but the date to EDWARD WILDER
is given as 1652 in his patent of the same land)

1 May 1742   -   Rec. 1 Dec 1742 - WILLIAM SALMON, Planter to COL^O:
6 DB 169 PAc   ANTHONY WALKE, GENT:...... 150 acres ... all that plan-
              tation whereon said WILLIAM now lives.

2 Aug 1739   - Rec 5 Jan 1742/3 - I, ANTHONY WALKE JUNR: of KING
6 DB 170 PAc   WILLIAM COUNTY, Merchant am held and firmly bound unto
              THOMAS WALKE, Mariner of Princess Anne County in the
just sum of £ 250.......... am obligated to said THOMAS........ 300
acres of land joyning Sly on the EASTERN BRANCH, Wly on BROAD CREEK,
ELY on MR: EDWARD HACK MOSELEY & Nly on EDWARD BARYS land.

30 Nov 1742 - Rec 1 Dec 1742 - JOHN LAMOUNT to JOHN MUNDEN.... 50 acres
6 DB 171 PAc   on the EASTERN SHORE of Princess Anne County. (Bounds are
              given but don't help in locating this land)

8 Nov 1742 - Rec 1 Dec 1742 - CAPT: JOHN HUTCHINGS of Norfolk Co.
6 DB 173 PAc   to WILLIAM ROBINSON son of WILLIAM ROBINSON late of
              Princess Anne County decd .... 3 lotts & 1/2 lot of
land in NEWTOWN .... (bounds are given)

1 Dec 1742 - EDWARD IDLE?, Seaman in County of Norfolk
6 DB 175 PAc   wd 22 Sep 1742 wp 1 Dec 1742 Exor: friend JAS: TIMBERLAKE
              wife's father HENRY? HOLMES, my wife's gold ring & said
ring not to be parted without from the name of HOLMES so long as the
ring doth last......to brother in law JOHN HOLMES my wearing clothes,
to SARAH TIMBERLAKE the wife of JAS: TIMBERLAKE .... to the 4
men undermentioned if they'll carry & assist me to my grave 20 shillings.
.... This will was proved by "both witnesses", GEORGE GRIFFIN and
GEORGE BALL. The four men referred to above were not named.

15 Nov 1742 - Rec 2 Feb 1742/3 - STEVEN PEW? & HUGH PEW? to SAMUEL
6 DB 176 PAc   BARINGTON..... 25 acres on South side of the EASTERN BRANCH.

2 Feb 1742/3 - PAUL DALE
6 DB 178 PAc   wd 17 Nov 1742 wp 2 Feb 1742/3
              Exor: Brother WILLIAM DALE & Kinsman WILLIAM BENSON
unto my dau MARY DALE 50 acres of Marsh that I bought of ROBERT RICHMOND
unto my dau RACHEL DALE 50 acres of Swamp land & my part of the Marsh at
CORATUCK INLET .... Unto my brother WILLIAM DALE the use of my
negro man Roger til my two daughters attain to age or day of marriage then
to my daughter RACHEL....... residue of estate to be sold & after debts
are paid to be divided between my two daughters.

1 Dec 1742 - Rec 2 Feb 1742/3 - Appraisal of the Estate of MR. FRANCIS
6 DB 178 PAc   SCOTT decd.   Total £ 31.19.6

6 Oct 1742 - Rec 2 Feb 1742/3 - Appraisal of the Estate of DAVID SCOTT
6 DB 178 PAc   decd.   Total £ 10.8.9

23 Feb 1742/3 - Rec 2 Mar 1742/3 - MATTHEW JAMES to ELIZABETH JAMES.....
6 DB 179 PAc   50 acres in the woods of the EASTERN SHORE of LYNHAVEN
              begin: at a Pine of WILLIAM FLANAGANS SWly to a gum th SE
.... th Ewardly ....

8 Feb 1742/3 - Rec 2 Mar 1742/3 - JOHN BUCKNER to HITELY ROE........
6 DB 181 PAc   100 acres including two necks of land, one called
                 BROAD NECK & the other LONG NECK begin: at the CAROLINA
LINE near the POCOSIN runing up the said CAROLINA LINE to WM: BRYANS
line.......so along said lines to the DIRT BRIDGE BRANCH to ROBERT REEDS
line......to the mouth of the said branch.

1 XXX 174X   - Rec 2 Mar 1742/3 - WILLIAM CREED (CREEDLES in the release)
6 DB 183 PAc   to THOMAS XXXXXX (There is a hole, but GARNER or GARNOR
                 is in the margin and GAINER in the body of the deed).....
50 acres at the HEAD of LINHAVEN RIVER according to the ancient bounds &
is the same land that KATHERINE CREEDLE purchased of JOHN THOROWGOOD the
only surviving son of COLL: ADAM THOROWGOOD by deeds dated 5 & 6 Apr 1726
(or 1736)

16 Feb 1742/3 - Rec 2 Mar 1742/3 - MR: KITELY ROE, GENT: of Princess Anne
6 DB 185 PAc   release to MR: ROBERT READ.....in his actual possession
                 50 acres in Princess Anne county.....(no bounds given)
The lease follows in this case on page 186....land called LONG & BROAD
NECKS.

2 Mar 1742/3 - GEORGE SIMMONS of PrincessAnne County
6 DB 186 PAc   wd 25 Jan 1742/3 wp 2 Mar 1742/3
                 Exor: wife (she is not named)
to eldest son THO^s: all my plantation & 1/2 the tract of land joyning
upon STEPHEN PICO?.....to other son LEMUEL the other part of the land
joyning upon THOMAS TURNER......daughters MARY, SARAH, EASTER?..........
residue to my wife..........

10 Feb 1742/3 - Rec 2 Mar 1742/3 - JOHN BUCKNER GENT: & SARAH his wife
6 DB 189 PAc   to ROBERT READE of Princess Anne County...50 acres......
                 (No bounds are given)

2 Mar 1742/3 - Rec 3 Mar 1742/3 - ARTHUR SAYER to WILLIAM MORRIS ......
6 DB 189 PAc   40 acres of Marsh in NANNYS CREEK and is part of a pattent
                 of 347 acres granted MR: JOHN FULCHER 20 Apr 1711........
(No bounds are given)

28 Feb 1742/3 - Rec 2 Mar 1742/3 - ADAM (X) KEELING to HENRY MOORE.......
6 DB 191 PAc   100 acres in Princess Anne County on the South side by a
                 pine parting the land of HENRY MOORES SENIOR & the said
tract by the SEA on the East & the DESERT on the North being the land formerly belonging to HENRY HARRIS....................

1 Mar 1742/3 - Rec 2 Mar 1742/3 - DANIEL LENARD & DINAH his wife to
6 DB 193 PAc   LEMUEL POWERS........50 acres upon a branch of LITTLE
                 CREEK called BELLEMIES COVE (BELLAMYS?) begin at a
chincopin standing in THOMAS IVYS LINE........JONATHAN MARTINS corner tree
........being the same land that was granted to DANIEL LENARD, father of
the aforesaid DANIEL by patent 28 Apr 1712...(bounds are complete)

            This book is now beginning to have holes in the pages
and parts of the pages torn away.

18

2 Mar 1742/3 - ABRAHAM LEGRAVE
6 DB 195 PAc   wd 23 Feb 1742/3 wp 2 Mar 1742/3
                    (This appears to be a nun-cupative will and is signed by
JACOB ELLEGOOD. The page is damaged and is hard to read)
...to JN°: KEELING Ł 5 and the rest of my estate to xxxxx WOODHOUSE.......
RUTH SPARKS............PAT MURPHY's wife...................................

Xx Feb 1742/3 - Recorded 2 Mar 1742/3 - Estate of MRS: MARG^t: MALBONE, decd
6 DB 196 PAc   (Parts of this are missing)

3 Feb 1742/3   - RICHARD CORBETT to JOHN HUTCHINGS of Burrough of Norfolk..
6 DB 196 PAc   xxxxxxxxxxxxxxxx w hich I bought of JOHN KNOWIS xxxxxxxxxx
                    (There are holes in this deed)

5 Apr 1743   - Recorded 6 Apr 1743 - TULLY WILLIAMSON to ARTHUR SAYER
6 DB 197 PAc   190 acres in Princess Anne County......the same land that
                    ROGER WILLIAMSON gave to said TULLY WILLIAMSON xxxxxxxxxxxx
deed of gift xxxxxxxxxxxxxx (Both the lease and release are partially missing
but a studied comparision of the two may result in a better picture)

27 Mar 1742/3 - XXXXXXXX LESTER lease to TULLY WILLIAMSON ..... 100 acres
6 DB 199 PAc   (after the word one hundred is missing - it may be more
                    than 100 acres. Most of the record is missing)

5 Apr 1743   - Recorded xxxxxxxxxx HENRY MOORE lease to HENRY WOODHOUSE,
6 DB 201 PAc   Mariner xxxxxxx Land on Eastern Shore xxxxxxxxxxxxxxxxxxxxxx

6 Apr 1743   - Recorded 6 Apr 1743 - THOMAS MORGAN to MICHAEL SHERWOOD
6 DB 203 PAc   (This is full of holes)

xx Apr 1743   - ANNE TREVETHAN
6 DB 205 PAc   wd 18 Mar 1743 wp xx Apr 1743
                    to my gr-dau ELIZABETH SCOTT the wife of MR: THOMAS SCOTT
xxxxx the money due to me in ENGLAND xxxxxxxxxxxxxx to my gr-dau MARY ANNE
THOROWGOOD .... to my gr-son RODERICK CONNER...under 21 years.......
my two gr-children KATHERINE xxxxxxx and JOHN WRIGHT.........(there are more
relationships given in this will but it would require a lot of study to
work it out because of illegible parts)

2 Apr 1743   - Recorded 6 Apr 1743 - Inventory of GEORGE SIMMONS decd....
6 DB 206 PAc   signed by SARAH SIMMONS ....

6 Apr 1743   - The Audit of the Estate of JAMES WHIREHURST decd
6 DB 207 PAc

5 Feb 1742/3   - Recorded xx May 1743 - CHRISTOPHER PHILPOT to ADAM TOOLY
6 DB 207 PAc   25 acres in Princess Anne County........................

12 Mar 1742/3 - Recorded xx May 1743 - ROBT: RICHMOND lease to JOHN KEELING
6 DB 209 PAc   (The lease is illegible. the release follows) 6 DB 210
                    50 acres of Swampland at the EASTERN SHORE of LINHAVEN PAR-
RISH at a place called the BROAD RUN & known by the name of the HOLLOW POPLAR
which said land ROBERT RICHMOND decd bought of HENRY WOODHOUSE..............

3 May 1743   -   Recorded 5 May 1743 - THOMAS HENLY & RICHARD (R) BRINSON to
6 DB 211 PAc   JOHN KEELING 50 acres   near BRINSONS INLET joyning on the
                  South side of the Pond. Given by JOHN BRINSON the elder to
be divided between his 2 sons MATT^W: & ADAM BRINSON. The said ADAM conveyed
his part to the said MATT^W: BRINSON which xxxxxxx powered the said THOMAS
HENLY to convey the whole title &c...

2 May 1743   -   ROBT: BROUGH of ELIZABETH CITY COUNTY & XXXXXXX his wife to
6 DB 213 PAc   MR: TULLY ROBINSON (space is left blank where the wife's
                  name would be in both the lease and release) ....
xxxxxxxx part of the same land that was formerly xxxxxxxxxxxxxx WILLIAMSON
decd. to ELINOR his wife by his last will dated 16 Apr 1711 xxxxx part of the
land lately recovered by the said BROUGH xxxxxxx the said ROBINSON & JAMES
WILLIAMSON as heir at law to the said ELINOR...............................

2 May 1743   -   MR: ROBT: BROUGH of ELIZABETH CITY COUNTY to JAMES WILLIAMSON
6 DB 216 PAc   of Princess Anne County, Planter....43 1/2 acres of land in
                  Princess Anne County & is part of the same land that formerly
JAMES WILLIAMSON devised to ELINOR his wife by his last will 16 Apr 1711 &
part of the same land recovered by the said BROUGH from the said JAMES WILLIAM-
SON to MR: TULLY ROBINSON ....A bond follows this on p 218 signed by
ROBERT BROUGH. (In all of the above records the name of ROBT: BROUGH's wife
is indicated by a blank space.)

3 May 1743   -   Recorded 4 May 1743 - COCKROFT (X) OLD to ROGER HATTON.......
6 DB 219 PAc   50 acres........ beginning at the HEAD of BURNT HOUSE XXXXX
                  (There are holes in the paper)

25 Mar 1742/3 - Recorded 4 May 1743 - MATTHEW BRINSON & ADAM BRINSON of ONSLOW
6 DB 220 PAc   COUNTY, NORTH CAROLINA...Power of Attorney to THOMAS HUNDLEY
                  of PAco.

4 May 1743   -   Recorded 4 May 1743 - DORCAS BROUGHTON...Deed of Gift to her
6 DB 221 PAc   son EDWARD BROUGHTON .... 25 acres on the Western Shore & is
                  the same land whereon the said DORCAS BROUGHTON now lives.....

4 May 1743   -   DORCAS BROUGHTON... Deed of Gift ... to her 3 sons, EDWARD,
6 DB 222 PAc   JAMES & THO^S: BROUGHTON.......stocks of cattle xxxxxxxxxxxxxx

xx Apr 1743   -   Recorded 4 May 1743 - Inventory of the Appraisal of THOROWGOOD
6 DB 222 PAc   KEELING decd Estate.

1 Jun 1743   -   ISAAC WHITE
6 DB 223 PAc   wd 16 May 1743 wp 1 Jun 1743
                  Exor: brother-in-law FR^a: CAREY to have guardianship of my
two daughters.....dau SARAH WHITE my plantation of 150 acres whereon I now
live....dau ELIZ^a: WHITE my plantation whereon ROBT: BURROUGHS now lives 150
acres........Residue to be divided between my two daughters..................

1 Jun 1743   -   MATT^W: ELLEGOOD of Princess Anne County
6 DB 223 PAc   wd 2 Apr 1743 wp 1 Jun 1743   Exix: wife MARGT:
                  ... son PETER NORLY ELLEGOOD the plantation whereon I now live

with reversion to my daughter MAXXXXX ..... wife MARGT: ELLEGOOD ....
sister SARAH ELLEGOOD reversion to my cousin REBECCA ELLEGOOD daughter of
JACOB ELLEGOOD.

18 Apr 1743 - Rec 1 Jun 1743 - GEORGE MOSELEY to JAMES MOORE .... 275 Acres
6 DB 224 PAc   of land the said GEORGE MOSELEY now lives on according to the
   most antient bounds thereof .....(no bounds are given)

14 May 1743 - Rec ? Jun 1743 (date is missing) Inventory of the estate of
6 DB 225 PAc   ROBERT RICHMOND decd.

1 Jun 1743 - Inventory of the Estate of JOHN ASHMAN decd..................
6 DB 226 PAc

1 Jun 1743 - JAMES NIMMO to CHARLES SMYTH in Newtown.... a Schoolhouse
6 DB 226 PAc   upon xxxxxxxxxxxxxx in lott belonging to me xxxx upon the same
   xxxxxxxx COL: EDWd: MOSELEY late of the said County of Princess Anne decd transferred to me by a Deed of gift near the lott that was
formerly JAMES IRDELLS? decd.......(a lot of this is missing)

1 Jun 1743 - LANCASTER LOVETT
6 DB 227 PAc   wd 4 Apr 1743 wp 1 Jun 1743 by MATTHEW PALLET & THO: HENLEY
   Exor: son JOHN & wife MARY Wit: THOs:(T) HENLY, MATHw: PALLET
& WILLIAM COX. .... eldest son JOHN LOVETT the plantation whereon I now live
with 350 acres of land joyning to the same.....wife to have 1/3 part during
her life...to son WILLIAM LOVETT the plantation where GEORGE NORRIS settled
& cleared with 350 acres.... to son LANCASTER LOVETT the plantation LEM1:
XXXXX (name may be JONES?) cleared & settled with 300 acres..... to son
HENRY LOVETT the plantation at the FRESH POND that I bought of JOHN BURFOOT
with 350 acres....... to son REUBIN LOVETT my POPLAR RIDGE plantation & all
the land belonging to the same....... to my 4 sons: JOHN WILLIAM, LANCASTER &
HENRY LOVETT my WESTERN SHORE swampland........wife MARY....................

4 May 1743 - Rec 1 Jun 1743 - Appraisal of the Estate of THOMAS IVEY decd.
6 DB 228 PAc   (There is very little left of this Inventory)

5 Jul 1743 - Rec 6 Jul 1743 - WM: WEBLIN to ANTHONY LEGGETT ....
6 DB 229 PAc   land in the EASTERN SHORE known by the name of KIN(?)ONS IS-
   LAND being by estimacon 130 acres.... bounds are partially
given. ('Alot of the lease and release are missing)

5 Jul 1743 - Rec 6 Jul 1743 - WILLIAM (W) BROCK to JOHN BURFOOT... 96 acres
6 DB 231 PAc   in the EASTERN SHORE of Princess Anne County xxxxxx a corner
   tree of JAMES LAMOUNTS in his XXXXERY NECK XXX ....a corner
tree of JOHN BRINSONS...............

29 Jun 1743 - Rec 6 Jul 1743 - RICHARD LESTER SENR:, Planter... Deed of Gift
6 DB 233 PAc   to my brother WILLIAM OAKHAM SENR: .... 60 acres ... half of a
   certain tract of marsh by virtueof a pattent granted to said
RICHARD LESTER dated 1741 .... lying on the West side of said OAKHAMS land.

1 Jun 1743   -   Rec4 Jul 1743 - Appraisal of the Estate of LANCASTER LOVETT
6 DB 234 PAc   decd.   Total ℔ 176.15.4 Taken by JOEL CORNICK, THOMAS (T)
                    HENLY & ffRA: WOODHOUSE.

X Jul 1743   -   EDWD: GIZBURN
6 DB 234 PAc   nun-will 5 May 1743 wp (6?) Jul 1743
                    AUGUSTUS LANE & JOHN SIMMONS of BLACK WATER PRECINCT came
before his Majestys Justices .... that they xx called & devised by
EDWD: GIZBURN on the 4th Instant to bear witness xxxx the said EDWD: GIZBURN
did freely give unto ELIZABETH his wife his xxxxxxxxxxx saddle, bridle &c .
..... said EDWD: GIZBURN did xxxxxxxx the said LANE & SIMMONS to witness that
he xxxx to his son THOROWGOOD GIZBURN one black yearling heifer & that (it
was) his will that his wife ELIZA: GIZBURN & son THOROWGOOD should divide the
personal estate...............witnessed by ANTHONY WALKE....................

3 Aug 1743   -   Rec 3 Aug 1743 - Bond of THOMAS WALKE, GENT. to the King on
6 DB 235 PAc   his appointment as SHERIF of Princess Anne County..........

3 Aug 1743   -   Rec 3 Aug 1743 - Audit of the Estate & Inventory of CAPT:
6 DB 235 PAc   JOHN IVY decd.... The Inventory as per list in the office
                    ℔ 69.10.

6 Jul 1743   -   Recorded 3 Aug 1743 - Inventory of the Estate of EDWARD GIZ-
6 DB 236 PAc   BURN decd.................Total ℔ 64.9.6

6 Sep 1743   -   Rec 5 Oct 1743 - THOMAS PURDY, Marriner, son of GEORGE PURDY
6 DB 236 PAc   late of Princess Anne County to JAMES KEMPE, XXubleman? of
                    PAc..... 100 acres .... half of one plantation ....
adjoyning to the land of said JAMES KEMPE which was devised by the said GEORGE
PURDY in his last will in 1730 to the said THOMAS PURDY & JOHN PURDY equally
to be divided ....(parts of this are missing).......................

3 Oct 1743   -   Rec 5 Oct 1743 - MARK POWELL to HENRY BARLOW, Clerk... 50
6 DB 238 PAc   acres on the WESTERN SHORE of LINHAVEN RIVER ....begin at MRS:
                    THOROWGOODS .... distance from her gate ......along
GEORGE WEBLINS land .... along RICHARD DUDLEY .....(bounds are given)

27 Jan 1743/4- Rec 1 Feb 1743/4 - GEORGE MOSELEY to NATHANIEL NEWTON........
6 DB 239 PAc   2(50?) acres on the Westward side of SAMUEL BENNETS CREEK....
                    which GEORGE MOSELEY decd father of the abovesd GEORGE pur-
chased of (JOB?) KEMPE, ROBERT THOROWGOOD & EDWARD MOSELEY as by their several deeds recorded in Princess Anne County.......p 241 - MARTHA MOSELEY wife
of said GEORGE MOSELEY being sickly & impotent..... was privily examined 28
Jan 1743/4.....(The name (JOB?) must be JAMES but it looks like JOB)

                    (The above two items seem out of place in the book. but the
dates are clearly 1743 which should mean 1743/4 for the months ot Jan & Feb?)

4 Oct 1743   -   Rec 5 Oct 1743 - MARK POWELL to HENRY BARLOW... 50 acres in
6 DB 241 PAc   the WESTERN SHORE of LINHAVEN... (bounds are given)

3 Sep 1743   -   Rec 5 Oct 1743 - CAPT: ANTHONY MOSELEY to MR: ISAIAH NICHOLAS,
6 DB 243 PAc   Marriner.... one lott, 1/2 acre of land, in NEWTOWN which
                  CAPT ANTHONY MOSELEY bought of COLL: EDWD: MOSELEY decd xxxx
                  next to the lotts that was formerly BENJA: MOSELEYS in the
letter E according to the platt of the said town......bounds are given.

] Nov 1743   -   Rec 2 Nov 1743 - LEMUEL CORNICK & FRANCES his wife to EDWD:
6 DB 245 PAc   ATTWOOD.....100 acres joyning on the said EDWARD ATTWOODS
                  land given by EDWARD ATTWOOD the Elder to his two sons THOMAS
& WILLIAM ATTWOOD & in case either of them should die without heirs of their
body ..to the survivor & his heirs & the said FRANCES claiming the said land
as one of those feeofees.................

? Jul 1743   -   Rec 2 Nov 1743 - RICHASON MORSE of PAc, Planter gives Power
6 DB 246 PAc   of Attorney to WM: BODMAN.

no date given-   Rec 2 Nov 1743 - Appraisal of the estate of ISAAC WHITE decd
6 DB 247 PAc   taken by WM: KEELING, WILLIAM COX & LAML: CORNICK.

5 Dec 1743   -   Rec 8 Dec 1743 - WILLIAM BALL of Norfolk County to WILLIAM
6 DB 248 PAc   PURDY of PAc .... 50 acres bounded as mentioned in & by
                  Indenture of release thereof made by MOSES BALL & ELIZ: his
wife unto the said WILLIAM BALL dated 1 Jun 1737 duly recorded in PAc.

7 Dec 1743   -   Rec 7 Dec 1743 - REOD^S: MALBON, Mariner of Norfolk County
6 DB 249 PAc   to THO^S: HILL SENR & THO^S: HILL JUNR ... 81 acres of Marsh
                  lying in the TABLE OF PINES & being the proportionable part
that his father REOD^S: MALBON gave him by his last will...................

7 Dec 1743   -   HENRY WOODHOUSE
6 DB 251 PAc   wd 15 Nov 174X wp 7 Dec 1743   Wit: names are missing
                  Exor: wife MARY & son-in-law CHARLES HILL
wife MARY.... negroes her natural life ...after her decease said negroes &
their increase to be equally divided among my four children: WILLIAM,
HORATIO, HENRY & MARY WOODHOUSE .... to my dau AMY HILL... negroes & 100
acres in the EASTERN SHORE SWAMP joyning on the xxxxxxx to my gr-dau MARY
HOxxxx .... to my son xxxxxx the plantation whereon I now live & the land
adjacent to it along the POND SWAMP to the CROSS ROAD that leads to the DAMS
thence xxxxxxx MAINLAND to PHILIP WOODHOUSES land ....to my two sons
WILLIAM & HENRY all my land xxxxxxx not already given away lying in the
EASTERN SHORE SWAMP....... to my son HORATIO WOODHOUSE my plantation at the
xxxxxx xxxxxx xx now lives also all my land on the WESTERN SHORE xxxxxxxxxxx
my four children when they shall come of age or marry......................

7 Dec 1743   -   Appraisal of the Estate of EDWARD OLD decd.................
6 DB 252 PAc   (Most of this is missing)

4 Jan 1743/4 -   Inventory of the Estate of MR: HENRY WOODHOUSE.............
6 DB 252 PAc   (Most of this is missing)

4 Jan 1743/4 -   Inventory of the Estate of ABRAHAM LEGROSS decd............
6 DB 253 PAc   (Most of this is missing)

1 Nov 1743   - Rec 4 Jan 1743/4 - ARTH^r: SAYER to CHARLES SMYTH... one lott
6 DB 254 PAc   or half acre of land in NEWTOWN............................

17 Jan 1743/4- Rec 1 Feb 1743/4 - JAMES WILSON, Planter & ELIZA: his wife
6 DB 255 PAc   of Norfolk County to JOHN WICKENS of PAc .... 50 acres in
               PAc upon the CYPRESS SWAMP running up the GUMM SWAMP to the
one that was called BIGGS LINE.......joyning upon the land of the said JOHN
WICKENS.............

31 Jan 1743/4- Rec 1 Feb 1743/4 - THOMAS CORPREW & JANE his wife of BLACK-
6 DB 258 PAc   WATER in PAc to JOHN SIMMONS .... 250 acres from wards? the
               Mouth of BLACKWATER RIVER to HENRY SOUTHERNS Line ....
mentioned in THOMAS CORPREWS will dated 10 Mar 1721/2 being all that plantation that my father gave me as appears in the abovesaid will..............

1 Feb 1743/4 - ffRANCIS ACKISS
6 DB 260 PAc   wd 21 Feb 1742/3 wp 1 Feb 1743/4
               Exor: wife ANNE & CAPT: JAMES KEMPE
to son JOHN ACKISS the plantation whereon I now live called POSCOSIN QUARTER
& 50 acres of Swamp part of the land purchased by me of MAXIMILLIAN BOUSH ..
... the South side thereof.... to son GEORGE my plantation called HOLLAND &
the land joyning thereto except the 50 acres above given containing 360 acres
..... he left negroes to his 2 sons JOHN & GEORGE .....wife ANNE ....
residue to wife & sons JOHN & GEORGE......................................

1 Feb 1743/4 - Audit of the Estate of MR: JAMES LAMOUNT decd...............
6 DB 261 PAc   Total ₴ 12.4.2

6 Jan 1743/4 - JAMES GRIFFIN
6 DB 261 PAc   Nun.wd 3 Jan 1743/4 wp 6 Jan 1743/4 or after (date not on
               the"order to be recorded")
Brother HENRY GRIFFIN to take all that belongs to him excepting 2 Guines and
a pare of Silver shoe buckles which he gave to JAMES GRIFFIN his brother JOHNS
son ..... this happened Tuesday 3 Jan 1743/4 and he departed this life Friday
the 6 following................. signed MARTHA B xxxxx

7 Jun 1743   - Rec 7 Sep 1743 - Inventory of MR: MATTHEW ELLEGOODS Estate...
6 DB 261 PAc   (These dates are not in order but, even though blurred I can
               make nothing but 1743 out of them.)

Missing 1743 - Rec 7 7ber 1743 - DENNIS CAPPS of NORTH CAROLINA to JOHN RUS-
6 DB 263 PAc   SELL of PAc .... 100 acres in PAc in the UPPER PRECINCT of
               the EASTERN SHORE on NANXXS CREEK (NANNYS?) beginning at JOHN
BURFOOTS Line ...... according to the ancient bounds that the said WM: CAPPS
SENR: laid off to THOMAS WEBB by deed of sale it being part of CAPPS PATTENT
dated xx xxx xxxx granted to him for 500 acres of land......................

17 Feb 1743/4- Rec No date given - JAMES MOORE of Norfolk County............
6 DB 264 PAc   Whereas GEORGE MOSELEY of PAc by mortgage deed 18 Apr 1743 for
               ₴ 50 by me paid ..... sould unto me that plantation in PAc
containing 260 acres ..... taken in my name for MAJOR NATHANIEL NEWTON ....

4 Mar 1743/4 -   (AN?)DREW PEACOCK
6 DB 264 PAc   wd 30 Jan xxxx/x wp 4 Mar 1743/4
                I give & bequeath xxxxxxxxxxxxxxx Estate to my wife ANNE
my whole and sole Executrix...................

7 Mar 1743/4 - Rec 7 Mar 1743/4 - LANCASTER LOVETT to HENRY LAMOUNT .....
6 DB 265 PAc   50 acres of Swamp land on the EASTERN SHORE & binding on the
                lands of CAPT: MOORES & PHILLIP WOODHOUSES..................

31 Jul 1743 - Rec 7 Mar 1743/4 - REODOLPHUS MALBONE to MATT^W: PALLET
6 DB 266 PAc   (Couldn't read this one)

10 Dec 1743 - Rec 4 Jul 1744 - (The date is written as shown) ABRAHAM
6 DB 268 PAc   WILLEROY of PAc, Planter to COLL: ANTHONY WALKE, GENT:.......
                75 acres in PAc on the South side of the EASTERN BRANCH com-
monly called by the name of the CYPRESS & bounded as mentioned in deeds of
lease and release made by WM: ffENTRISS decd to ABRAHAM WILLEROY dated 7 & 8
Dec 1743 .... & negroes ....

7 Dec 1743   - Rec 7 Mar 1743/4 - JOHN BUCKNER to JOHN SWENY .... 100 acres
6 DB 270 PAc   & bounded as followeth upon WILLOUGHBY MERCHANTS land along
                the dams to the pocoson & so along the side of the pocoson
to KEADOR? MERCHANTS line ....&c................

16 Mar 1743/4- Rec 7 Mar 1743/4 - WILLIAM (GUTTON?) WHITE to CAPT: WILLIAM
6 DB 272 PAc   KEELING ..... 50 acres binding on CAPT: WILLIAM KEELINGS land
                (Parts of this are missing)

6 Mar 1743/4 - Rec 7 Mar 1743/4 - PETER JOLLIFF (JOLLEY in margin) to NATH-
6 DB 274 PAc   ANIEL MARTIN .... 57 acres on the EASTERN SHORE in the Parrish
                of LINHAVEN & is the same which PETER -missing- bought of JOHN
SWEENEY & being the same which THO: MOORE left in his -missing- & Testament to
be sold at Public Sale ....

6 DB 275 PAc - The handwriting changes on the following release.

6 Mar 1743/4 - Release - PETER JOLLIFF to NATHANIEL MARTIN .....(see above
6 DB 275 PAc   item)lying upon the NORTHERN BRANCHES xxxxxatural in LYNHAVEN
                PARRISH ..... along JOHN CIVALLS line .... JAMES MOORES line...

xx Feb 1743/4- Rec 7 Mar 1743/4 - WILLIAM PURDY & URSULLA his wife to ARTHUR
6 DB 276 PAc   ..... URSULLA is sister and co-heir of xxxxx IVY...(this lease
                is just scraps) - the release on pp 277 & 278 shows - ....all
that the said part in 3 parts to be divided of that Plantation of land whereon
JOHN IVY father of the said URSULLA lately lived .... containing 600 acres
in the EASTERN BRANCH of ELIZABETH RIVER........(What is left of this is hard
to read)

7 Mar 1743/4 - Audit of the Estate of MRS: MARGARET MALBONE ....
6 DB 279 PAc

6 Mar 1743/4   - Rec 7 Mar 1743/4 - THO: HILL SENR: to JOHN BONNEY & JOHN
6 DB 280 PAc   HILL ..... 20 acres of Marsh near the TABLE of PINES form-
                  erly sold by REODOLPHUS MALBONE, Mariner to the said THOMAS
HILL.....................................

6 Mar 1743/4   - Rec 7 Mar 1743/4 - LANCASTER LOVETT to PHILLIP WOODHOUSE
6 DB 282 PAc   50 acres of Swampland on the EASTERN SHORE & binding on the
                  lands of CAPT: BOUSHES & RICHMONDS & HENRY LAMOUNTS ....

6 Mar 1743/4   - Rec 7 Mar 1743/4 - THO^S: LANGLEY to JOHN HUNTER ....
6 DB 284 PAc   50 acres of the remaining part of the Marsh commonly called
                  the GREAT MARSH .... which Marsh COL^O: GEORGE NEWTON
bought of REASON? (or BASON?) MORSE in PAc xxxx pattent granted to CAPT: FRAN-
CIS MORSE decd dated 2X Apr 1711 better known by the name of SURRY (or SWENY?)
PLANTATION, said pattent   752 acres of land & Marsh ....

4 Jun 1743   - Rec 4 Jul 1744 - (dates between pages 261 & 309 are not in
6 DB 286 PAc   cronological order) ....WILLIAM BROCK to JAMES FITZ-
                 GARRALD ..... 81 acres of land on the EASTERN SHORE PRECINCT
....beginning at a gum & running xxx lines to the BAY SIDE...................

4 Jul 1744   - HENRY GRIFFEN (H)
6 DB 288 PAc   wd 18 Apr 1744 wp 4 Jul 1744 by ABIGAIL GRIFFEN & MARTHA
                 HOLMES (or HOLMAN?) Exix: wife MARGARET
..to son HENRY GRIFFEN the land & Plantation I now live on...................
residue to wife MARGARET GRIFFEN during her natural life.....................

XX May 1744   - Rec 4 Jul 1743 (sic) Division of the negroes belonging to
6 DB 288 PAc   the Estate of MR: WILL^m: LILBURN DECD & have alloted to the
                 said OLIVE LILBURN one negro wench et als .... & OLIVE
LILBURN to pay her brother ABRAHAM LILBURN 40/. (It was thought that this
name should be GISBURN, but it does not look like it in any of the spellings)

6 Jun 1744   - Rec 4 Jul 1744 - THO^S: GARNOR to JOHN BURFOOT ..... 25 acres
6 DB 288 PAc   ..... at a stake standing by the Road .....to an oak stand-
                 ing at the head of the Branch............................

4 Jul 1744   - GEORGE WEBLIN SENR:
6 DB 291   wd 21 Feb 17XX wp 4 Jul 1744 Exix: wife & kinsman GEORGE
                 WEBLIN. .... to son JOHN WEBLIN my Plantation
joyning on a Plantation called BIDDLES MYES? PLANTATION known by the name of
CODDS & 50 acres of Swamp that joyneth HOLLAND .... & slaves.....&c......
wife MARY......... xxx younger children .... four daughters ELIZA:, MARY,
HESTER & SUSANNAH WEBLIN............(The right side of this will is missing.)

4 Jul 1744   - Inventory of xxxxxx LANGLEY decd Estate (first name missing)
6 DB 291 PAc   (Hard to read, very short, and is probably an addition to an
                 earlier Audit)

4 Jul 1744   - MR: HENRY WOODHOUSE ESTATE, additions to the Inventory of
6 DB 291 PAc

4 Jul 1744   -   JAMES FENTRISS
6 DB 292 PAc   wd 8 Apr 1743 wp4 Jul 1744 Witnesses names are missing.
                  Exor: THOS: WALKE & EDWD: MOSELEY (X)
"April the 8 day which was my birthday and to the best of my remembrance I
am 60 years of age".   Wife: ELIZA:......... dau LEAH FENTRISS reversion to
her ..... sister SARAH ANN FENTRISS ...... sons ABSALOM FENTRISS, JAMES FAN-
TRISS, HORATIO FENTRISS & (PHARO?) FENTRISS ..... daus ELIZABETH, TAMOR and
PAELOM? EDGAR.... 3 gr-children MASON?, WILLXXX, and MARY XDGAR...........4
daus LEAH, SARAH ANN, ELIZAth:, TAMER FENTRISS when they come of age........

25 May 1744   -   Rec 4 Jul 1744 - COL: ANTHONY WALKE, GENT: to LEML: CORNICK
6 DB 293 PAc   40? acres xxxxxxxxxxxxxxx and along said LANCASTER LOVETTS
                  line .... & the land JOHN xxxxxxx sold to WILLIAM
ATTWOOD ..... being a tract of land which LEWIS xxxxxxxxsold JOHN FULCHER
JUNR: by a deed 1 Mar 16XX/X (Parts of this are missing, but a study of this
and the release may reveal more- see what follows)

The release of the above gives bounds: beginning at a pine XXXX of LANCASTER
LOVETTS formerly FRANCIS BONDS line and along said LOVETTS xxxxxxxxx Chinco-
pine a corner tree of said LOVETTS then along a line of mkd trees to BROCKS
SWAMP that divided this land & the land JOHN WOODHOUSE sold xxxx LOVETT to
EDWD: ATWOODS line along ATWOODS line to a mkd red oake xxxx along the line
that divides this land JOHN WOODHOUSE sold to WILLIAM xxxxod? to the first
station being part of a tract of land which LEWIS PURVINE (sold?) JOHN FULCHER
JUNR: by a Deed bearing date 1 Mar 1698.....................................

3 Jul 1744   -   Rec 4 Jul 1744 - CAPT: LEML: LANGLEY of Norfolk County to JOHN
6 DB 295 PAc   HENLY   xxxxx   60 acres .. an equal half part of a plantation
                  in PAc. The release on p 296 gives more information.   ANN
LANGLEY acknowledged the release.

3 Jul 1744   -   Rec 4 Jul 1744 - ROBERT THOROWGOOD to ADAM THOROWGOOD 100
6 DB 297 PAc   acres in LYNHAVEN PARISH..(The release is on p 298 recorded
                  the same day. The bounds are given, however, both sides of
the page are torn off).

7 Dec 1743   -   Rec 4 Jul 1744 - WILLIAM FENTRISS SENR: to ABRAHAM WILLEROY
6 DB 299 PAc   70 acres of land in PAc on the South side of the XXXXXXXXXX
                  Branch called by the name of the CYPRESS xxxxxxx xxxxxxxxx
a corner tree of TULLY MOSELEYS ....(The release follows on the next page)

(NOTE: The dates change here to April 1744 which is out of place and may be
explained by the factthat the middle of this book is badly torn and has been
restored, and the pagination is new.)

4 Apr 1744   -   WILLIAM (W) CAPPS of Lynhaven
6 DB 301 PAc   wd 11 Oct XXXX wp 4 Apr 1744   Exor: son GEORGE CAPPS
                  Wife ELIZA: sons JOHN under age, FRANCIS CAPPS, HENRY CAPPS,
GEORGE CAPPS, RICHARD CAPPS, HORATIO underage and my son XXXX ... dau SARAH....

4 Apr 1744   -   BENJAMIN CUMMINGS of Blackwater
6 DB 301 PAc   wd XX Feb 1743/4 wp 4 Apr 1744   .. wife ELIZA: ....
                  sons MARTIN CUMMINGS, BENJA: CUMMINGS.......................

20 Feb 1743/4 - Rec 4 Apr 1744 - ROBT: TODD, Merchant to EMPEROR MOSELEY ....
6 DB 302 PAc   North East lotts in the Division B in NEWTOWN lying on the
                West xxxx of the Street going down to the KETCH LANDING.

4 Apr 1744   - Rec 4 Apr 1744 - JAMES SMITH to SIMON WHITEHURST ... 75 acres
6 DB 303 PAc   in the NORTHWOODS of PAc.... page 306 - MARY Mother of and
               SARAH wife of JAMES SMITH relinquished all their right thereunt

4 Apr 1744   - Rec 4 Apr 1744 - THOMAS CONNER to ROBT: JONES ... 60 acres ....
6 DB 306 PAc   joyning upon THOS: HENLYS & ABROSE (AMBROSE?) BURFOOTS & HENRY
               CORNICKS lines..............

12 Mar 1743/4 - Rec 2 May 1744 - Audit of the EState of PALMER MOSELEY decd...
6 DB 308 PAc   To sundry debts in the office   Ł 6.1.8 12
                To D⁰   paid the widow   3.5.0
                Balance due to the Estate   53.9.7 1/2
                (Estate had been sold at outcry)   Ł62.17.2

29 Apr 1744   - Rec 2 May 1744 - BENJAMIN CUMMIN(GS) decd - Inventory of his
6 DB 308 PAc   Estate was signed by ELIZ: (M) CUMINGS.

3 May 1744   - Appraisement of the Estate of MR: FRANCIS ACKISS decd in 1743.
6 DB 308 PAc

30 Apr 1744   - Rec 3 May 1744 - RICHD: (R) CAPPS, Planter to GEORGE CAPPS
6 DB 309 PAc   40 acres in MUDDY CREEK & is the same 40 acres lately devised
                to said GEORGE CAPPS in the last will of his father WILLIAM
CAPPS decd.

24 Jul 1744   - Rec 1 Aug 1744 - WILLM: MOSELEY to CHARLES SMYTH, GENT: One
6 DB 311 PAc   lott or 1/2 acre in NEWTOWN beginning at a stone upon the
                Northmost side of the BACK STREET in the xxxx ....

30 Jul 1744   - Rec 1 Aug 1744 - SOLOMON WILLYS (also spelled WILLE) of NORTH
6 DB 313 PAc   CAROLINA to MOSES ROBERTS of PAc.... 50 acres in PAc at a
                place called DAMN'D NECK (sic) .... bounded on the land of
THOS: TURNER on one part & joyning on the land of MOSES ROBERTS the now purchaser...........

30 Jul 1744   - Rec 1 Aug 1744 - Appraisal of the Estate of MR. GEO: WEBLIN
6 DB 315 PAc   decd...........

1 Aug 1744   - Rec 1 Aug 1744 - Audit of the estate of JOHN GRIFFIN decd
6 DB 316 PAc

4 Sep 1744   - Rec 5 Sep 1744 - WILLIAM WORMINTON of Norfolk County.......
6 DB 316 PAc   Whereas my father JOHN WORMINTON decd purchased of ADAM
                FORGESSON (FERGUSON?) 120 acres in PAc in precinct of BLACK-
WATER by Deed recorded in PAc 1 Oct 1710 ......Whereas my father did desire
by his nun-cupative will that his daughter GRACE WORMINTON & her heirs should
be possessed of said land........I the said WILLIAM for the love & affection
I bear to my said sister GRACE confirm a xxxxx of her title to the same......

1 Oct 1744   -   Rec 4 Oct 1744 - Audit of the estate of THOS: IVY decd ....
6 DB 317 PAc   To CAPT JOHN IVYS Estate....... By sale of Estate..........

26 May 1744 -   Rec 3 Oct 1744 - Audit of the Estate of ROBT: RICHMOND JUNR:
6 DB 317 PAc   decd........ to bill due to WILLIAM RICHMONDS decd Estate...
                (Estate was apparently sold or partially sold. There is a
long list of names, but the amounts are torn or illegible.)

30 Jun 1744 -   Rec 3 Oct 1744 - THOMAS OLD & LELIE? his wife of Blackwater
6 DB 318 PAc   (Her sign looks like Letia^a, could it be Letitia?)   to
                JOHN ELKS ... a parcell of land on the ASH BRANCH ....

6 Nov 1744   -   Rec 7 Nov 1744 - FRANCIS (F) SHIP to JOHN SHIP 200 acres on
6 DB 321 PAc   the South side of the EASTERN BRANCH called by the name of
                the CYPRESS NECK (more complete bounds are given in the re-
lease on page 322) DINAH wife of said FRANCIS relinquished her right of dower.

1 Sep 1744   -   Rec 7 Nov? XXXX (Must be 1744) LEML: WHITEHURST to COL^O: ANTH-
6 DB 323 PAc   ONY WALKE ... 150 acres on the South side of the EASTERN
                BRANCH of Elizabeth River & is the same land which THOS:
WHITEHURST decd gave in his last will dated 9 Jan 17X7/8 to the abovesaid
LEML: WHITEHURST his son........................

XX XXX 1744 -   Rec (1744 is the only date showing) Audit of the Estate of
6 DB 324 PAc   LANCASTER LOVETT decd......... to be divided between his
                xxxe (wife?) & 7 children according to the said decedents last
will according to sale & appraisement due to his widow - torn - Total to be
divided was Ƚ 118.19.9 (There is more of this, but the page is partially
missing.)

6 Nov 1744   -   Rec 7 Nov 1744 - JOHN BURFOOT & JAMES ALBRITTON to JOHN
6 DB 325 PAc   BUSHBY SENR: 131 acres on the East side of BROCKS BRIDGE.....
                ELIZA: wife of the said JAMES relinquished all her right &c...

3 DB 327   -   The bottom and sides of this page are missing and the writing
                that is left is blurred. It is the beginning of JOHN NICHOLAS
                will, the remnants of which follow:

7 Nov 1744   -   JOHN NICHOLAS
6 DB 328 PAc   wd 22 Mar 1744 (1743/4?) wp 4 Jul 1744 by EDWD: HACK MOSELEY
                and THOMAS WALKE
The executor thereto refusing to take the burthen thereof the heir at law being summoned & having nothing to say why the said will should not be proved &
admitted to record... at a Court held 7 Nov 1744 administration granted to
MRS: YATES NICHOLAS his widow.   .... the youngest (ANN) underage .....
two daughters ELIZA: & ANN.........the Lott in NEWTOWN to be sold ....
if the two daughters die then estate to be divided between my two sxxxxxx
(sisters?) xxxx & ELIZA: & my brother ISAIAH NICHOLAS.......................
Executors: brother ISAIAH NICHOLAS & NATHL: McCLANAHAN.

14 Sep 1744 -   Rec 2 Jan 1744/5 - JOHN RUSSELL to JAMES JACKSON of Norfolk
6 DB 329 PAc   County ... 35 acres one certain Point of Land & Marsh upon
                NANNYS CREEK (bounds are given) ....to the outside line
of said RUSSELLS land that he bought of DENNIS CAPPS ......running upon
CORNICKS line.............

20 Dec 1741   - Rec 2 Jan 1744/5 - CAPT: ANDREW NICHOLAS to MR: ROBERT
6 DB 331 PAc   TODD, Merchant .....Deed of sale of negroes..........

29 Nov 1744   - Rec 2 Jan 1744/5 - CAPT: GEORGE WISHART to JOHN RUSSELL
6 DB 332 PAc   100 acres of Marsh being near KNOTTS ISLAND PARRISH of
                 PAc .... REV. HENRY BARLOWS CREEK thence across
OYSTER SHELL CREEK ....binding on XXXX Marsh of RICHD: POOLE decd
formerly bought of ROBERT DUDLEY ....(There are missing parts
in both the lease and release, however, a careful study might possibly give
the complete bounds)

29 Dec? 1744 - Rec 2 Jan 1744/5 - JAMES NIMMO to CAPT: JAMES KEMPE   300
6 DB 335 PAc   acres of Marsh in NAXXXX CREEK in Lynhaven Parrish upon a
                 Creek that makes out of DOLLEYSBAY xxxx ..... to SANDYS
COVE xxxxxxx to the GREAT NARROWS that makes into the said BAY including
an Island lying Easterly from said NARROWS & binding upon DOLLEYS BAY about
50 acres .... xxxx NANNYS CREEK BAY to a cove called GREEN? KILL? COVE
(Parts of both pages missing)

3 Dec 1744   - Rec 5 Dec 1744 - Inventory of the Estate of THOS: HARRISON
6 DB 337 PAc   decd. (This was presented in Court 5 Dec 1744)

3 Feb 1744/5 - Rec 6 Feb 1744/5 - COL: ANTHONY WALKE to MR: WILLIAM CART-
6 DB 338 PAc   WRIGHT   670 acres in the WESTERN XXXXX of the Parrish of
                 Lynhaven whereon xxxxxxx formerly lived & is the same land
said COL: ANTHONY WALKE purchased of CASON XXXXX (MOORE?) & MARY his wife
1 Apr 1741..............(Bounds are not given.)

Date Missing - Rec 6 Feb 1744/5 - ROGER HATTON to AQUILA MUNDEN... Bounds
6 DB 340 PAc   are given, but large pieces of this are missing.

6 Feb 1744/5 - Rec 6 Feb 1744/5 - JOHN MUNDEN to MOSES ROBERTS 75 acres
6 DB 342 PAc   (There are missing pieces of these pages)

7 Aug 1742 - Pvd 7 Nov 1744 - Rec 6 Feb 1744/5 - FRANCES CORBETT late the
6 DB 345 PAc   wife of RICHD: CORBETT decd to COL: ANTHONY WALKE who lately
                 purchased of RICHD: CORBETT son & heir of abovesaid RICHD:
CORBETT decd 240 acres in Lynhaven Parrish 7 Aug 1742 receipts whereof the
said FRANCES CORBETT hereby acknowledges................

3 Feb 1744/5 - Rec 6 Feb 1744/5 - MR: WILLIAM CARTWRIGHT to CAPT: JAMES
6 DB 346 PAc   KEMPE 150 acres in the EASTERN BRANCH PRECINCT ... 100 acres
                 of which was purchased by ROBERT CARTWRIGHT father of the
abovesaid WILLIAM CARTWRIGHTof THOS: SOLLEY as by deed 2 Oct 1684 and the
other 50 acres purchased by abovesaid WILLIAM CARTWRIGHT of WILLM: PURDY by
deed 6 Feb 1732? ......(No bounds given)

4 Feb 1744/5 - Rec 6 Feb 1744/5 - JOHN BURFOOT to WILLIAM WEBLIN... 96
6 DB 348 PAc   acres on the EASTERN SHORE......(Bounds are given)

29 Jan 1744/5 - Rec 6 Feb 1744/5 - JOHN BRINSON only son and heir at law
6 DB 351 PAc   of THOS: BRINSON & MARY his wife who was one of the two

sisters and co-heirs of EDWD: LAND JUNR: decd to CAPT: GEORGE WISHART 170 acres .... the full tract & equall half of all that plantation in the WESTERN SHORE in Lynhaven Parrish whereon EDWD: LAND grandfather of the said JOHN BRINSON party to these presents formerly lived ....

3 Feb 1744/5   -   Rec 6 Feb 1744/5 - CAPT: JAMES KEMPE & wife FRANCES to COL:
6 DB 354 PAc   ANTHONY WALKE 400 acres in LITTLE CREEK & is the same land
                    whereon CAPT: GEO: HANCOCK decd formerly lived & died......

3 Dec 1744   -   Rec 6 Feb 1744/5 - MATHEW PALLET deed of gift to "My loving
6 DB 357 PAc   friend" JOHN SWENY.... a parcel of land near JOB GASKINGS..

6 Feb 1744/5   -   THOMAS (+) TAYLOR
6 DB 358 PAc   wd 29 Dec 1744 Codicile 31 Dec 1744 wp 6 Feb 1744/5 by
                    JONAS TAYLOR & THOS: BUTT & also at a Court held 8 May 1745
was further proved.   Exor: wife SARAH & friend ANTHONY MOSELEY
...wife SARAH use & labor of negroes & Plantation during my son WILLM: TAYLORS
minority...and other things..... my youngest dau ANN TAYLOR... son THOS: TAY-
LOR...... WILLIAM not to be possesses of some of his legacies "until his
mother-in-law removes all out of my Dwelling House"... son JOHN TAYLOR my
Plantation in Norfolk County at the head of JULIANS CREEK.....son JAMES TAYLOR
...daus MARTHA TAYLOR, MARY TAYLOR when she is 21 years of age, ELIZA: TAYLOR
underage, ANN TAYLOR........ my wife to keep my dau ELIZA: & my son JAMES & my
dau MARTHA & MARY....He left ship carpenters tools and a lot of slaves........

6 Feb 1744/5   -   THOMAS (X) WILES SENR:, Cordwainer
6 DB 361 PAc   wd Not given wp 6 Feb 1744/5 Exors: sons THOS: & SAML:
                    son ANTHONY WILES, Mariner [who settled in the City of BRIS-
TOL in GREAT BRITAIN] one gun of the value of 40/ in full of his part of my
estate..... sons THOMAS, LEMUEL & SAMUEL WILES & my 3 daus SARAH ANN, MARY &
ELIZA: [my six children] all the lands to them severally given in a Deed of
Gift dated 7 May 1735............

6 Feb 1744/5   -   MARTIN BURROUGHS
6 DB 362 PAc   wd 2 Feb 1743/4 wp 6 Feb 1744/5   Exor: cousin JOHN BROWN
                    to RACHEL DALE .... to ELIZA: KEELING dau of WILLIAM KEELING
.... to BETTY DALE dau of WILLIAM DALE .... to WILLM: DALE .... to ANTHONY
BURROUGHS JUNR: .... to ELIZA: SHEPHERD dau of SMITH SHEPHERD .... to WILLM:
CROMPTON .... to my cousin JANE BROWN 15/ out of my estate to buy a gold ring
for MARY ANN DALE dau of PETER DALE .... to my cousin EZEKIALL BROWN a cow at
JOHN WILBORES .... to my cousin JOHN BROWN all the remainder part of my estate
paying all my debts &c ....

5 Mar 1744/5   -   Rec 6 Mar 1744/5 - COLL: JACOB ELLEGOOD to ELIZA: WHITE one
6 DB 363 PAc   of the daughters & co-heirs of ISAAC WHITE late of PAc decd
                    150 acres [the half part of 300 acres] on the EASTERN SHORE
which said ELLEGOOD purchased 16 Oct 1741 of ISAAC WHITE & SARAH his wife &
is the same land which said ISAAC WHITE gave to his daughter ELIZA: in & by
his last will .... being the plantation whereon ROBT: BURROUGHS lived.....
lying on the EASTERN SHORE in Lynhaven Parrish................................

5 Mar 1744/5 - Rec 6 Mar 1744/5 - COLL: JACOB ELLEGOOD to SARAH WHITE one
6 DB 365 PAc   of the two daughters & co-heirs of ISAAC WHITE ...150 acres
                  ... SARAHS half part of the land in the previous deed .....
(These deeds of lease and release are practically duplicates of those to her
sister ELIZA:)

8 Feb 1744/5 - Rec No Court Date Given - JOHN THOROWGOOD JUNR: as inter-
6 DB 368 PAc   marrying with MRS: MARY ANNE THOROWGOOD...Whereas JOHN WILSON
                  by Mortgage Deed 4 Feb 1741 for Ł 20 to him in hand paid by
MRS: ANNE TREVATHAN in trust for the abovesd MARY ANNE THOROWGOOD sold unto
the said ANNE TREVATHAN in trust 400 acres at the BACK BAY .... Whereas
DENNIS CAPPS has lately purchased the Fee Simple estate in the said land from
the said JOHN WILSON as by Deeds unto the said DENNIS CAPPS may appear......&
for the better securing the said JOHN WILSON & his heirs....&c...............
                                    signed: JOHN THOROWGOOD

19 Feb 1744/5 - Rec 6 Mar 1744/5 - JOHN (I) WILSON to DENNIS CAPPS 380 acres
6 DB 369 PAc   in the UPPER PRECINCT of the EASTERN SHORE of PAc at the BACK
                  BAY .... 300 acres of which said JOHN WILSON bought of
CAPT: GEORGE WISHART & CAPT: JAMES KEMPE ... the other 80 acres being that
land sold by order of Court at Public Sale by WM: ROBINSON Sheriff that formerly belonged to WM: FLEAR..................

26 Dec 1742   - Rec 6 Mar 1744/5 - THOS: (T) PERRY SENR: & MARY his wife to
6 DB 372 PAc   JOSIAS MORRIS 100 acres being part of a xxxx called DABBS
                  RIDGE ....EASTERN SWAMP .... GREEN POND...........

5 Mar 1744/5 - Rec 6 Mar 1744/5 - THOROWGOOD BRINSON to HARRISON BANKS 100
6 DB 374 PAc   acres .... which CASON MOORE the ELDER bought of EDWD: HAYES
                  in the EASTERN SHORE of Lynhaven Parish ..... joyning on the
land that THOMAS HENLY SENR now lives on...................

No date   - Rec 6 Mar 1744/5 - Audit of the Estate of ROBT: RICHMOND
6 DB 377 PAc   SENR: decd .... to WILLIAM RICHMOND his Exor............
                  To ELIZA: RICHMOND part of her legacy left her by ESTHER
POOLE Ł 13.5 .... By Inventory appraisal amounts to Ł 97.14.6.......

Rec 6 Mar 1744/5 - Audit of the Estate of WILLIAM RICHMOND decd.............
6 DB 378 PAc   To CAPT: WILLIAM KEELING his Exor...... To ELIZA: BOUSH per
                  order .... Paid ROBT: RICHMOND JUNR: his proportion of
his fathers Estate Ł 16.13.10.

2 Apr 1745   - Rec 3 Apr 1745 - JOHN (Ŧ) CAPPS to THOS: LANGLEY 100 acres
6 DB 379 PAc   .... a Plantation on the EASTERN SHORE in Lynhaven Precinct
                  & is the same which HENRY DAULEY sold to JOHN CAPPS.......

10 Mar 1744/5 - Rec 3 Apr 1745 - WILLIAM MOSELEY of Norfolk Borough, Mariner
6 DB 382 PAc   to EDWD: HACK MOSELEY of PAc, Merchant 35 acres on the
                  North side of the EASTERN BRANCH of ELIZA: RIVER & is bound-
ed beginning at a black beech near a Branch that has a Bridge over it & runs
along the ROAD to NEWTOWN NE by E 80 poles to HANCOCKS Line in WHITE PINE
NECK & so along the said HANCOCKS Line & the said road leading to IVYS S by E
to a large white oak a corner tree & th SWbyW to a corner tree th NbyW 5° W

70 poles to the first station.

2 Apr 1745   -   Rec 3 Apr 1745 - JAMES WILLIAMS to JOHN AIRES (HARRIS?)   70
6 DB 385 PAc   acres in Lynhaven Parish & is the same land which JAMES WIL-
               LIAMS decd bought of JOB? BROOKS as by Deed 31 Oct 1698.....

2 Apr 1745   -   Rec 3 Apr 1745 - JOHN CAPPS to THOROWGOOD BRINSON   60 acres
6 DB 387 PAc   ...a plantation at a place called MUDDY CREEK & is the land
               that RICHD: CAPPS his father lived on.....................

3 Apr 1745   -   CAPT: HENRY MOORE SENR:
6 DB 390 PAc   wd 27 Aug 1742 wp 3 Apr 1745 by FRANCIS MALBONE & COL:
               JACOB ELLEGOOD.   Exor: wife MARY
wife MARY the whole use & benefit of my Plantation whereon I now live......
during her widowhood........ also 5 negroes: Tom, Wend, Moll, Jemmy & Judy
to her and hers forever....& residue of Estate......son HENRY MOORE the
Plantation & negro boy Africa....son THO: MOORE the Plantation whereon he
now lives also negro woman Jenny ...... to sister Sean^a: (Susana?) CHESHIRE
negro man Philip .... to son JAMES MOORE my Plantation in the Swamp called
BEAR QUARTER also my negroman Mingo .....to dau SARAH MOORE my negro Charles
& Nanny & Benny .... to my 2 sons WOODHOUSE & CASON MOORE my negro woman
Bess & her 2 children Cuffy & Jasper ...... to son ANTHONY MOORE my Planta-
tion in the swamp called LITTLE POPLAR RIDGE ..... to dau SUSANNA MOORE
negro girl Pegg ..... to my 5 youngest children named ANTHONY, XXXX, EDWD:
SUSANNAH & CHARLES all underage, negroes.........

6 Feb 1744/5 -   Taken 14 Feb Rec 3 Apr 1745 - Appraisal of THOS: TAYLOR decd
6 DB 391 PAc   Estate .... Figures are not totaled.

4 Jan 1744/5 -   Rec 1 May 1745 - ISRAEL SLAUGHTER (signature is SLATTER) &
6 DB 392 PAc   his wife LIDIA to LAWRENCE DOYLEY   60 acres in BLACKWATER
               called LANDING NECK beginning AT A Creek runing E ....

30 Apr 1745 -   Rec 1 May 1745 - WILLIAM RICHMOND (signature RICHMAN), Planter
6 DB 395 PAc   · to JOHN RAINEY, Planter 50 acres of Marsh & Sand Banke lying
               between LYNHAVEN BAY & LONG CREEK being part of the Marsh MR:
ROBT: RICHMOND decd gave to him in his will.................................

3 Mar 1744/5 -   Rec 1 May 1745 - WILLIAM MARTIN & wife ANN Deed of Gift to
6 DB 397 PAc   her loving son JOHN ACKISS... a negro girl .... if JOHN ACKISS
               should die under lawful age without issue .... said negro to
descend to GEORGE ASKISS brother of the said JOHN if both die underage ....
negro to return to the said ANN wife of said WILLM:..........

1 May 1745   -   WILLM: SMITH
6 DB 398 PAc   wd No date on will wp 1 May 1745   Exor: wife ANN & son
               SOLOMON .... to wife ANN SMITH my Riding horse........
to son WILLM: SMITH .... to daus WINNE SMITH, SARAH SMITH, ELIZA: SMITH &
SUSANNA XXXX (her last name is not Smith) .... to sons THOS: & SOLOMON SMITH
... to my four daughters four pewter dishes.............................

1 May 1745   -   Rec 1 May 1745 - Audit of the Estate of EDWARD GISBURN
6 DB 399 PAc   To the widow .... By sale of the Estate ₤ 17.9.4
                  By ELIZ: GISBURN ₤ 10...... Total ₤ 44.14.4.............

3 Apr 1745 - Taken 1 May 1745 & Rec. same day - Audit of the Estate of
6 DB 400 PAc   WILLIAM GORNTO decd to MARGARET GORNTO administrator.....
                  Appraisal amounted to ₤ 32.16.6.............

30 Apr 1745   -   Rec 5 Jun 1745 - THOS: MOORE to JAMES MOORE 75 acres in the
6 DB 400 PAc   UPPER PRECINCT of the EASTERN SHORE being the Southward part
                  of the said THOS: MOORES plantation......................

18 May 1745   -   Rec 5 Jun 1745 - MR: LEWIS CONNER of Norfolk County to
6 DB 403 PAc   THOMAS WALKE of PAc ... 350 acres, a certain parcel & Island
                  & Marsh in PAc in a place called the TABLE OF PINES .... be-
ing all that remains not sold by him ... of a certain parcell & Island &
Marsh purchased by said CONNERS Father from EDWARD LAMOUNT in 1708 containing
1775 acres & bounded .... at a place called MALBONES UPGOING? ....
bounding on the said LAMOUNTS MARSH .... to the BACK BAY thence bounding
on the BACK BAY & LONG ISLAND CREEK including LITTLE CEDAR ISLAND & another
Island to the NW of LITTLE CEDAR ISLAND....&c.. bounds given in full........

5 Jun 1745   -   Rec 5 Jun 1745 - MARY (H) WALKER now the wife of GEORGE WALKER
6 DB 406 PAc   with the consent of my son JAMES OAST to GEORGE WALKER........
                  a Plantation of land which descended to the said MARY from
XXXX SMITH her father by the last will of RICHARD XXXXXX decd dated 27 Jan
1688/9.....(This is very hard to read)

2 Jul 1745   -   Rec 3 Jul 1745 - COL: ANTHONY WALKE to THOMAS WALKE one lott
6 DB 409 PAc   & a half or 3/4 acre bounded Northerly on CAPT: JAMES KEMPES
                  Land, Ely & Sly on said COL: ANTHONY WALKES Land Wly on XXXX
& Head of the EASTERN BRANCH.............................

4 Jun 1744   -   Rec 3 Jul 1745 - JOHN SWENY (Slaymaker?) to RICHARD TAYLOR,
6 DB 411 PAc   Joyner ..... 100 acres in BLACKWATER & is the same land said
                  JOHN SWENY PURCHASED OF JOHN BUCKNER by Deed 8 Dec 1743.

Rec 3 Jul 1743   WILLIAM GOOCH appointing Sheriff of PAc. (This is a bond
6 DB 414 PAc   and it is almost impossible to read)

6 Aug 1745   -   Rec 7 Aug 1745 - JOSIAS? MORRIS to FRANCIS SHIPP 100 acres
6 DB 414a PAc   in the UPPER PRECINCT of the EASTERN SHORE.................

7 Aug 1745   -   RICHARD TAYLOR
6 DB 416 PAc   wd 1 Jul 1745 wp 7 Aug 1745   Exor: Part of will is missing.
                  ... son ROBERT TAYLOR all that I am possessed with with rev-
ersion to my sister MARY - can't read the name - ....

6 Aug 1745   -   SAMUEL BARRINGTON of Norfolk County to ABEL EDMONDS 25 acres
6 DB 417 PAc   on the South side of the EASTERN BRANCH bounded on East by a
                  run that divides this land from land of MRS: ELIZA: McCLANA-
HAN on the No by land of HUGH WHITEHURST, on W by land of CAPT: JOHN NICHOLAS
.................(the record gets blurred)

34

21 XXX 1744   -   Rec ? - WILLIAM WHITES Mortgage Deed to WILLIAM KEELING
6 DB 419 PAc   (This is badly blurred with parts missing)

6 Jul 1745   -   Rec 7 Aug 1745 - JAMES BROUGHTON & ANN his wife of Norfolk
6 DB 421 PAc   County to DOC^{tr}: GEORGE RAMSEY of the Borrough of Norfolk.
                  150 acres of land, a Plantation in BROAD CREEK & is the
same Plantation devised to the said ANN wife of said JAMES BROUGHTON by the
last will of WILLIAM MARTIN late of Princess Anne County decd 8 Jun 1714...
excepting 99 acres formerly sold to THOS: TAYLOR decd by the said JAMES &
ANN his wife...............

3 Sep 1745   -   Rec 4 Sep 1745 - JOHN AIRES (HARRIS?) & RUTH his wife to
6 DB 425 PAc   SOLOMON WHITEHURST...... 50 acres ..... & is part of the
                  same land which PETER CRA(SH?)LY gave to his daughter,ANN,
the wife of MICHAEL EATON, in his last will........(In the margin of the
release the name is spelled AIRSI and in the release the bounds are given
but are very hard to read.)

No date   -   Rec 4 Sep 1745 - THOS: (X) MOORE Indebted to JAMES MOORE
6 DB 428 PAc   in the sum of ₺ 20 in lieu thereof 40 acres in the UPPER
                  of the EASTERN SHORE being the same land which the said
THOS: MOORE bought of JOHN DYER & his wife .... to which payment will
be truly made..................

3 Sep XXX4   -   Rec XX XXX 1745 - Appraisal of the Estate of XXXX SMITH
6 DB 429 PAc   (SMYTH in margin) There are a lot of holes in this.

27 Jul 1745   -   Rec 4 Sep 1745 - Audit of the Estate of HENRY MOORE decd.
6 DB 430 PAc   Signed by MARY MOORE.

4 Sep 1745   -   ANN (X) COLLINS
6 DB 431 PAc   wd 25 Dec 1738? wp 4 Sep 1745 Presented in Court by JAS:
                  CHAPMAN.   Exor: my brother MARK POWELL
dau SARAH COLLINS ...son GEORGE COLLINS ..brother MARK POWELL.............

7 Oct 1745   -   The Bond of WILLIAM COX, GENT: appointed Sheriff of PAc
6 DB 431 PAc   by WILLIAM GOOCH ESQR:

5 Nov 1745   -   Rec 6 Nov 1745 - CHARLES SMYTH to GEORGE JAMMESON........
6 DB 432 PAc   one Lott in Newtown......................................

3 Sep 1745   -   Rec 6 Nov 1745 - JOHN KEELING & ANN his wife to JOHN WHICH-
6 DB 435 PAc   ARD (sic) 50 acres near BRINSONS INLET and is the same land
                  said JOHN KEELING had of THOS: HENLY & RICHD: BRINSON by a
deed dated 3 May 1745...........

6 Nov 1745   -   Rec 6 Nov 1745 - JOHN (X) BUSKEY SENR: & SARAH (X) his wife
6 DB 438 PAc   to JOHN BURFOOT ..... 80 acres in PAc ..... at the head of
                  the REEDY BRANCH... South to the MAIN ROAD................

2 Apr 1745   -   Rec 6 Nov 1745 - JOHN (X) LESTER of NANSEMOND COUNTY to RICHD:
6 DB 442 PAc   LESTER of PAc.... 100 acres in the UPPER PRECINCT of PAc......
                  bounds are given.

21 Aug 1745 - Rec No date given - Should be 6 Nov 1745 - JOHN THOROWGOOD
6 DB 444 PAc   JUNR: GENT: to ANTHONY WALKE SENR: ... Whereas said JOHN
              THOROWGOOD by virtue of his marrige with MARGARET WALKE
on the 12 Oct 1743 was entitled to 5 negroes & their increase, 1 silver
tankard, 12 silver spoons, 1 silver can, 1 piece of gold, 1 pair of gold
earrings, 1 Pearl necklace, 1 Cxxt hoopring, 1 trunk of her mothers cloaths,
sundry books, also Ł 150 which the said ANTHONY WALKE gave to his daughter
MARGARET WALKE by a deed of gift 12 Jun 1719..............................
Acknowledged in Court by JOHN THOROWGOOD the receipt of the above to the said
COL: ANTHONY WALKE.

21 Oct 1745 - Rec 6 Nov 1745 - RICHD: CORBETT to JOHN HUTCHINGS of Norfolk
6 DB 446 PAc   County ...... 130 acres in BLACKWATER & 30 acres is the same
              land RICHD: CORBETT purchased of JOHN KNOWAS? 3 Dec 1740 &
100 acres CORBETT bought of OWEN JONES 5 May 1742..........................

2 Sep 1745 - Rec xx xxx 1745 - GEORGE EILAND (this name is clearly written)
6 DB 449 PAc & SARAH his wife to SAML: MACASSTON? 300 acres bounded on
              SE on the land of JAMES HEATH to the NE by land of JONATHAN
JACKSON to NW on land of PETER JOLLY & on the SW on the NORTH RIVER said lamd
formerly called by the name of BLACK CHARLES and being sold & bought sundry
times untill it became the Proper Estate of RICHD: EILAND, who by his last
will dated 7 Mar 1733/4 bequeathed it to the aforesaid GEORGE EILAND. (Could
this name be IRELAND?)

5 Nov 1745 - JAS: MOORE to FRANS: WOODHOUSE 100 acres where JAS: MOORE
6 DB 453 PAc now lives & is called by the name of BEAR QUARTER .....JOHN
              GORNTOS LINE .....a persimmon run .... to the CYPRESS SWAMP.

5 Sep 1745 - Rec 6 Nov 1745 - WM: RICHMOND, Planter to JOHN KEELING 80
6 DB 456 PAc acres on the EASTERN SHORE of Lynhaven Parish & joining on
              LYNHAVEN RIVER the one side & on the lands of MR: ADAM KEELING
.... on the lands of MR: ROBT: RICHMOND & is now in the possession of JAS:
HAYNES & is the same land whereon the said JOHN KEELING now lives according
to the ancient & reputed bounds thereof as the same hath hitherto formerly
been held by WILLM: RICHMOND SENR: decd...................................

11 Sep 1745 - Rec 6 Nov 1745 - Inventory of the Estate of WILLM: SMITH decd.
6 DB 459 PAc Total Ł 22.4.9 .... Taken by JOEL CORNICK, JOHN LEGETT &
              JOHN LOVETT.

6 Nov 1745 - HENRY WOODHOUSE
6 DB 460 PAc Nun.w. 1 Sep 1745 wp 6 Nov 1745
              Deposition of JOHN FLEAR of full age saith that he heard MR:
HENRY WOODHOUSE decd declare on his death bed that he desired MRS: MARY WOOD-
HOUSE should have after his decease his PRIZE MONEY and he believes he was
in his perfect senses & further saith not.... Sworn to in Court 6 Nov 1745.
Then came JOHN FLEAR & SARAH SIMMONS before me & made solomn oath that yesterd
being the first day of September they heard HENRY WOODHOUSE, Marriner now decd
say that it was his desire that MRS: MARY WOODHOUSE might have all the prize
money and that he was in his perfect sense..... sworn before me 2 Sep 1745
              Signed: JOHN (X) FLEAR & WILLIAM KEELING SENR:

4 Sep 1745   -   Rec 6 Nov 1745 - MR: GEORGE RAMSEY of Norfolk County,
6 DB 461 PAc   Practitioner of Physick & chyrurgey & SARAH his wife to
                MR: PETER DALE of Norfolk County 184 acres of land lying
upon BROAD CREEK in the parish of Lynhaven & County of Princess Anne and is
the same land which the said MR: GEORGE RAMSEY lately purchased of JAS: BROUGH-
TON & ANN his wife .... beginning at a pine upon a Point opposite to a white
oak in BRAYS LINE by a cove that makes out of the said BROAD CREEK thence
binding by the said Cove by its natural bounds to a Point upon the said Creek
thence binding upon the said Creek to another point where a Branch of said
Creek makes up between the said land & the land of SIMMONS thence binding
upon the said Branch by various courses to a Red Oak over a fork of the said
Branch thence running NE 66° 68 poles to a pine thence NE 85° 105 poles to a
corner pine adjoyning MOSELEYS LAND thence thence binding S upon said MOSELEYS
LAND 122 poles to a white oak thence binding NWly 80° upon the said MR: PETER
DALES 99 acres formerly sold out of the said tract to THOS: TAYLOR decd & from
the said TAYLOR conveyed to the said DALE down to the first mentioned cove·
thence down the said cove to the first mentioned pine ....
(This property is very close to what was known as Poplar Hall the home of
THURMER HOGGARD and is the reason the bounds have been given in full. My
research of Poplar Hall isthe reason, after all, for the abstracting of these
records)

6 Nov 1745 - RICHARD (R) LESTER
6 DB 464 PAc   wd 19 Dec 1742 wp 6 Nov 1745 by WM: OAKHAM & JOHN RUSSEL
                Exix: wife DARCAS..... to dau ISABEL one shilling ....
to son RICHARD LESTER 1/ ...... to son JOHN LESTER 1/ ...... to son ABELL LES-
TER the plantation where I now live on with the land houseing & orchards & if
he should die before he comes to the age of twentyone years it shall fall to
my next youngest son .... & to son ABELL 30 acres of land & marsh lying
on the NNE side of NORTH RIVER falling upon WM: OAKHAMS LAND ......reversion
to youngest son .... and also 35 acres lying between the land that I had
of EDWD: & my coisons JOHN LESTERS LAND .... to son WILLM: LESTER all my
land lying upon the S fork of NANIES CREEK with the houseing & orchards......
if he should die before he comes to age it shall fall to my youngest son.....
Residue of Estate to my wife DARCAS.....Codicile: As far my two daus, MARY &
ELIZA: LESTER 2 heifers apiece ....

6 Nov 1745 - PAUL RIGBY (X) of Princess Anne County
6 DB 465 PAc   wd xx not given wp 6 Nov 1745 by DINAH WARD & OMY? PATERSON
                Exor: friend JOHN WHITEHEAD
tc the child that my wife now goes with all my land if he be a man child month
of January next & if she brings a female the said land is to be divided into
3 parts namely between MARTHA MORSE the wife of THOS: MORSE & JOYCE SCARBORNE
the wife of CHARLES SCARBORE in PASPETANK (PASQUOTANK, N. C.?) & with that
promise that said female so aforesaid shall be born in the month of January
before mentioned to be left to them & their heirs forever with that provision
that either this male or female be itwhich comes in the said month is to be
cast off with a shilling .... a cow & calf to ANN SENICER the dau of NATHL:
SENICA, likewise to MARY SENICA sister to said ANN one Ewe & lamb ....to
WILLM: PATERSON one heifer ..... Residue to be divided between them aforesaid
my wife MARY & MARTHA MORSE & JOYCE SCARBORE................................

6 Nov 1745   - Rec 6 Nov 1745 - JOHN HARPER the Elder deed of gift to his
6 DB 466 PAc   son JOHN HARPER the Younger .... one moyty or half part of
                 all that plantation in quantity & quality known by the name
of ASHEN SWAMP near the NEGRO SWAMP in the Parish of Lynhaven..............

3 Dec 1745   - Rec 4 Dec 1745 - CASON BUSKEY & MARY his wife, which MARY
6 DB 467 PAc   was only daughter of JOHN CANNON & ELIZA: his wife who was
                 one of the two sisters & co-heirs of EDWD: LAND JUNR: decd
to COLO: ANTHO: WALKE the equall half of 100 acres in the WESTERN SHORE of
the Parish of Lynhaven ...... & is the same land which EDWD: LAND the Elder
bought of HENRY SNAILE & given by him in his last will to his son the above
named EDWD: LAND JUNR:..

3 Dec 1745   - Rec 4 Dec 1745 - WILLIAM PURDY & URSULLA his wife & one of
6 DB 471 PAc   the - xxxxxxx - sisters & co-heirs of ALIPH late wife of
                 MATTHIAS MILLER of Norfolk County, Mariner to ARTHUR SAYER
GENT: of Princess Anne County .... the half part of one individual plantation
of land containing 600 acres in 3 parts to be divided whereon JOHN IVY, the
father of said URSULLA lately lived & was seized thereof including that part
where WILLIAM McCLANAHAN lives according to the several bounds thereof and
after whose decease the same descended to THOMAS IVY his son & heir who died
seized thereof without issue after whose decease the same descended unto the
said URSULLA, ALIPH & HANNAH IVY sisters & co-heirs of the said THOMAS IVY
who became seized thereof and 1/3 part thereof said ALIPH died so seized
leavinge issue one daughter named MARY which soon after also died after whose
decease the said one third part descended & came unto the said WILLIAM PURDY
& URSULLA his wife in right of the said URSULLA & to the said HANNAH IVY as
sisters & co-heirs of the said ALIPH & of which said undivided moity or half
part of one undivided third part of the said land & appurtenances the whole
in 3 parts to be divided, the said WILLIAM PURDY, URSULLA his wife are siezed
as aforesaid.........(Parts are missing from the lease - most of the above
was taken from the release).

3 Dec 1745   - Rec 4 Dec 1745 - WILLIAM COX & ANN his wife one of the daug-
6 DB 475 PAc   ters & co-heirs of WILLM: LOVETT decd of PAc to THOS: WALKE
                 50 acres in Lynhaven Parish & near the head of BOWRINS? RIVER
in the WESTERN SHORE SWAMP it being part of a larger tract of land now in the
possession of MRS: MARY WOODHOUSE one of the daughters & co-heirs of the said
WILLM: LOVET decd ....

3 Dec 1745   - Rec 4 Dec 1745 - SOLO: WOOD to SAMUEL FENTRISS 61 acres at a
6 DB 479 PAc   place called DAM NECK (the release gives this description):
                 61 acres on the South side of the head of the EASTERN BRANCH
of ELIZABETH RIVER ...... begin at a gum by the Dams... bounds are given.

6 Nov 1745   - Rec 4 Dec 1745 - Inventory & Appraisal of the Estate of MR:
6 DB 482 PAc   JOHN JAMESON decd........ Total ₤ 37.16.00 ....

Rec 4 Dec 1745   Inventory of the Estate of RICHARD LESTER decd. It is signed
6 DB 483 PAc   by DORCAS LESTER.

Rec 4 Dec 1745   Appraisal of (PAUL?) RIGBY decd. (This is blurred and the
6 DB 483 PAc   name may or may not be PAUL).

Rec 4 Dec 1745 - Audit of the Estate of MR: BARON MORSE decd.....By amount
6 DB 484 PAc   of Sales Ret^d: per Sheriff Ł 36.2.3

31 Dec 1745   - Rec 1 Jan 1745/6 - HENRY MOORE & SARAH his wife to MATTHEW
6 DB 484 PAc   PALLET ... the plantation whereon CAPT: HENRY MOORE lived
                the same being the equal half part of a tract of land given
by CASON MOORE the father of CAPT: HENRY MOORE containing 330 acres..........
on the EASTERN SHORE of Linhaven Parish & joyning on the FRESH POND the one
side and on LINKHORN BAY the other side & on the land that THOS: MOORE SENR:
now lives on ....

31 Dec 1745   - Rec 1 Jan 1745/6 - JOHN BURFOOT & PRUDENCE his wife to
6 DB 486 PAc   HENRY MOORE 200 acres which WILLIAM CAPPS the Elder gave
                to SAML: BROCK according to the most ancient bounds being
on the EASTERN SHORE of Lynhaven Parish joyning on SPRATTS OLD MILL DAM the
said lying & being in a NECK commonly known by the name of FINKLEYS NECK...

1 Jan 1745/6   - Rec 1 Jan 1745/6 - THOROWGOOD BRINSON & ELIZA: his wife to
6 DB 488 PAc   JOHN MARSHALL 60 acres at a place called MUDDY CREEK in
                Princess Anne County & is the same land THOROWGOOD BRINSON
bought of JOHN CAPPS.

1 Jan 1745/6   - SOLOMON WATERMAN
6 DB 491 PAc   wd 30 Nov 1745 wp 1 Jan 1745/6   Exix: wife (not named)
                ... son CHARLES, underage, all my land with the appurte-
nances thereof..... my wifes widowhood in the land..... to son SOLO: ......
to daughters MARY & FRANS:...

8 Jun 1745   - Rec 22 Mar 1745/6 - Whereas MR: ANTHONY WALKE of PRINCE
6 DB 492 PAc   GEORGE COUNTY by his Indentures of Bargain & Sale dated the
                30 & 31 Oct 1740 have conveyed unto CAPT: THOS: WALKE of
Princess Anne County the fee simple Estate of 300 acres of land with the
appurtenances in PAc & Whereas it appears that ANN WALKE wife of the said
ANTHONY WALKE.... cannot travel to PAc Court to acknowledge the conveyance
...... she was examined privily......... and relinquished her dower right..

4 Nov 1745   - Rec 5 Feb 1745/6 - THOS: GARDNER, Planter to RICHARD GARDNER
6 DB 493 PAc   50 acres in the Parish of Lynhaven.... in the VALLEY by the
                RIVER..........Bounds are partially given.................

4 Feb 1745/6   - JOHN LAMOUNT to SAML: GRIFFIN one certain WATER MILL being
6 DB 497 PAc   on the EASTERN SHORE of PAc ...... joining to the land where-
                on JOHN LAMOUNT now liveth & from thence across the DAMS to
LWML: CORNICKS LAND..............

5 Feb 1745/6   - Rec same day - Audit of the Estate of HENRY & ANN COLLINS
6 DB 500 PAc   decd..... By amount of sale after deduct: Ł 72.19.82

5 Feb 1745/6   - Inventory of the Estate of SOLOMON WATERMAN decd presented
6 DB 500 PAc   in Court by MARGT: WATERMAN. A short list, no value given.

3 Feb 1745/6   -   WILLIAM BONNEY
6 DB 501 PAc   wd 8 Aug 1745 wp 3 Feb 1745/6   Exix: wife (not named)
                    ...My land to be equally divided between my two sons JOHN
& THOS: BONNEY only my son JOHN BONNEY to have the Plantation whereon I now
reside......... to my daughters JEAN BONNEY, BETTY BONNEY .... residue to
wife................

5 Feb 1745/6   -   NATHANIEL LILBURN, Mariner
6 DB 501 PAc   wd 10 Feb 1741/2 wp 5 Feb 1745/6 by CASON MOORE
                    Exor: MR: JOSIAH SMYTH in Norfolk County
"now taking a voyage to Sea &c.... I give & bequeath unto sister CATHARINE
LILBURN one negro boy Cote & one negro girl Moll & after her death to her
son ROBERT........ to sister OLIVE LILBURN a negro with reversion to my
brother ALEXANDER LILBURN.... my sister SHOE? BUCK? and since CUCKELS? and
STOCK CUCKLE? I gave unto HENRY CHAPMAN son of NICHLIS CHAPMAN my Plantation
& my Mothers thirds of the negroes I gave unto my brother ALEXANDER LILBURN
the rest of my parson (personal?) Estate which is moveable I leave to be sold
.... after debts are paid the remainder to my brother ALEXANDER LILBURN....."
Will was presented in Court by MRS: MARTHA CONNYER appointed by the Court who
made oath thereto ....(Whether the above refers to names of persons
or not remains to be seen. This will is hard to understand)

4 Oct 1745   -   Rec 5 Feb 1745/6 Inventory of the Estate of MRS: MARY MOORE
6 DB 502 PAc   decd.. A fairly long Inventory which totals Ŀ 109.16.4.

18 Feb 1745/6 -   Rec 5 Mar 1745/6 - JOHN HARFORD, Millwright & ALIPH his wife
6 DB 504 PAc   to EDWD DENBY ... one Lott or half acre of land in NEWTOWN
                  which formerly belonged to JAMES ISDELL and since conveyed
by the aforesaid DENBY unto aforesaid JOHN HARFORD & ALIPH his wife the 4 Oct

4 Mar 1745/6 -   Rec 5 Mar 1745/6 - WILLIS PARSONS & DINAH his wife of Norfolk
6 DB 507 PAc   County to TULLY MOSELEY of PAc ... 50 acres of Swampland on
                  the South side of the EASTERN BRANCH OF ELIZABETH RIVER at a
place called the GUM SWAMP which land was given to the aforesaid DINAH by her
grand-father bounded as specified in a deed of lease and release between the
aforesaid parties dated 5 Mar 1745/6,,,,,,,,,,,,,,,,(Bounds are given in the
release and WILLIAM FENTRISS line and SAML: WILES line are mentioned.......)

1 Jan 1745/6 -   Rec 5 Mar 1745/6 - Appraisal of the Estate of MR: PHILIP
6 DB 510 PAc   DYSON taken at the late dwelling house of MRS: PHILIP DYSON.
                  Total of Inventory Ŀ 112.10.6

5 Mar 1745/6 -   Rec 2 Apr 1746 - Inventory of the Estate of NATHL: LILBURN
6 DB 511 PAc   Total Ŀ 8.0.7.   The Appraisal of his Estate follows on the
                  same page: Total 22.19.3.

1 Apr 1746   -   Rec 2 Apr 1746 - MICHL: FENTRISS to CHAS: EDWARDS 50 acres
6 DB 512 PAc   in the NORTHWOODS between the land of abovesaid CHARLES
                  EDWARDS & LEML: HARGROVE.................................

1 Mar 1745/6 -   Rec 2 Apr 1746 - CHARLES EDWARDS & SARAH his wife to WILLM:
6 DB 516 PAc   75 acres joyning the land whereon the said WILLIAM FENTRISS
                  now dwells begin at the HORSE BRIDGE RUN ....

4 Nov 1745   —   Rec 2 Apr 1745 - Appraisal of MARTIN BURROUGH decd.........
6 DB 519 PAc   Estate in the hands of JOHN BROWN Exor.....................

19 May 1745   —   Rec 20 May 1746 - (date 1745 should probably be 1746)
6 DB 521 PAc   MRS: MOLLY BRAY, one of the daughters & co-heirs of EDWD:
                  BRAY of Princess Anne County to MR: TULLY ROBINSON SMYTH ..
The 1/3 part, the same in 3 parts to be divided, of a certain plantation
containing 200 acres in PAc on a Creek called BROAD CREEK & is part of a
tract of land patented by ARTHUR MOSELEY in the year 1670 containing 540
acres according to the most ancient bounds thereof... Page 522 - the release
gives: bounding on BROAD CREEK ....with the appurtenances. (No real
bounds to help locate the exact site)

19 May 1746   —   Rec 20 May 1746 - WM: FENTRIS & MARTHA his wife to ARTHUR
6 DB 524 PAc   FRIZLE ... 50 acres in the NORTHWOODS in PAc & joyning on
                  THOS: SCOTT & JAS: COLLINS LAND..........................

19 May 1745   —   Rec 20 May 1746 - JOHN SMITH & ELIZA: SMITH his wife of
6 DB 527 PAc   BLACKWATER, PAc., to BENONY HEATH 50 acres....that Planta-
                  tion being a part of a patent of JOHN CELIA that he sold to
THOS: DOBS afterwards transferred to JAMES KEATON then to JOHN SMITH & now
to BENONY HEATH... It being all that dividend that JOHN CELIA sold to THOS:
DOBS the E part of the tract binding on BLACKWATER RIVER &c...............

19 May 1746   —   Rec 20 May 1746 - WILLIAM FENTRISS & MARTHA his wife to
6 DB 531 PAc   JAMES COTTON 50 acres in the NORTHWOODS in the County of
                  Princess Anne & joyning on ARTHUR FRIZLE & the said JAMES.

3 Sep 1745   —   Rec 5 Mar 1745/6 - WILLM: SUTTON WHITE to WILLIAM COX
6 DB 534 PAc   (Dates are out of place in book, but see Marginal note below)
                  105 acres in the EASTERN SHORE of Lynhaven Parish & joyning
on the land of CAPT: WM: KEELING on one side & on the lands of MAXM: BOUSH
on the other side now in the possession of the REV: HENRY BARLOW & is the
same land whereon the said WILLM: SUTTON WHITE now lives....The release page
536 gives: 105 acres johning on LINKHORN BAY & on the land of CAPT: WILLM:
KEELING according to the ancient bounds..... excepting the 50 acres that the
said WILLM: SUTTON WHITE sold to CAPT: WILLIAM KEELING whereof the said WILLM:
SUTTON WHITE hath any estate of freehold....&c.......NOTE IN MARGIN: 20 Apr
1747 then came ELIZA WHITE wife of said WILLM: SUTTON WHITE into Court & relinquished all her right of dower &c..

20 May 1746   —   JOHN SMITH of Blackwater
6 DB 537 PAc   wd 19 Feb 1745/6 wp 20 May 1746 by PETER HARBERT, BERNARD
                  BANGER & JOHN GISBORN   Exix: wife ELIZA:
..to my son SAML: SMITH the Plantation I now live on ... all my Smiths tools
..to my son JOHN SMITH...... to my son SETH SMITH ... residue to wife ELIZA:

20 May 1746   —   BENONY HEATH
6 DB 538 PAc   wd 3 Feb 1745/6 wp 20 May by PETER HERBERT & JOHN GISBORN
                  Exix: wife VILAR?
... my brother JAMES HEATH all my land .... wife VILAR? HEATH all my
personal estate during her widowhood.....................................

20 May 1746 - MARTHA CREED
6 DB 539 PAc   wd 15 Mar 1737/8 wp 20 May 1746 by JNO: BONNEY SENR: Will
                  was presented in Court by JOHN BRAY the Executor. The
other witnesses were: LANCASTER LOVETT & JOHN BERRY. Exor: named in will
son-in-law JOHN BRAY & JOHN BONNEY....... to dau MARY BRAY 12 pence........
to daus MARTHA ROBINSON, DINAH COOPER, & EASTER FISHER 12 pence each.......
residue to be divided between my two younger children JOHN CREED & REBECAH
CREED............

16 Jun 1746 - Rec 17 Jun 1746 - WILLIAM RICHMOND, Planter to CAPT: WILLIAM
6 DB 539 PAc   COX 50 acres of Marsh Land in PAc at a place called the SALT
                PONDS near LYNHAVEN RIVER and next adjacent to the Marsh that
his brother ROBT: RICHMOND decd formerly held together with all houses &c....

19 May 1746 - Rec 17 Jun 1746 - FRANS: SHIPP & DINAH his wife to JOHN WHITE-
6 DB 543 PAc   HEAD   50 acres on the Upper Precinct of the EASTERN SHORE of
                PAc...... being part of a Patent granted to JOHN RICHASON &
from him conveyed to JOHN OAKHAM & binding .... at a mkd tree on the E side
of JOHN BOOTHS land .... Wly......being the South end of the Patent.......

19 Dec 1744 - Rec 17 Jun 1746 - SOLO: WILLEY of NORTH CAROLINA to YATES NICH-
6 DB 546 PAc   OLSON administrator of JOHN NICHOLAS decd 45 acres in PAc
                joyning to the land formerly belonging to WILLM: NICHOLAS decd
.....in YATES NICHOLAS actual possession ...... joyning the land whereon
RICHARD SCOTT now lives ....

10 Jun 1746 - Rec 17 Jun 1746 - JOSIAH (J) MORRIS to JAMES JACKSON 100 acres
6 DB 549 PAc   joyning upon the South fork of NANNYS CREEK...bounds are given.

1 Apr 1746 - Rec 17 Jun 1746 - JAS: NIMMO to THOROWGOOD SPRATT 254 acres
6 DB 552 PAc   of Upland and Marsh the upland containing 104 acres the marsh
                containing 150 acres. Bounded: the 102 acres of upland ad-
joyning to the Northmost line ...... the 100 acres of land which the said JAS:
NIMMO formerly bought of MAJOR HENRY SPRATT decd thence along said line to the
head corner tree thence for breadth from the lowermost markt pine next to the
Marsh to a markt pine in the head of a Valley next to JOHN WILLIAMS & to con-
tinue same breadth from the Marsh to the head line being the same 100 acres
that said JAS: NIMMO bought of MR: HENRY WHITE and the said THOROWGOOD SPRATT
be the same more or less together with 2 acres of land binding square Souther-
ly out of the said 100 acres ....near to JOHN WILLIAMS LANDING..........

17 Jun 1746 - Audit of the Estate of WILLIAM DAVISS decd.....By sale of the
6 DB 556 PAc   Estate......₺ 11.18.8.

17 May 1746 - Audit of the Estate of JOHN HUGINS decd ... Amount of the sale
6 DB 556 PAc   ₺ 54.1.8.

17 Jun 1746 - ROBT: (X) DUDLEY
6 DB 557 PAc   wd 17 Apr 1746 wp 17 Jun 1746 by WILLIS SIMONDS & CORNELIUS
                (X) AUSTIN   Exix: wife ELIZA:
..to son ROBT: DUDLEY... a negro boy SAMBO &c....................................
..to son HENRY DUDLEY negro boy London ...... to dau ISABELLAH DUDLEY a negro
girl Cate reversion to sons ROBT: & HENRY & my two daus AMY & ELIZA:..........

...to dau AMY Ł 4.10/ out of the money due from my brother THOS:DUDLEY with
2 head of cattle..... to dau ELIZA: JACKSON Ł 4.10/ out of the money due
from my brother THOS: DUDLEY ...... residue to my wife ELIZA: DUDLEY.......

14 Apr 1746 - Rec 17 Jun 1746 - LEML: WHITEHURST, Planter to RICHD: DAVISS
6 DB 557 PAc   of Norfolk Borough 150 acres joining to the land of -hole-
COLO: ANTHO: WALKE now liveth & devised to me by the last will of my father
THOS: WHITEHURST decd with houses &c......(No release given on this deed)

17 Jun 1746 - Audit of the Estate of ROBT: RICHMOND decd to WM: RICHMOND
6 DB 559 PAc   his Executor.... to ELIZA: RICHMONDS part of her legacy from
ESTHER POOLES Estate 13/5 ......Total 97.14.6.......This Audit is combined
with WILLIAM RICHMONDS Audit... see what follows.

17 Jun 1746 - Inventory of the Estate of WILLIAM RICHMOND decd to CAPT:
6 DB 559 PAc   WILLIAM KEELING his Executor... To CAPT: WM: KEELING for his
                trouble & sale of the Estate Ł 5.6.7......To ROBT: RICHMONDS
Estate Ł 83.11.5. Total 127.10.5. By paid ROBT: RICHMOND -?- & brother of
An mony? & part of his fathers Estate......(not given in full)

19 May 1746 - Rec 17 Jun 1746 - GEORGE SHIRLEY...Mortgage Deed to COLO:
6 DB 560 PAc   ANTHO: WALKE, Merchant 298 acres whereon the said GEORGE
                SHIRELY now lives .... Bounds not given.

15 Apr 1746 - Rec 16 Jul 1746 - RICHD: GARNOR & ELIZA: his wife... Deed of
6 DB 562 PAc   Gift to dau MARY GARNER at the age of 21 years or day of mar-
                riage 80 acres known by the name of CREEDLES which was pur-
chased of THOS: GARNER Being bounded by water in the head of LYNHAVEN RIVER
.... joining on LAWSONS LINE down in a .....Bounds given in full.

13 Jul 1746 - Rec 15 Jul 1746 - ALEXANDER POOLE to JAMS: WMSON: SENR: one
6 DB 563 PAc   lot or half acre in NEWTOWN .... begin: at the corner stone
                of the lott of MRS: YATES NICHOLAS... Bounds are given.......

14 Jul 1746 - Rec 15 Jul 1746 - ABIA COX & ELLEN his wife to CASON MOORE
6 DB 566 PAc   100 acres beginning at a Cedar on the East side of LINKHORN
                BAY & runing & joining on the land that THOS: MOORE now lives
on by the courses near E then along the SEABOARD ro JAMES LAMOUNTS Line formerly called & joining on the land whereon ROBT: JONES now lives down to the said
BAY again by the course as it stands near W situate lying & being on the EAST-
ERN SHORE OF LINHAVEN PARISH........&c......................................

14 Jul 1746 - Rec 15 Jul 1746 - JOHN KEELING, Planter to ADAM KEELING 6
6 DB 569 PAc   acres on LINKHORN BAY begin at a stake the head of a Cove in
                the Marsh thence to a mkd pine at the head of a Marsh thence
to a corner tree in a valley & so binding on said ADAM KEELINGS Land........

14 Jul 1746 - Rec 15 Jul 1746 - AMBRUS (AMBROSE?) BURFOOT & MARY his wife to
6 DB 572 PAc   THOROWGOOD BRINSON 60 acres binding on STIRRINGS LINE former-
                ly so called & in OLD POPLAR RIDGE & in BOUSKEY RIDGE on the
EASTERN SHORE of Lynhaven Parish...

15 Jul 1746 - Rec 15 Jul 1746 - AMBRUS BURFOOT & MARY his wife to JAMES
6 DB 575 PAc   HARRISON ... There are holes in the Feoffment (or Deed)
                There is no lease or release.

15 Jul 1746 - WILLIAM BODNAM
6 DB 578 PAc   wd 3 Dec 1745 wp 15 Jul 1746 by JOEL CORNICK & WILLIAM SMITH
                Exix: wife KEZIA ... unto my wife KEZIA BODNAM all my negroes
(7 are named).... my plantation whereon I now live & all my personal estate.

9 Jul 1746   - Rec 15 Jul 1746 - SARAH (X) TAYLOR... Deed of Gift to her
6 DB 578 PAc   children... to son RANDALL JONES & dau ANN TAYLOR.... to
                son RANDALL JONES one bed &c...... to ANN TAYLOR one cow &
calf &c ..... reserving the use of the above legacies my natural life........

19 Mar 1745/6 - Rec 19 Aug 1746 - WILLIAM MOSELEY, Mariner of Norfolk County
6 DB 579 PAc   to CHARLES SMYTH one lott or half acre in NEWTOWN. Bounds
                are given in the release on page 581.

19 Aug 1746 - Rec 19 Aug 1746 - HENRY MOORE & SARAH his wife to AMBRUS BUR-
6 DB 582 PAc   FOOT 100 acres on the EASTERN SHORE of Linhaven beginning at
                a pine by the MAIN ROAD side & runing by the MAIN ROAD thence
along the LITTLE OLD ROAD near SW down to MAIN line joining to JOHN LAMOUNTS
line.........

19 Aug 1746 - WILLIAM GISBURN of Blackwater
6 DB 585 PAc   wd 6 May 1746 wp 19 Aug 1746 by JOHN GISBURN & JAS: RANDOLPH
                Exix & Exor: wife MARY GISBURN & Father GILES RANDOLPH
..to bro EDWD: GISBURN 50 acres being all that end of my plantation where I
now live.... to dau MARY GISBURN all the rest of my plantation & land and all
the rest of my estate to my beloved wife MARY GISBURN......................

19 Aug 1746 - RICHARD SMITH of Blackwater
6 DB 586 PAc   wd 24 Apr 1746 wp 19 Aug 1746 by JOHN GISBURN & ELIZ: OLIVER
                Exor: wife & son RICHARD
.. to son RICHARD SMYTH my plantation at the head of BLACKWATER RIVER........
.. to son JAMES SMITH my Maner Plantation whereon I now live..... to dau SARAH
WHITE one Roan mare &c ...... to wife ELIZA SMITH the residue during her widowhood then to be equally divided among my five least? children...............

18 Aug 1746 - Rec No date given - Dated 1745 - Audit of the Estate of WILL-
6 DB 587 PAc   IAM SMITH.... to paid ROBT: TODD his assump[n]:? for his son
                SOLO: SMITH..... to paid CHARLES SMYTH per acct..... to the
Estate of JAMES GAINES which is charged to JACOB ELLEGOOD but SMITH had the
effects. Inventory amounted to Ь 22.14.9.

15 Sep 1746 - Rec 16 Sep 1746 - WILLIAM (W) SALMON & ABIAH his wife to
6 DB 587 PAc   LEM: HARGROVE 20 acres beginning at a maple on the North
                side of the HORSE BRIDGE RUN standing in the said WILLM:
SALMONS line .... by mkd trees across said WM: SALMONS Land to a white gum
in the dividing line between him and his uncle JOHN SALMONS Land thence to a
Holly in the line that divides said WM: SALMONS & LEML: HARGROVES land to a
Creek ....

30 Aug 1746 - Rec 16 Sep 1746 - MR: GEORGE PURDY, Mariner of Norfolk
6 DB 590 PAc   County to MR: JAMES HUNTER of PAc 47 acres in Lynhaven
                Parish & is the same land which GEORGE PURDY decd devised
to abovesaid GEORGE PURDY his son by his last will & joining on the lands
of COLO: ANTHY: WALKE, BENJA: MOSELEY, formerly JAS: DOLLARS & LEML:
THELABALLS ....

16 Sep 1746 - Rec 16 Sep 1746 - JOHN SWENY & KATHERINE his wife to
6 DB 593 PAc   WILLIAM MAYE, Blacksmith .. 30 acres in PAc near LONDON
                BRIDGE at the head of LYNHAVEN RIVER begin at a stake in the
line of ROGER FOUNTAINE....... SEly 45 ^{o} 58 poles to a stake by LYNHAVEN
RIVER thence begin: at the first station & runing on a line of mkd trees
dividing this land and the land called SMYTHS SWly 61° 72 poles to a white
oak in said SMYTHS Line & a corner tree of COOKS Land along COOKS line SEly
25° 24 poles to a gum at the head of the MIRE BRANCH thence down said
branch SEly 9° 32 poles to LYNHAVEN RIVER thence down said river to the
first station.

6 Jun 1746   - Rec 16 Sep 1746 - JAMES WILLIAMSON, Inventory of his Estate
6 DB 596 PAc   The Inventory is a full page long... Total ₤ 107.14.22.

16 Sep 1746 - JEFFREY DUNCKLIN
6 DB 598 PAc   Nun.wd 26 Apr 1746 Recorded 16 Sep 1746
                .... SARAH BARNES made oath that she heard JEFFREY DUNCKLIN
sayth at day he dyed & severall times before that it was (his) will & desire
that THAMAR BARNS should have all of his Estate after his just debts were
paid....Sworn to before me 26 Apr 1746 signed: JACOB ELLEGOOD

20 Oct 1746 - Rec 21 Oct 1746 - CAPT: JOHN THOROWGOOD & MARY ANN his wife
6 DB 598 PAc   to MR: WILLIAM NASH, Ship Carpenter of Norfolk County......
                448 acres in PAc whereon JAMES PATREE now liveth & is the
same land that MR: JOHN THOROWGOOD decd, father of the abovesaid JOHN THOROW-
GOOD Devised to him in & by his last will........known by the name of PUGGETS
NECK joining on the lands of CAPT: JOHN IVY decd, MR: WILLIAM HANCOCK, ANTHY:
LAWSON & THOS: TAYLOR decd..........No bounds given.

20 Oct 1746 - Rec 21 Oct 1746 - ANTHY: WHITEHURST son of JAS: WHITEHURST
6 DB 601 PAc   decd & ANN his wife to MOSES FENTRISS son of JOHN FENTRISS
                50 acres at a place called THREE RUNS joyning Nly on the said
MOSES FENTRISS own land Ely on JOHN WHITEHURST & Sly on WILLIAM PARSONS land.

20 Oct 1746 - Rec 21 Oct 1746 - The Estate of WILLM: HORSLEY decd to ARTHR:
6 DB 604 PAc   SAYER his Administrator.... To WILLIS & MARTHA GWIN orphans
                of JOS: GWIN ₤ 4.11.4......Sundry goods sold by the Admin-
istrator ₤ 13.10.4 ....

21 Oct 1746 - Inventory of the Estate of RICHARD SMYTH decd...this covers
6 DB 605 PAc   half a page and contains shoe makers tools...............

14 Nov 1746 - Rec 18 Nov 1746 - RICHARD (R) WHITEHURST, Planter to MICHL:
6 DB 605 PAc   FENTRISS, Planter 100 acres being the same land as was de-
                vised to said MICHL: FENTRISS in fee tail by the last will
of his father MICHL: FENTRISS decd as by the said will recorded in Norfolk
County .... and all houses ....No bounds given............

7 Oct 1746   - Rec 18 Nov 1746 - JOSIAH (J) MORRIS to WILLIAM MORRIS
6 DB 608 PAc   300 acres in NANNYS CREEK in the Upper Precinct of the EAST-
                ERN SHORE begin: at a red oak in a Branch joyning to THOS:
MORSES land & runinge ESE to a gum standing in a branch joining to CAPT:
ARTHUR SAYERS land thence runing S to the mkd trees the other bounds of a
new survey thence to a pine in the WESTERN SWAMP .... to the first station
Part is of a NEW PATENT & part out of a bill of sale of CAPT: JOHN THOROWGOOD.

16 Sep 1746 (& 23 Sep 1746) Rec 16 Dec 1746 - Inventory & Appraisal of the
6 DB 613 PAc   Estate of MRS: MARGARET ELLEGOOD decd.... Furniture, Silver,
                China and Pewter are listed and et als..... Total ₺ 16.18.2.

16 Dec 1746   - Rec Same day - Audit of the Estate of MR: JOHN WISHART decd
6 DB 614 PAc   To CAPT: JAMES KEMPE his administrator for Sundry payments
                made by him ....₺ 90.3.?. ......Balance due to Estate
from JAMS: KEMPE ₺ 1.5.5 ...... Total ₺ 91.9.4 1/4

16 Dec 1746   - SARAH HARVEY
6 DB 614 PAc   Nun.wd 21 Nov 1746 wp 16 Dec 1746 by THOS: HUNTER& SARAH
                HARVEY......."Memo: of SARAH HARVEYS verball will to ELIZA:
OMERRY I give one mare & 1 pair Harrow hoes present MR: THOS: HUNTER.......
also all her wearing cloaths in presents of SARAH TOMLINGSON" This is the
entire will.

19 Jan 1746/7 - Rec 20 Jan 1746/7 - THOMS: WALKE & MARGT: his wife to EDWARD
6 DB 615 PAc   HACK MOSELEY, GENT: 300 acres, reserving out of the said
                300 acres forty feet square for a burying place to the use
of the said THOMAS WALKE & his heirs, which said 300 acres is part of a pattent of 540 acres granted by SIR WILLIAM BARKLEY Knt &c to ARTHUR MOSELEY
of NORFOLK COUNTY dated 20 Oct 1670 & by the said ARTHUR MOSELEY sold &
conveyed to THOS: WALKE father of COLO: THOS: WALKE the fatherof the now
vendor as by his deed bearing date 16 Mar 1691 & recorded in Norfolk County
& by the said COLO: THOS: WALKE devised to ANTHY: WALKE his son & heir as by
the will of the said COLO: THOS: WALKE recorded in Princess Anne County &
by said ANTHONY son & heir of said COLO: THOMAS WALKE sold & conveyed to THOS:
WALKE party hereto as by a lease & release dated 30 & 31 Oct 1740 & recorded
in PAc same is expressed & bounded in & by the Deed of ARTHUR MOSELEY to
THOMAS WALKE.

15 Jan 1746/7 - Rec 20 Jan 1746/7 - MOSES FENTRISS son of JOHN FENTRISS, to
6 DB 619 PAc   JOHN WHITEHURST JUNR: 25 acres at a place called the THREE
                RUNS joyning & lying between said MOSES FENTRISS & JOHN
WHITEHURSTS land ..... being 1/2 of 50 acres lately purchased by the said
FENTRISS of ANTHONY WHITEHURST.............

19 Jan 1746/7 - Rec 20 Jan 1746/7 - WILLIAM KEELING JUNR & MARY his wife which
6 DB 621 Pac   said MARY is one of the two daughters & co-heirs of MR: JOHN
                THOROWGOOD decd. to MR: WILLIAM ROBINSON 375 acres all that
one half, in two parts to be divided, of that plantation whereon the abovesaid
JOHN THOROWGOOD father of said MARY lived & died containing 750 acres in Linhaven Parish on the WESTERN SHORE PRECINCT & is the Easternmost part of said
land according to the most ancient & known bounds... From the Release: On
the Western Shore begin: at the Wmost end of a ditch binding up on MARK POW-

ELLS land thence N 22 degrees Ely to the RIVER through a small cove near
the cornfield...................

19 Jan 1746/7 - Rec 20 Jan 1746/7 - MAJ: NATHL: NEWTON, GENT: & ELIZA: his
6 DB 625 PAc   wife to THOMAS WALKE 97 acres at a place called the NEGRO
                SWAMP near BOWINES? (BOWRINGS?) RIVER begin at a Holly of
GEORGE KEMPES PATTENT runing SW 43° 105 poles to a corner pine in said
KEMPES PATTENT thence S 44 1/2° E 40 poles to a gum in said KEMPES line
thence S 75° W 190 poles to a gum in EDWARD DAVIS line thence S 40 poles
on said DAVIS line to a pine a corner tree of said DAVIS & JOHN CARAWAY
thence E 22 poles to a poplar said CARRAWAYS corner tree thence N 26° E
93 poles to a holley in LOVETTS line the said CARRAWAYS corner tree thence
bounding on said LOVETTS line N 40° E 167 poles to the first station.

16 Jan 1746/7 - Rec 20 Jan 1746/7 - WILLIAM ROBINSON to WILLIAM KEELING JUNR:
6 DB 628 PAc   200 acres on the EASTERN SHORE bounded on the land of ADAM
                KEELING on the S & on the land that was MATTW: ELLEGOODS on
the W on the land of WILLIAM KEELING SENIOR on the N & on the BAY on the E
& is that same land that MR: WILLIAM ROBINSON father of the above WILLIAM
ROBINSON bought of JOHN HANCOCK & gave to his son WILLIAM..................

20 Jan 1746/7 - Rec 20 Jan 1746/7 - EDWARD HACK MOSELEY & (Deed of partition
6 DB 631 PAc   to each other) HENRY HOLMES & -hole in paper- JAMESON.......
                250 acres of MARY -missing- xxxxx being an ISLAND by the
name of CASONS ENTRY adjoyning to -xxxx- ISLANDS in the Parish of Lynhaven
.... Know ye that since the death of the said JOHN -xxxxxxx- the joint title
now remains in the said MR: EDXXXX MOSELEY & HENRY HOLMES as Survivors, Now
..........Marsh ...... to have equal moity ..... MOSELEY to have half of the
said ISLAND next to the RAGGED ISLAND...(One side of this page is missing)

20 Jan 1746/7 - JOHN MARSHALL
6 DB 632 PAc   wd 13 Jun 1746 wp 20 Jan 1746/7 by JOHN CAPPS & THOS: (T)
                LANGLEY.   Exor: wife & CAPT: WILLIAM KEELING
.. to wife PEMBROKE MARSHALL my lands & Plantation in MUDDY CREEK during
her life and after her decease to be divided between her two eldest sons...
residue to wife.........

15 Dec 1746 - Dates in Margin: 2 Mar 174X, May, Jun 25, Jul 23 1742 & 1741
6 DB 633 PAc   to 1745. (Your Editor has no idea why these dates are scatt-
                ered in the margin unless they are dates of the accounts listed)
To Capt:GEORGE WISHART per account & receipts for sundry clothing for his
daughter MARY   ᵽ 5.4.0..... To MR: CORKER for schooling his daughter 4/2
Total ᵽ 91.9.4 1/4........

7 Feb 1746/7 - LEML: THELABALL
6 DB 634 PAc   wd 24 Mar 1745/6 wp 7 Feb 1746/7 by HENRY SNAILE & JAMES SMITH
                Exor: brothers LEWIS & THOS: THELABALL
"Now goin to sea do make this my last will.....to brother LEWIS THELABALL..
with reversion to brother NATHL: THELABALL with reversion to brother LEWIS...
Brother THOS: THELABALLS daughter ABIGAIL THELABALL .. a negro girl.........

5 Feb 1746/7 - Rec 7 Feb 1746/7 - SARAH (S) CONDON Deed of Gift to her son-in-
6 DB 635 PAc   law ROBT: PATERSON .. all my lands with all houses &c.... re-
                taining the whole use of them to myself during my natural life..

xx Feb 1745/6 - Ordered 6 Nov 1746 - Rec 17 Feb 1746/7 - Inventory of the
6 DB 637 PAc   Estate of CAPT: JAMES CONDON decd. (This is a full page)

22 Aug 1746   - Rec 2 Feb 1746/7 - Further proved 17 Feb 1746/7 - CASON
6 DB 637 PAc   MOORES mortgages to DOCT: JAMES BLAIR... his moity or part
                of a certain parcell of Negroes bequeathed in and by the
last will of CAPT: HENRY MOORE his father decd between him the said CASON
& WOODHOUSE MOORE his brother .... Slaves are named......................

17 Feb 1746/7 - Rec Same day - JOB GASKINGS SENR: & MARTHA his wife & CHARLES
6 DB 638 PAc   his sone to ROBERT HUGGINS 175 acres on the EASTERN SHORE
                125 acres of which is that land that the aforesaid JOB GAS-
KINGS formerly purchased of COCKROFT OLD by deeds dated 4 & 5 May 1736 the
remaining 50 acres as the property of CHAS: GASKINGS was granted him by
ADAM HAYES in a Deed of Gift dated 5 Aug 1739.....Release gives: begin at
a Cove & binding Sly on a Cove formerly belonging to JOHN MUNDEN thence Wly
on said MUNDEN & COCKROFT OLDS own land thence Nly on a Cove & on ADAM HAYES
to the first station the said land commonly known by the name of THE OLD
PLANTATION..... bounds of the 50 acres are given...........................

16 Mar 1746/7 - Rec 17 Mar 1746/7 - WILLIAM GARTON & MARY his wife to JOHN
6 DB 641 PAc   TURNER 37 acres on the head of the EASTERN BRANCH of ELIZA:
                RIVER ..... begin at an Oak near a Branch runing up to the
dwelling house thence along by the natural courses of said branch to a white
myrtle in the midst of the branch near the house thence to a gum by the side
of the branch thence E by N 52 poles to.......&c..........................

17 Mar 1746/7 - Rec 17 Mar 1746/7 - JOHN KEELING & ANN his wife to ADAM
6 DB 644 PAc   KEELING 73 acres binding on part of LYNHAVEN RIVER & is the
                same land that JOHN KEELING party hereto bought of WM: RICH-
MOND.......The Release: & is bounded begin at a pine in ADAM KEELINGS line
runing thence a Wly course to a pine near the head of a Marsh thence along
by a small piece of Marsh to LYNHAVEN RIVER & so bounded by the natural
courses of the said river to the first station.....

26 Jun 1746   - Rec 17 Mar 1746/7 - JOHN CANNS mortgage deed to JACOB ELLEGOOD
6 DB 647 PAc   100 acres being that parcel of land which said CANN bought of
                WILLIAM RUTLAND as also the following slaves: Peter, Coffie,
Betty & her child named London all which named slaves said CANN bought of
THOMAS GARDNER & also JASPER which CANN bought of READ: MALBONE.............

17 Mar 1746/7 - Rec 17 Mar 1746/7 - HENRY MOORE & SARAH his wife to JOHN
6 DB 649 PAc   KEELING 150 acres in the EASTERN SHORE and is the same land
                that HENRY MOORE purchased of JOHN BURFOOT ..... Release: ..
near the EASTERN SHORE CHAPPEL at a place called the MILL DAM & runing E by
S along one of the Prongs of the said Dam 140 poles to an oak on the head
of the South fork runing thence S 86 poles to an oak a corner tree of MR:
SIMMONS thence along said SIMMONS line untill you meet with the line of
AMBROSE BURFOOT which said line is that line that separates the 70 acres
that AMBROSE BURFOOT lately purchased of HENRY MOORE from the aforesaid tract
thence along the boundaries round the said 70 acres to an -blank- in AMBROSE
BURFOOTS Old line.........corner tree of WILLIAM COTTLES...................

17 Mar 1746/7 - JOHN (X) BUSKEY ... Deed of Gift to his son WILLIAM BUSKEY
6 DB 652 PAc   & my grandson JOHN BUSKEY son of CASON BUSKEY alias KEELING.
                To WILLIAM my plantation whereon my son JOHN BUSKEY now lives
containing 130 acres... only reserving the whole use & benefits of the same
to myself during my natural life & to my grandson JOHN BUSKEY my Plantation
whereon my son CASON BUSKEY alias KEELING now lives containing 100 acres also
one negro woman called Rose.... only reserving the whole use & benefits of
both land & negro & her increase to his father CASON abovesaid during his
natural life ....

12 Feb 1746/7 - Rec 17 Mar 1746/7 = Audit of the Estate of JOHN RUTLAND decd
6 DB 652 PAc   By amount of sales as per list in the Office Ł 25.15.9.

17 Mar 1746/7 - Inventory of the Estate of JOHN MARSHALL signed by PEMBROOK
6 DB 653 PAc   MARSHALL.   No value is given.

xx Feb 1746/7 - Rec 17 Mar 1746/7 - Audit of the Estate of FRANCES MOSELEY
6 DB 653 PAc   decd...... to MRS: MARGT: SAYER per account 7/4............
                Credit by the return of sales Ł 25.7.3....................

xx Feb 1746/7 - Rec 17 Mar 1746/7 - Audit of the Estate of JOHN HARVEY decd
6 DB 653 PAc   By amount of the sales Ł 42.2.3.....Amount of claims lodged
                in the office Ł 7.4.6.

20 Jan 1746/7 - Rec 17 Mar 1746/7 - Audit of the Estate of MRS: ELIZ: GISBURN
6 DB 654 PAc   decd... The amounts of Sales & Cash Ł 51.8.3..............

18 May 1747   - Rec 19 May 1747 - MR: JEREMIAH LANGLEY of NORFOLK COUNTY to
6 DB 654 Pac   THOM: WALKE of PAc .... (the lease is hard to read) From the
                Release: 100 acres of land & Marsh upon the SEASIDE bounding
on the N side of LAMOUNTS PASTURE & is the same Moytie or 100 acres of Marsh
which JACOB JOHNSON the ELDER in his last will devised to his grandsons WM:
& JACOB JOHNSON by deed dated 27 May 1710 and purchased by the aforesaid
JEREMIAH LANGLEY from CAPT: JAMES NIMMO and MARY his wife as per deed dated
20 Jun 1727.......

18 May 1747   - Rec 19 May 1747 - JOHN WHITEHEAD & MARGT: his wife to ERASMUS
6 DB 658 PAc   HAYNES   100 acres near MACHIPONGO LANDING begin: at the Head
                of a Branch & Runing E along a line of markt trees to the
Patent line thence runing S to a gum thence by a line of mkd trees a Wly
course to the Plantation & so binding on a Valley to a gum on the NORTH RIVER.

22 Oct 1746   - Rec 19 May 1747 - Inventory of the Extate of ROBT: DUDLEY
6 DB 659 PAc   decd..... This is a small 1/2 page listing with no value given.

16 Jun 1747   - NATHANIEL NICHOLAS SENR:
6 DB 662 PAc   wd 23 Feb 1746/7 wp 16 Jun 1747 y ARTH: SAYER & JAMES KEMPE
                Exix: wife SARAH .... to wife SARAH the whole use & benefit
of the house and lott of land whereon I now live during her natural life and
after her decease to my daughter MARY NICHOLAS..... to my son NATHL: NICHOLAS
my plantation whereon he now lives................

6 DB 663 PAc - A Plat of the land of JAS: HUNTER & JOHN HUNTER

14 Jun 1747 - Rec 16 Jun 1747 - WILLIAM CARTWRIGHT & MARY his wife to
6 DB 664 PAc   CAPT: JAMES MOORE 167 3/4 acres being part or divident of
                that land lately divided between the said WILLIAM CARTWRIGHT
& GEORGE WISHART begin: upon the MAIN ROAD that leads from NEWTOWN by CAPT:
LANDS Plantation 54 1/2 poles from a corner oak by JAMES BANNISTERS fence
being a straight line of mkd trees NE 42° along to JACOBS corner tree thence
along said MAIN ROAD by various courses to the fork of the road that leads
to the FERRY BRIDGE thence along said FERRY ROAD till it intersects a mkd
line that leads from a gum at the head of a branch that parts this divident
of land & the land of the said JACOBS thence along said line NWly 87° 34 po
to an oak thence NW 41° 85 po to first mentioned corner tree of said JACOBS
thence along first mentioned line of mkt trees SWly 42° 297 po to the first
beginning.......

15 Jun 1747 - Rec 16 Jun 1747 - MR: CHARLES NICHOLSON whose mother ELIZA:
6 DB 667 PAc   & his wife MARTHA relinquished their rights thereunto......
to COLO: ANTHONY WALKE 20 acres ... being part of the land
whereon the said XHARLES NICHOLSON now lives ..... near the MAIN ROAD thence
by several bounds binding on the said MAIN ROAD to MAJR: FRANCIS MOSELEYS line
thence along said line S ...... (the full bounds are given)

16 Jun 1747 - WM: WEBLIN
6 DB 669 PAc   wd 23 May 1747 wp 16 Jun 1747 by RICHARD DUDLEY SENR & JUNR:
                Exor: Presented in court by SARAH WEBLIN appointed by the
Court..... The entire will follows: "In the name of God Amen I give and if
my wife be with child I leave plantation whereon I now live to my child & all
the rest of my estate between my wife& child, but if my wife be with child
I except my negro Tom & him I give to my brother GEORGE WEBLIN at a year old
this my last will & testament signed this 23 day of May 1747. I leave it
with RICHD: DUDLEY to prove.

15 Jun 1747 - Rec 16 1747 - Audit of the Estate of GEORGE BROWN decd - There
6 DB 670 PAc   is not much listed on this faded entry. The only figure seems
to be Ł 16.3.8.

24 Apr 1747 - Rec 16 Jun 1747 - JOHN CHAPMAN .. Mortgage Deed to DOCTR:
6 DB 670 PAc   GEORGE RAMSEY of NORFOLK COUNTY 250 acres of land the said
                JOHN CHAPMAN now lives on in Lynhaven Parish according to the
most ancient known bounds.....

16 Jun 1747 - Rec 16 Jun 1747 - YATES NICHOLAS Deed of Gift to "my two
6 DB 672 PAc   children ELIZABETH & ANNE NICHOLAS as also for their future
                support....... pursuant to my husbands, JOHN NICHOLAS decd,
last will do give & grant unto my said children, after my decease not before,
45 acres on the S side of the EASTERN BRANCH it being the same land which my
husband bought of SOLOMON WILLEY but never was acknowledged in his lifetime
& since his decease was made over to me the said YATES admx: to the said
JOHN NICHOLAS decd as by deeds dated 19 & 20 Dec 1744 ....

16 Jun 1747   -   THOS: HUNTER his bond as Sherif of Princess Anne County
6 DB 673 PAc

14 Jun 1747   -   Rec 21 Jul 1747 - WILLIAM PURDY & URSLEY his wife (she signed
6 DB 674 PAc   URSULA) to CHARLES KITLEY   50 acres of Marsh in the Upper
                Precinct of the EASTERN SHORE lying in the GREAT MARSH
PASTURES which MAJR: SOLOMON WILSON bought of the Executors of BARON MORSE
decd being half of 100 acres which JOHN IVY father of the abovesaid URSLEY
bought of said BARON MORSE in his lifetime........

1 Jan 1746/7   -   Rec 21 Jul 1747 - JAMES FITZGARRALL & FRAS: his wife to
6 DB 676 PAc   WILLIAM COTTLE   95 acres joyning on the Eward side of
                LINKHORN BAY on the S side of the abovesaid COTTLES Land
(Bounds are given) which land did formerly belong to SAMUEL BROCK & by him
divided unto   his son WILLIAM BROCK & by him conveyed unto said JAMES FITZ-
GARRELL with all houses &c..............

7 Aug 1745 - Returned14 Jul 1746 - Rec 21 Jul 1747 - Audit of the Estate of
6 DB 678 PAc   CAPT: JOHN NICHOLAS DECD.... Total ₺ 146.6.72 ....
            ₺ 49.0.7 1/2 due from MRS. YATES NICHOLAS as adm. to the
said estate.

17 Aug 1747   -   Rec 17 Aug 1747 - EDWARD (X) KEELING late of NORTH CAROLINA
6 DB 679 PAc   to BATSON WHITEHURST   100 acres on the Head of LINHAVEN RIVER
                joyning on the said BATSON WHITEHURST land down to ....
Bounds are partially given & are hard to read.   The release is not any clearer.

16 Aug 1747   -   Rec 17 Aug 1747 - CASON MOORE to THOMAS MOORE   100 acres
6 DB 681 PAc   which CASON MOORE bought of ABIA COX being on the EASTERN
                SHORE of Linhaven Parish.....Bounds are not given.

Order 17 Nov 1747 (1746?) Rec 16 Aug 1747 - Audit of the Estate of THOMAS
6 DB 683 PAc   CLAY decd...................................

6 DB 663 PAc -   Plat of NIMMO/HUNTER

17 Aug 1747?   -   No dates on this - Inventory of the Estate of CHARLES HENLEY
6 DB 683 PAc   decd..........

18 Aug 1747   -   Rec same day - Audit of the Estate of JAMES WILLIAMSON decd
6 DB 684 PAc   Amount of sales   ₺   79.10.7.

21 Jul 1747   -   Taken 30 Jul 1747 - Rec 18 Aug 1747 - Inventory & Appraisal
6 DB 684 PAc   of the Estate of WILLIAM WEBLIN decd.... Total ₺ 28.17.2.

25 Aug 1747   -   Rec 15 Sep ;747 - THOMAS MOORE & SARAH his wife to ROBERT
6 DB 685 PAc   JONES   125 acres a parcell of land which CAPT   HENRY MOORE
                decd devised to his son THOMAS MOORE, in the EASTERN SHORE
of Linhaven joyning on MATTHEW PALLETS line & on LINKHORN BAY & is the land
THOMAS MOORE now lives on.....Bounds are not given.....

14 Sep 1747 - Rec 15 Sep 1747 - WILLIAM GASTON & MARY his wife, which said
6 DB 687 PAc   MARY is one of the two sisters & co-heirs of JOHN CARTWRIGHT
                decd to JOHN TURNER.... being all that one moyity or full
half, in two parts to be divided, of that plantation whereon WILLIAM CART=
WRIGHT father of the said MARY lived containing 74 acres on the WESTERN
SHORE according to the bounds by which the same now is....................
Partial bounds are given.

15 Sep 1747 - Audit of the Estate of JOHN BARNS decd Total ℔ 19.15.8.
6 DB 689 PAc

Rec 12 Apr 1748 (This date is out of place) MR: JOHN SIMMONS & MARY his
6 DB 690 PAc   by their xxxx dated 3 Jul 1706 have conveyed unto THOMAS
                SCOTT SENR: the Fee Simple Estate of 125 acres & also another
piece of land containing 62 1/2 acres also 2 acres purchased of DANIEL
DOUGLYS in all 197 1/2 acres of land ..... Whereas it appears that said
MARY cannot conveniently travell to our Court of PAc to acknowledge the conveyance.........................

19 Oct 1747 - Rec 20 Oct 1747 - JACOB ELLEGOOD to JOHN BONNEY 600 acres
6 DB 691 PAc   in Uper Precinct of the EASTERN of PAc bounded on WILLIAM
                DYERS, WILLIAM CARRELLS & THOMAS FRANKLANDS land & its own
natural bounds. No bounds are given.

19 Oct 1747 - Rec 20 Oct 1747 - JOHN BONNEY & SARAH his wife to JAMES MOORE
6 DB 693 PAc   60 acres whereon said JAMES MOORE now lives ..... some bounds
                are given which don't give much information.

19 Oct 1747 - Rec 20 Oct 1747 - GEORGE WEBLIN to HENRY TROWER ... in the
6 DB 695 PAc   EASTERN SHORE..... near land of AMBROSE BURFOOT & JOHN BRIN-
                SONS & WM: BROCK........ Bounds are given.

Junly 1744 - 20 Oct 1747 - Audit of the Estate of RICHARD TAYLOR decd
6 DB 697 PAc   Total ℔ 31.12.2. (Date in margin is 1744)

20 Oct 1747 - Rec Same day - GEORGE HOLMES of NORFOLK COUNTY to LEMUEL
6 DB 698 PAc   HOLMES of PAc 87 acres.....by the BEAVER DAMS...... ROBERTS
                Line...... GUYS ...... the same dividend of land lately set
apart to the said GEORGE by virtue of an order of PAc Court dated 21 May
1746 for 87 acres...............

24 Aug 1747 - Rec 17 May 1748 WILLIAM COX SENR: bill of Sale to JOHN
6 DB 701 PAc   MOORE .... all my personal estate....but the said WILLIAM
                COX SENR: for himself doth further ..... reserves the use
thereof for his natural life & the natural life of his wife ANN............

20 Oct 1747 - MARTHA CREED decd, The Inventory of signed by JOHN BRAY.
6 DB 701 PAc   A short list of items.

19 Oct 1747 - Rec 20 Oct 1747 - ROBERT THOROWGOOD & BLANDINAH his wife to
6 DB 702 PAc   GEORGE WEBLIN one lott in NEWTOWN & is the same lott which
                the aforesaid BLANDINAH purchased formerly of BENJA: MOSELEY
& whereon they, the said ROBT: & BLANDINAH lately lived...................

1 Jun 1747   -   Rec 17 Nov 1747 - TULLY ROBINSON SMYTH Mortgage of £155.
6 DB 704 PAc   to TULLY ROBINSON 130 acres of land which the said SMYTH
                  now lives in which formerly belonged to EDWARD BRAY decd as
also the following slaves....... stock .... plate......silver spoons
marked T^{R}S...........

4 Sep 1745   -   Rec 4 Dec 1745 - Appraisal of the Estate of JOHN NICHOLAS
6 DB 706 PAc   decd. Total of this Inventory £ 57.12.4.

17 Nov 1747   -   Rec 17 Nov 1747 - JOHN HARRISON & RACHEL his wife to ROBT:
6 DB 706 PAc   JONES 100 acres on the EASTERN SHORE of Linhaven a pcell
                  of land which CAPT: HENRY MOORE decd bought of JAMES HARRISON
...... JOYNING ON THE LAND THOMAS MOORE now lives on............

17 Nov 1747   -   CHARLES HENLY
6 DB 708 PAc   wd 29 Sep 1747 wp 17 Nov 1747 by SARAH & JNO: (or JAS:) CASON
                  Exor: son JOHN   ...... to wife my bed I lie on with the
furniture belonging to it & ...... to son JOHN ..... negro & .... all my
lands & houses & orchards & all the rest of my estate to be equally divided
to my three daughters FRANCES, SARAH & MARY.................

25 Aug 1747   -   Rec 17 Nov 1747 - ROBERT JONES & MARY his wife to ERAPRADITUS
6 DB 709 PAc   MUNDEN 61 acres known by the name of BUSKEY RIDGE on the
                  EASTERN SHORE of Linhaven Parish joyning to the land that
HENRY CORNICK now lives on.... No bounds are given.

16 Nov 1747   -   Rec 17 Nov 1747 - THOMAS LESTER & MARY his wife to WILLIAM
6 DB 711 PAc   HARPER 50 acres part of a dividert of land whereon ROBERT
                  THOROWGOOD now liveth....... The bounds are given.

17 Nov 1747   -   HENRY SOUTHERN
6 DB 713 PAc   wd ? Jan 1745/6 wp 17 Nov 1747
                  ... to son HENRY SOUTHERN the plantation whereon I now live
reversion to dau ELIZA:..... if they should both die my Plantation & all
other estate should be taken care of by the GENT: of the VESTRY ...to be
disposed of yearly for the Education of children .... and the benefits for
the people of BLACKWATER.........

1 Apr 1747   -   Rec 17 Nov 1747 - ANTHONY WALKE Deed of Gift to his son
6 DB 714 PAc   ANTHONY WALKE the Younger 100 acres of land which said
                  ANTHONY WALKE the Elder purchased of JOHN IVY also one
other tract which ANTHONY WALKE the Elder purchased of WISHAM PURDY containing
64 acres also one other tract of 50 acres which ANTHONY WALKE the Elder purchased of THOS: MARTIN one other tract of 60 acres purchased of GEORGE WEBLIN.

21 Oct 1747   -   Rec 17 Nov 1747 - ANTHONY WALKE to SARAH NICHOLAS widow &
6 DB 715 PAc   relict of NATHL: NICHOLAS decd & MARY NICHOLAS dau of said
                  SARAH & NATHL:... Whereas SAID NATHL: NICHOLAS in his lifetime
purchased of said ANTHONY WALKE a lot or half acre on or near the head of the
EASTERN BRANCH of ELIZ: RIVER joyning on the land of said ANTHONY WALKE begin:
at a corner stone lying at the fork ot the NORTH LANDING ROAD th along said
road ....(bounds are continued) .... & whereas the said NATHL: departed
this life before conveyance was made to him by said WALKE... he made his last
will 23 Feb 1746/7 and gave to his wife SARAH the said land during her natural

life & after her death to his daughter MARY...........

19 Jan1747/8 - WOODHOUSE MOORE, NORFOLK BOROUGH
6 DB 716 PAc   wd 9 Sep 1746 wp 19 Jan 1747
         ... having been left by my father HENERY MORE a negro wench
called Bess, the said negro & her increase to be equally divided between me
and my brother CASON MORE therefore it is uncertain whether I may ever return
in case I should not or should die ......my part of said negro to wholly belong to my brother CASON MORE ....

30 Oct 1747 - Rec 19 Jan 1747/8 - JAMES CHAPMAN to HENRY CHAPMAN 100 acres
6 DB 717 PAc   ... and is the same land whereon the said JAS: CHAPMAN now
                liveth & is the land whereon JAMES CHAPMAN decd father of
the said JAMES CHAPMAN formerly lived............

19 Jan 1747/8 - JOHN NICHOLAS
6 DB 718 PAc   wd 30 7br 1747 wp 19 Jan 1747/8   Exor: SAMUEL BOUSH
          ..unto MR: SAMUEL BOUSH my tract of land lying upon BROAD
CREEK containing 130 acres which I escheated from MR: HUGH CAMPBELL to him
& his heirs forever & 118 acres joyning to the tract where my brother NATHL:
NICHOLAS lived & 50 acres of swamp which I purchased of THOS: E. DAVIS joining upon a place called the GUM BRANCH to him & his heirs forever & my negro
George, my riding horses, all my stock of cattle, sheep, hoggs & all my
household goods with all my real & personal estate that is mine or can be
made out to be mine.......

6 Dec 1747   - Rec 19 Jan 1747/8 - JOSIAH SMITH of NORFOLK COUNTY to GEORGE
6 DB 719 PAc   OLDNER of PAc   One lott of land in NEWTOWN & is the same the
                Said JOSIAH SMITH purchased of LUKE MOSELEY ....

30 Dec 1747 - Rec 19 Jan 1747/8 - GEORGE OLDNER to JOSIAH SMITH one lott
6 DB 721 PAc   or parcel of land with the dwelling house &c........ in
                NEWTOWN being the same that said JOSIAH SMITH sold to the said
                GEORGE OLDNER (see p 719 above)

At a Court held 18 Nov 1747 - Then came JANE CORBETT wife of RICHD: CORBETT
into Court & being first privily examined relinquished all her right of dower
in the 240 acres of land sold by said RICHARD TO COLLO: ANTHO: WALKE.
                        . signed: ARTH: SAYER CL CUR
This is the last item in the book.

MINUTE BOOK 6 - PRINCESS ANNE COUNTY, VIRGINIA
++

1744 - 1753

6 Mar 1744/5 - THELABALL's Estate - On petition of JAMES THELABALL &
  6 MB 4 PAc   ELIZA: his wife tis ordered that they have their porpor-
                tionable parts of ROBT: & WM: RICHMOND's Estates sold at
outcry & logged in the office.

6 Mar 1744/5 - In the motion of ARTHUR SAYER liberty is given him to
  6 MB 5 PAc   turn the road that leads through that part of his land
                called xxxxxx Neck leading to NEWTOWN down by the back
of the Public Warehouse & across the Eastern Branch & across his cleared
ground & to go between him and TULLY ROBINSON till it intersects the
Main Road again providing he make the new road according to law.

1 May 1745   - JOSIAH BUTT & MARY his wife, MAX: BOUSH, FREDERICK BOUSH,
  6 MB 11 PAc   & ELIZA: BOUSH &c against LEMUEL BOUSH in Chancery.
                    ANTHONY WALKE, JAMES KEMPE, JNO: THOROWGOOD, XXXXXXXXX
XXXXXXXXX or any 3 of them to make division of the xxxxxxxxx (probably
negroes) contained in the Compltts: bill xxxxxxx negroes belonging to
xxxxxx xxxxxxx COLL: MAX: BOUSH decd. except only the widows. (This
item was almost impossible to read. It is apparently the division of
slaves belonging to the Estate of COLL: MAX: BOUSH decd. AGW).

7 Aug 1745   - DINAH SHIPP wife of ffRA: SHIPP mentioned.
  6 MB 20 PAc

6 Nov 1745   - Ordered that the Sheriff summon: SARAH ROD, JNO: LEONARD,
  6 MB 26 PAc   THO: LANGLEY, THO: BROUGHTON & HIS WIFE, JOHN SHERWOOD &
                HIS WIFE, PHILLIP WOODHOUSE, ROBERT WOODSIDES, ROBT:
ALLEN & HIS WIFE, MARY SMITH wido:, MARY PEAD wife of JOHN PEAD, JOHN
ROBINSON & HIS WIFE, THO: BALLENTINE, MARY GROUNDSELL, ELIZA: OLIVER,
JOHN HUDLESTON & MARY NASH commonly called MARY GARDNER to answer the
presentment of the Grand Jury.

1 Jan 1745/6 - Ordered that the sheriff sell all the Estate of ffRANCIS
  6 MB 31 PAc   MOSELEY decd...

2 Apr 1745   - Petition of CAPT. SOLOMON EDY & HANNAH his wife.....the
  6 MB 42 PAc   Clerk to deliver to them their part of CAPT: (name may
                be JNO: CAPPS but I cannot be sure) Estate sold at out-
cry and lodged in   the office & further tis ordered that WILLIAM
PURDY pay them their part of THO: IVY's Estate in his hands. (There
is a question as to whether this is Thos: Ivy or not, but nothing more
likely could be made of it. AGW)

20 May 1746 - Ordered that the Sherif sell all the Estate of WILLOUGHBY
  6 MB 43 PAc   HARBERT decd.

20 May 1746 - Sale of FRANCIS MOSELEY decd his estate being returned
  6 MB 44 PAc   is ordered to be lodged in the Clerks office for benefit
of his children.

16 Sep 1746 - MR: JOB GASKINS SENR: adm: of MRS. MARGARET ELLEGOOD,
  6 MB 59 PAc   ROBERT PATERSON, LEMUEL CORNICK, & WM: KEELING JR: or
                any two of them to appraise the said decd. estate......

16 Sep 1746 - MR: JOB GASKIN SENR: next of kinn to MRS: MARGARET
6 MB 59 PAc   ELLEGOOD came into Court and made oath that the said
               MARGARET departed this life without making any will so
far as he knew. Certificate is granted him for obtaining letters of
administration &c..

16 Sep 1746 - On the motion of CAPT: JAMES NIMMO to turn the Road
6 MB 59 PAc   that leads through his plantation from MR: SAMUEL
               BOUSHES over JOHNSONS Bridges it's ordered that COLL:
ANTHONY WALKE chosen by the Court, MR: EDWARD HACK MOSELEY chosen by
MR: SAML: BOUSH & ARTHUR SAYER chosen by the sd: CAPT: JAMES NIMMO view
where the new road is to go and report same to the next Court.

16 Sep 1746 - The sale of WILLOUGHBY HARBERTS & BENONY HEATHS Es-
6 MB 62 PAc   tates being returned is ordered to be lodged in the Clerks
               Office for benefit of their creditors.

21 Oct 1746 - Sales of GEORGE WALKER, WILLIAM GISBURN & WILLIAM JOLLIFFS
6 MB 63 PAc   Estates being returned is ordered to be lodged in the
               Clerks Office for benefit of their creditors.

21 Oct 1746 - CAPT: ANTHONY WALKE, MR: EDWARD HACK MOSELEY & ARTHUR
6 MB 64 PAc   SAYER appointed to view CAPT: JAMES NIMMOS new road that
               leads from the Bayside over JOHNSONS BRIDGES have return-
ed their report in these words: ...in obedience to an order of Court 16th
instant this day met & reviewed the Road proposed to be made by CAPT:
JAMES NIMMO leading from MR: SAMUEL BOUSHES to the bridges called JOHN-
SONS BRIDGES were of the opinion that when the road is made good and
passable it is reasonable that it should be received......22 Sep 1746.
......Liberty is therefore given CAPT: JAMES NIMMO to turn the said road...

30 Oct 1746 - CAPT: JAMES NIMMO, Kings Attorney paid 1000 l tob out of the
6 MB 65 PAc   County Leavy.

10 or 18 Nov 1746 - THOMAS OWENS son of ELIZ: GASTON decd: came into
6 MB 66 PAc   Court & made oath that sd: ELIZ: departed this life
               without making any will.....Certificate granted him for
obtaining letters of administration.

20 Jan 1746/7 - Last will and Testament of THOMAS SPRATT was presented
6 MB 69 PAc   in Court by his Exix: MARY SPRATT ...... probate granted
               to her.

20 Jan 1746/7 - Probate of will of JOHN MARSHALL decd., PEMBROKE MAR-
6 MB 70 PAc   SHALL his Exix. Will proved by JOHN CAPPS, THOMAS
               LANGLEY witnesses thereto.

17? Jan 1746/7- WILLIAM MORRIS & ISBELL his wife it's ordered that the
6 MB 77 PAc   clerk deliver to them their part of their fathers, JNO:
               GISBURNS Estate sold at outcry and lodged in the office.

17 Jan 1746/7 - ffRANCIS ffRIZELL & MARGARET his wife ordered that the
6 MB 77 PAc   Clerk deliver to them their part of their fathers xxxx
                xxx, lands, Estates sold at outcry & lodged in the off-
                ice.

17 Jan 1746/7 - The will of LEMUEL THELABALL decd presented in Court by
6 MB 77 PAc   THO: & LEWIS THELABALLS his exors & being proved by the
                oaths of all the witnesses.

7 Mar 1746/7 - On motion of SAMUEL SMITH its ordered that PETER HARBERT
6 MB 79 PAc   be appointed his guardian during his minority & to take
                care of him & his estate giving bond & security in the
sum of ₺ 50.

21 Apr 1747   - SAMUEL WILES Appointed Constable in the Eastern Branch
6 MB 83 PAc   Precinct. CHARLES GASKING Constable in the Western
                Shore precinct.

21 Apr 1747   - On petition of JOHN JAMES, AMY JAMES, SUSANNAH JAMES &
6 MB 84 PAc   JANE JAMES its ordered that the clerk deliver to them
                their proportionable parts of JANE HUTCHINSONS Estate
sold at outcry & lodged in the office.

19 May 1747   -- JOHN CONNER bound over by warrant under the hand of
6 MB 89 PAc   ANTHONY WALKE to answer the complaint of ELIZ: WILES
                wife of THOMAS WILES.........can't read the rest of this.

20 Aug 1747   - JOHN HUNTER & JACOMINE his wife vs JAMES NIMMO & MARY
(Date is out   his wife: This suit has been continued for a long
of Place)   time. It is finally being given, but is almost impossi-
6 MB 91 PAc   ble to read. I think it is about land in Nansemond Co.

21 Jul 1747   - FRANCIS FARQUHASSON & DEBORAH FRANKS FARQUHASSON his wife
6 MB 97 PAc   agst: EMPEROR MOSELEY & ELIZ: his wife....argued, dismist.

21 Jul 1747   - In the Petition of JOHN HUNTER to turn the road that
6 MB 98 PAc   leads through his plantation over JOHNSON's BRIDGES it's
                ordered that BARTHOLOMEW WILLIAMSON, JOHN THOROWGOOD JUNR
& SAML: BOUSH GENT view the sd road & report the same to the next Court.
(See also p 109 - nothing further on the bounds)

21 Jul 1747   - MRS. YATES NICHOLAS having provd her acct for nineteen
6 MB 100 PAc   pound 12 shillings for Sundry Clothing bought for ELIZ:
                & ANNE NICHOLAS daughters of CAPT: JOHN NICHOLAS decd.
Ordered that she be allowed out of that decedants Estate as her cost.

13 Aug 1747   - The sale of JOHN SMITHS Estate being returned is ordered
6 MB 102 PAc   to be lodged in the office.

15 Sep 1747   - On the petition of JOHN BROWN & ELINOR his wife it's
6 MB 104 PAc   ordered that the Clerk deliver to them their part of
                JOHN BASON's Estate sold at outcry & lodged in the office.

15 Sep 1747   - Sale of JOHN SMITH's Estate being returned is ordered
 6 MB 105 PAc   to be lodged in the Clerks Office for the benefit of
               his creditors.

15 Sep 1747   - ....Laying off the streets of NEWTOWN "finding the
 6 MB 105   platt of said town so imperfect & inconsistant........
               to the next court........

3 Oct 1747   - At a Court for laying the Leavy:
 6 MB 106 PAc   To CAPT: JAMES NIMMO, Kings Attorney   1000
               To COLO: ANTHONY WALKE for Record Book 4000
               There were 1543 Tythables

20 Oct 1747   - JOEL CORNICK apptd guardian of MAXIMILLIAN BOUSH during
 6 MB 107 PAc   his minority giving bond & security in the amount of
               Ł 500.

20 Oct 1747   - ROBERT THOROWGOOD & BLANDINAH his wife came into Court
 6 MB 107 PAc   and acknowledged lease & release for one lott of land
               to GEORGE WEBLIN.

20 Oct 1747   - On petition of SMITH SPARROW & MARTHA his wife its or-
 6 MB 108 PAc   dered that DAVID BALLENTINE deliver to them all the es-
               tate of the said MARTHA in his hands.   .

20 Oct 1747   - Sale of HENRY SOUTHERN's Estate being returned is order-
 6 MB 108 PAc   ed to be lodged in the Clerks Office for benefit of his
               Creditors.

11 Nov 1747   - On the motion of LEMUEL BOUSH it's ordered that JOSIAS
 6 MB 111 PAc   BUTT be appointed his guardian during his minority.
               Security Ł 200.

17 Nov 1747   - The sale of JOHN HARVEYS Estate being returned ordered
 6 MB 113 PAc   to be lodged in the office for the benefit of his
               creditors.

15 Dec 1747   - The sale of GEORGE MUNTGOMERYS Estate being returned is
 6 MB 116 PAc   ordered to be lodged in the Clerks Office for benefit
               of his creditors.

19 Jan 1747/8 - JOHN WILLIAMSON bound over by warrant under the hand of
 6 MB 120 PAc   NATHANIEL NEWTON GENT: to answer the complaint of MARY
               WILLIAMSON his wife who is afraid that he would xxxxxxx
               xxxxxx maim or kill her. Court is of the opinion &
therefore order the Sherif to take him in custody untill he enters into
bond with security Ł 100 for his good behavior for 12 months.

15 Mar 1747/8 - On the motion of DANIEL WHITEHURST its ordered that the
 6 MB 122 PAc   Clerk deliver to him his part of his fathers Estate
               lodged in the office.

15 Mar 1747/8 - ELIZABETH LOVETT wid^{o}: of WILLIAM LOVETT decd came into
6 MB 123 PAc   Court and made oath that sd. WM: departed this life
                 without making any will.....Certificate is granted her
for obtaining letters of Administration.

15 Mar 1747/8 - On petition of ARJANT? (ARGENT?) FENTRIS its ordered
6 MB 124 PAc   that the Clerk deliver to her her part of her Father's
                 Estate sold at outcry & lodged in the office.

19 Apr 1748   - LANCASTER LOVETT & ALIFF his wife selling 100 acres of
6 MB 127 PAc   land to MAJOR THOMAS WALKE.

19 Apr 1748   - Estate of THO: WHITEHURST to be sold at public outcry
6 MB 127 PAc

19 Apr 1748   - Sale of JOHN SMITHS Estate returned & ledged in the
6 MB 130   Clerks office for benefit of his creditors.

19 Apr 1748   - JOHN SULLIVANT to be delivered his part of his fathers
6 MB 131 PAc   estate sold at outcry & lodged in the office.

17 May 1748   - Sale of THOMAS WHITEHURST returned & lodged in the
6 MB 134 PAc   clerks office for benefit of his Creditors.

17 May 1748   - SIMEON? JONES Estate returned & lodged in the office.
6 MB 134

17 May 1748   - DOCT: ROBERT PATERSON apptd: guardian to SUSANNAH LAM-
6 MB 134 PAc   OUNT dau of THOS: LAMOUNT decd during her minority....
                 he to take care of her estate....bond for same ⊢ 100.

17 May 1748   - WILLIAM LAND & MARY his wife selling 50 acres to
6 MB 135 PAc   WILLIAM GUY. FRANCES mother of sd MARY relinquished
                 all her right of dower thereto as did MARY.

21 Jun 1748   - SARAH NICHOLAS given liberty to keep an ordinary for
6 MB 136 PAc   one year. On motion of JOSIAH NICHOLAS its ordered
                 that the Sherif sumon JOHN INCE & YATES his wife to
the next court to shew why they do not return an Inventory of CAPT: JOHN
NICHOLAS Estate.

21 Jun 1748   - On the motion of MARY MORRISET its ordered that JOHN
6 MB 136 PAc   BONNEY, PETER MALBONE, TULLY WILLIAMS & WILLIAM DYER
                 or any three of them appraise the Estate of PETER
                 MORRISET.

21 Jun 1748   - Appraisal of EDWARD KEELINGS Estate being returned is
6 MB 136 PAc   ordered to be recorded.

21 Jun 1748   - MAXIMILLIAN BOUSH orphan to be bound to JOHN ELDRIDGE
6 MB 137 PAc   untill he be 21 years old to be taught to read & write
                 and the trade of a Joyner.

60

21 Jun 1748　－ Appraisal of WM: LOVETTS Estate returned & ordered to
6 MB 137 PAc　be recorded.

21 Jun 1748　－ MR: TULLY ROBINSON & ARTHUR SAYER to audit the Estate
6 MB 138 PAc　of THOMAS WALSTON.

21 Jun 1748　－ THOMAS LANGLEY given liberty to keep an Ordinary for
6 MB 138 PAc　one year.

21 Jun 1748　－ COL: ANTHONY WALKE to audit the Estate of DAULEY LATTER
6 MB 138 PAc　decd.

19 Jul 1748　－ JEREMIAH HANLYS Estate to be appraised by JOHN GORNTO
6 MB 139 PAc　JUNR:, JOEL CORNICK, MOSES ROBERTS & JOHN MUNDEN.
　　　　　　　　　Administration granted to SARAH HENLY wido:.
JEREMIAH HENLY departing this life without making a will.

16 Aug 1748　－ FRANCES MOSELEY to be paid Ŀ 4.10 out of the Estate of
6 MB 141 PAc　JAMES WILLIAMSON, decd for keeping 2 of his children
　　　　　　　　　to this time.

16 Aug 1748　－ Appraisal of THOMAS LAMOUNTS Estate returned.
6 MB 143 PAc　Appraisal of JEREMIAH HENLYS Estate returned.

16 Aug 1748　－ HENRY BARLOW & SUSANNAH his wife selling 100 acres of
6 MB 143 PAc　Marsh to JOHN SHIPP.

16 Aug 1748　－ Negroes in Estate of CAPT: JOHN NICHOLAS decd divided
6 MB 144 PAc　between ELIZA: & ANNE NICHOLAS & JOHN INCE & YATES his
　　　　　　　　　wife.

16 Aug 1748　－ HENRY BARLOW & SUSANNAH his wife sold 300 acres of
6 MB 144 PAc　Marsh to WM: CORNICK

20 Sep 1748　－ Ordered that MAXIMILLIAN BOUSH be bound to MR: MORDICA
6 MB 145 PAc　BOUSH untill he be 21 years old & to be taught to read
　　　　　　　　　& write & the art or mistery of Navigation............

20 Sep 1748　－ JOEL SIMMONS & AMY his wife agst LANCASTER LOVETT con-
6 MB 146 PAc　tinued.

10 Oct 1748　－ At a Court for Laying the Leavy:
6 MB 148 PAc　To CAPT: JAMES NIMMO, KINGS ATTORNEY　　　　1000
　　　　　　　　　To ANTHONY WALKE, THO: WALKE & JAMES KEMPE towards build-
　　　　　　　　　ing a bridge over the Head of the Eastern Branch 5000.

18 Oct 1748　－ Sherif ordered to sell all the perrishable Estate of MRS:
6 MB 150 PAc　SARAH THOROWGOOD decd at Public Outcry.

15 Nov 1748　－ JOHN & HENRY SNAILE agst THOMAS LANGLEY & BRIDGET his
6 MB 152 PAc　wife.　Continued.

15 Nov 1748   - Ordered that the Sheriff summon GEORGE OLDNER, PHILIP
6 MB 153 PAc   WOODHOUSE & his wife, JAMES JONES, ABRAHAM WILLEROY &
   -155   his wife, SOLO: WOOD & his wife, THOMAS WHITEHURST SENR.
& his wife (living at three runs), ABRM: POWERS, JOHN CAVENDER & his
wife, JOHN BRINSON JUNR: & his wife, THO: ASHEAL & his wife, OZBURN
BAINS & his wife, MARGARET GARNOR, JOHN MOORE, ELIZA: LOVETT, MARTHA
ROBINSON, THO: LANGLEY & his wife,(at the North Landing). The overseer
of Muddy Creek Road, HESTER SEADY & JOHN STOKES to appear at the next
Court to answer presentments for not going to Church.   .

15 Nov 1748   - CAPT: SOLOMON EDEY & HANNAH his wife acknowledged Lease
6 MB 154 PAc   & release for 300 acres to ARTHUR SAYER...............
                Just below the above:
CAPT: SOLOMON EDEY & HANNAH his wife - 50 acres of Marsh to THO: WARD.

17 Jan 1748/9 - JAMES WHITE son of JOSEPH WHITE decd....ordered that
6 MB 157 PAc   the Clerk deliver to him his part of his Father's &
                Mother's Estate sold at Public Outcry & lodged in the
                Office.

17 Jan 1748/9 - On motion of LEMUEL COLLINGS its ordered that the Clerk
6 MB 157 PAc   deliver to him his part of his fathers estate sold at
                outcry & lodged in the office.

17 Jan 1748/9 - TULLY ROBINSON SMYTHs Lease & Release for 2/3 of 200
6 MB 158 PAc   acres of land to LEWIS THELABALL.....ordered to be
                recorded.   (No bounds are given)

17 Jan 1748/9 - MRS: JACOMINE BRAY acknowledged lease and release for
6 MB 158 PAc   one/third part of 200 acres to LEWIS THELABALL.

10 Feb 1748/9 - Division of CAPT: JOHN NICHOLAS decd, his land between
6 MB 159 PAc   JOHN INCE & YATES his wife adm: of said JOHN & ELIZABETH
                and ANNE NICHOLAS. JOHN NICHOLAS former husband of said
                YATES.   (This included Land and Houses in Newtown)

10 Feb 1748/9 - JOHN MORISS petition for his part of his fathers
6 MB 159 PAc   estate abated by will?

21 Feb 1748/9 - FRANCES wife of TULLY ROBINSON SMYTH relinquished all
6 MB 160 PAc   her right of dower in & to 200 acres of land sold by sd:
                TULLY to LEWIS THELABALL.

21 Feb 1748/9 - CALEB WHITEHURST eldest brother of DAVID WHITEHURST
6 MB 160 PAc   decd. who departed this life without making a will,
                sd: CALEB granted administration.

21 Feb 1748/9 - Ordered that the Clerk deliver to CHRISTOPHER MOSELEY
6 MB 163 PAc   his part of his fathers estate sold at outcry & lodged
                in the office.

21 Feb 1748/9   - On Petition of ARON FENTRISS the Clerk is ordered to
6 MB 163 PAc   deliver to him his part of his fathers estate sold
                   at outcry and lodged in the office.

21 Feb 1748/9   - MR: TULLY ROBINSON GUARDIAN to ELIZ: MacCLANAHAN ROB-
6 MB 163 PAc   INSON......its ordered that he sell all the perrishable
                   Estate of sd: ELIZA: in his hands.

21 Mar 1748/9   - DOCTR: WILLIAM HAPPER to be paid ₤ 11.18.11 out of
6 MN 164 PAc   the Estate of MRS: SARAH THOROWGOOD decd.

21 Feb 1748/9   - Sheriff to sell all the Estate of JOHN OLIVER decd at
6 MB 164 PAc   Public Outcry & return to next Court.

21 Feb 1748/9   - JOHN BRAY decd. & on the same date
6 MB 164 PAc   p 167: Sale of JOHN BRAY's Estate ordered to be lodged
                   in the office for the benefit of his Creditors.

21 Feb 1748/9   - A Chancery suit betw: CHARLES GASKING agst: LEMUEL
6 MB 167 PAc   GASKING, HENRY GASKING & SARAH GASKING.

18 Apr 1748/9   - On the motion of COLL: JAMES MOORE to turn the Road
6 MB 169 PAc   that leads through his plantation to Norfolk........
                   GEO: WISHART, JAS: HUNTER & ROBT: MOSELEY to view &
report to the next Court.

14 May 1749   - SUSANAH MOORE to be bound to DOCTR: CHRISTOPHER WRIGHT
6 MB 172 PAc   & MARY his wife ... that they teach sd. orphan to read
                   sew, knit & spinn......and .....carry her to the
Clerk's Office & take indentures .... & further that they have the lab-
our of a negro girl, Pegg, belonging to the sd. SUSANAH during her
apprenticeship.

14 May 1749   - HENRY SPRATT's decd Estate to be app: by JNO: BONNEY
6 MB 174 PAc   SENR:, TULLY WILLIAMSON & JOHN RUSSELL.

14 May 1749   - Sale of JOHN OLIVER's decd. Estate being returned is
6 MB 175 PAc   ordered to be lodged in the office.

20 Jun 1749   - Clerk to deliver to GEORGE CHAPPEL his part of his
6 MB 177 PAc   fathers estate sold at outcry & lodged in the office.

20 Jun 1749   - SARAH KEELING presented for having a base born child
6 MB 177 PAc   & failing to appear it is ordered that she be attached.

20 Jun 1749   - On motion of BRIDGET LANGLEY there is sundry cattle
6 MB 177 PAc   belonging to her three children, FRAN:, MARY & HENRY
                   SNAILE & nobody to take care of them...its ordered
that the Sherif sell so many of them as MR: JOHN WHITEHURST shall think
necessary & return the money to the next Court.

20 Jun 1749 - Ordered that JOHN LOVETT deliver to WILLIAM COX his
 6 MB 178 PAc   wifes part of her fathers Estate in his hands accord-
                ing to Audit.

10 Jul 1749 - On Motion of 20 Jun 1749 THOROWGOOD SPRATT in behalf of
 6 MB 178 PAc   his brother ADAM SPRATT (p 178) who due to sickness was
                excused from paying leavy...........................
p 179: - HENRY SPRATTS appr. returned & recorded
p 179: - THOROWGOOD SPRATTS Deed of Gift to his 2 sons HENRY & ARGALL
SPRATT for 102 acres.

10 Jul 1749 - On petition of PETER SPARROW....the Clerk to deliver to
 6 MB 180 PAc   him KEZIAH WHITE's part of her mothers estate sold at
                outcry and lodged in the office.

15 Aug 1749 - WILLIAM KING, he being 6 years of age October last, to
 6 MB 182 PAc   be bound to JNO: FENTRIS untill he be 21 years old & to
                be taught to read & write & the trade of a Shewmaker.

15 Aug 1749 - Sheriff to sell all the estate of DUNCAN WHITE decd at
 6 MB 183 PAc   Outcry.

19 Sep 1749 - On petition of THOMAS CASON & SARAH his wife its ordered
 6 MB 185 PAc   that the Clerk deliver to them their part of RENATUS
                LANDS Estate sold at outcry & lodged in the office.

19 Sep 1749 - On Motion of CAPT: JAMES NIMMO in behalf of HENRY MOORE
 6 MB 185 PAc   to have MRS. ANN COX's Dower of the land whereon JNO:
                MOORE lived laid of(f), its ordered that COL°: JACOB
ELLEGOOD, CAPT: WM: KEELING, MAJR: NATHL: HUSTON & ARTHUR SAYER or any
three of them (the sd. ANNE being present & consenting thereto) lay off
& assign to the sd ANNE her dower according to last will of CASON MOORE
& report same to the next Court.

19 Sep 1749 - JOEL SIMMONS & AMY his wife acknowledge release of 46 acs
 6 MB 185 PAc   to JOHN THOROWGOOD.

19 Sep 1749 - Sale of DUNCAN KING Estate being returned to be lodged
 6 MB 186 PAc   in the office for benefit of his creditors.

Same date & - JOHN THOROWGOOD acknowledged lease & release for 28 acs
       page   to JOEL SIMMONS.

26 Oct 1749 - At a Court held for laying the leavy:
 6 MB 188 PAc   To CAPT: JAMES NIMMO, KINGS ATTY   1000
                There were 1629 Tythables.

21 Nov 1749 - Sherif to sell all the Estate of DINAH SULLIVANT at outcry.
 6 MB 189 PAc
21 Nov 1749 - Nuncupative will of DINAH SULLIVANT decd being pvd: by
 6 MB 190 PAc   oaths of THOMAS TURNER & MARK ROBERTS admitted to record.

21 Nov 1749 - On petition of LEWIS BAKER its ordered that the Clerk
 6 MB 190 PAc deliver to him his part of his fathers estate sold at
               outcry & lodged in the office.

21 Nov 1749 - On petition of WILLIAM MOSELEY its ordered that the Clerk
 6 MB 190 PAc deliver to him his part of his fathers Estate sold at
               outcry & lodged in the office.

21 Nov 1749 - Ordered that MR: WILLIAM HANCOCK be appointed surveyor
 6 MB 190 PAc of the roads on the North side of the Eastern Branch
               & the Bridges.

16 Jan 1749/50-On motion of SUSANNAH HANCOCK its ordered that HENRY
 6 MB 191 PAc HOLMES be her guardian during her minority.

16 Jan 1749/50-MRS: EDITH MOSELEY wife of CAPT: WILLIAM MOSELEY.
 6 MB 192 PAc came into Court and relinquished all her right of dower
               into some lots of land sold to GEORGE JAMIESON.

16 Jan 1749/50-The will of MRS: SUSANAH CHESHIRE presented in Court by
 6 MB 192 PAc MRS: ELIZ: CHESHIRE her Exix: & pvd by oaths of ANTHY:
               WALKE SENR: & ANTHY: WALKE JUNR: GENT: & MRS. MONICA
CONNER witnesses thereto.

20 Mar 1749/50-ANNE BLAIR WIdo of JAMES BLAIR......
 6 MB 194 PAc
 same page: The Sheriff is ordered to sell the:
20 Mar 1749/50-Estates of CHARLES MALBON decd., & WILLIAM PEED decd,,
               & WILLIAM LAWRENCE at public outcry.

20 Mar 1749/50-The sale of DINAH SULLIVANTS Estate being returned is
 6 MB 196 PAc ordered to be lodged in the office for benefit of her
               Creditors.

21 Mar 1749/50-LEVINAH (Susinah?) FOUNTAINE by ELIZA: FOUNTAINE her
 6 MB 198 PAc mother & next friend agst. SAMUEL HOLLOWELL & PRUDENCE
               his wife - Trespas.

21 Mar 1749/50-On motion of JAMES MOORE tis ordered that the clerk del-
 6 MB 198 PAc iver to him all the estate of his brother MOSES MOORE
               sold at outcry & lodged in the office.

21 Mar 1749/50-On the motion of THURMER HOGGARD its ordered that the
 6 MB 199 PAc Clerk deliver to him his wifes part of her fathers
               Estate sold at outcry & lodged in the office.

21 Mar 1749/50-EDWARD ABSALOM & SUSANNAH his wife complainants agst.
 6 MB 200 PAc EDWARD CANNON & als defts: in Chancery.   CAPT: WILLIAM
               KEELING, MR: JOEL & LEML: CORNICK should make division
of the negroes in the complts: bill.

15 May 1750 - Ordered that JOHN SULLIVANT be bound to ADAM DALE till
6 MB 201 PAc   he be 21 years old & to teach him to read & write and
               the trade of a Hatter.

15 May 1750 - JOHN TURNER's will proved
6 MB 202 PAc

15 May 1750 - The sale of JOSEPH HARMONS Estate being returned is
6 MB 202 PAc   ordered to be lodged in the Clerks Office for benefit
               of his creditors.

15 May 1750 - Sale of WILLIAM LAWRENCES Estate being returned ordered
6 MB 203 PAc   to be lodged in the officc....
               Ditto .... WILLIAM PEEDS Estate.......................

15 May 1750 - Clerk ordered to deliver to DAVID ffENTRIS his part of
6 MB 203 PAc   his fathers estate sold at ourcry and lodged in the
               office.
15 May 1750 - Clerk ordered to deliver to JOHN CUMBERFORD his part of
6 MB 204 PAc   his fathers estate.

15 May 1750 - EDMOND ABSOLUM & SUSANNAH his wife agst: EDWARD CANNON
6 MB 205 PAc   & ELIZA: his wife, EDWARD, KATHERINE, & ffRANCIS LAMOUNT
               in Chancery. LEMUEL CORNICK & WILLIAM KEELING GENT:
               two of the Comrs: apptd to divide the negroes in Complt:
bill. Assigned dower of THOMAS LAMOUNTS negroes to ELIZABETH now wife
of EDMD: CANNON which is Adam, he the sd. CANNON to pay 3/4 to sd LAM-
OUNTS Children & that EDMOND ABSOLUM who intermarried with SUSANAH one
of the daughters of afsd. THO: LAMOUNT to have negro Moody he paying
£ 10.16.8 to the younger children of LAMOUNT.

15 May 1750 - Sale of CHARLES MALBONE Estate returned & lodged in the
6 MB 205 PAc   office for benefit of his creditors.

6 Jun 1750 - BARBARA KEELING - that her son ALEX: KEELING is so infirme
6 MB 206 PAc   that he is not able to do anything towards getting his
               board.......He is to be excused from paying leavy during
his Inability.

16 Oct 1750 - Ordered that the Clerk deliver to FRANCIS LAND his part
6 MB 224 PAc   of his father RENATUS LANDS Estate sold at outcry & lodged
               in the office.

16 Oct 1750 - JOHN MOSELEY son of PALMER MOSELEY bound to JNO: WMSON:
6 MB 225 PAc   untill he is 21 years old & to teach him to read & write
               and the trade of a blockmaker.

20 Nov 1750 - Clerk to deliver to ROBERT DAVIS his part of his fathers
6 MB 226 PAc   Estate sold at outcry & lodged in the office.

18 Dec 1750 - Clerk to deliver to BURROUGH MOSELEY his part of his
6 MB 230 PAc   fathers Estate sold at outcry & lodged in the office.

18 Dec 1750   - On the motion of CAPT: JAS: KEMPE guardian of MRS: ELIZA:
 6 MB 230 PAc LOVETT its ordered that LANCASTER LOVETT deliver to him
               the sd ELIZABETHS part of her brother JOHN LOVETTS Estate
in his hands........LANCASTER being present & agreed thereto.

18 Dec 1750   - LEWIS THELABALL on a jury 18 Dec 1750. (He was alive at
 6 MB 231 PAc this date so couldn't have been SUSANNAH's father. She
               being the wife of THURMER HOGGARD)

16 Jan 1750/1- THO: EVERARD & JAMES NIMMO Exors of WILLIAM NIMMO decd.
 6 MB 238 PAc agst: JOHN KEELING dismist.

16 Jan 1750/1- Land purchased by MR: THO: HUNTER of HENRY MOORE on
 6 MB 240 PAc Lincholn Bay...... East side of......ANNE GILES to
               receive & hold her dower of the land and orchards.
               GERSHOM NIMMO was the Surveyor.

20 Feb 1750/1- JOHN HARPER agst: JOSIAH BUTT & MARY his wife, THOS:
 6 MB 246   THELABALL & ELIZABETH his wife, LEML: BOUSH, MAXM: BOUSH
               & FREDERICK BOUSH Infants by JOSIAH BUTT, THO: THELABALL
               & WM: KEELING their guardians in chancery..............
Depositions taken in the said cause should be read in order to make appear that MAXM: BOUSH in the bill mentioned was a Fraudulent purchaser
& had notice before the purchase made from MARK LOWELL that the property
of the slave in this bill was in compltts: ancester JAS: HARPER under
the will of ROBT: HARPER the compltts: grand father......Appealed to the
next Court. (see also p 256 CAPT: JAS: MOORE agst same as above & also
p 257 - above case to next court.)

19 Mar 1750/1- On petition of SARAH ANNE FENTRISS its ordered that
 6 MB 250 PAc ELIZA: FENTRISS pay her her part of her fathers, JNO:
               FENTRISS Estate with interest.

21 May 1751   - On the motion of ARGALL & ffRA: THOROWGOOD its ordered
 6 MB 258 PAc that LANCASTER LOVETT be their guardian during their
               minority.

21 May 1751   - MRS: ELIZABETH THELABALL wido: of MR: THO: THELABALL
 6 MB 259 PAc decd. came into Court & being first privily examined
               acknowledged her right of dower in & to 223 acres of land
formerly sold by COLL: MAXL: BOUSH her former husband decd to SAMUEL
BOUSH & by sd: SAMUEL lately sold to LEML: GASKING & ordered that the
Clerk make record thereof

21 May 1751   - Petition of MAJ: ffR: MOSELEY & others to turn the road
 6 MB 261 PAc that leads from Lynnhaven Bay to NEWTOWN.....to the next
               Court.

20 Aug 1751   - WM: LANGLEY Exor: of JEREMIAH LANGLEY decd.
 6 MB 267 PAc

16 Oct 1751   - ANNE COX alias GILES Exix: of JOHN MOORE decd.
 6 MB 275 PAc

19 Nov 1751   - MARG: ELLET Exor of PETER ELLET decd who died without
6 MB 275 PAc making a will. (see p 278)

17 Dec 1751   - CAPT: MARKHAM HERBERT agst: DAVID MUSSOR? to next Court.
6 MB 283 PAc

17 Dec 1751   - Judgmt: granted ANTHONY, THO: & CHARLES LAWSON for 35
6 MB 283 PAc shillings due from JAMES SHERWOOD.

27 Mar 1751/2- JOHN WHIDDON deed of gift for 1 negro girl named Pleasant
6 MB 293 PAc to JOHN CAWSON.

27 Mar 1752   - Ordered that ARGALL THOROWGOOD have his equall share of
6 MB 295 PAc two negroes Barrick & Cuffe sold by MR: WM: KEELING She-
              rif by order of this Court belonging to the Estate of
MR: FRA: THOROWGOOD decd.

21 Apr 1752   - Ordered that HEWLET MOSELEY be guardian to ABSOLUM MOSELEY.
6 MB 301 PAc

14 May 1752   - On the motion of HEWLET MOSELEY son of PALMER MOSELEY
6 MB 304 PAc decd. its ordered that NATHL: NEWTON, JAMES HUNTER,
              JONATHAN SAUNDERS & WILLIAM MOSELEY GENT: make division
of the negroes belonging to the decedents Estate.

14 May 1752   - JOEL SIMMONS Guardian to ANNE & FRA: THOROWGOOD during
6 MB 304 PAc their minority.....& enter into bond & security in the
              amount of ₤ 50.

16 Jun 1752   - CAPT: JAMES NIMMO ordered himself as special bond for
6 MB 314 PAc GEORGE ROUVIERE

21 Jul 1752   - On the petition of HENRY WOODHOUSE who marryd: ELIZA:
6 MB 322 PAc the daughter of THOS: HILL decd its ordered that AFFIAH
              HILL wido: of the decedant pay him his part of the said
HILLS Estate in her hands.

26 Sep 1752   - On the motion of SAML: EASTER its ordered that THOS:
6 MB 325 PAc WISHART, JAMES ASHLEY & THURMER HOGGARD audit & settle
              the estate of JAMES JONES & return the same to the next
              Court.

18 Nov 1752   - Court for laying the leavy: to CAPT: JAMES NIMMO, Kings
6 MB 332 PAc Attorney   1000.

18 Nov 1752   - JAS: LANGLEY decd....his will further proved ....
6 MB 337 PAc "reserving the use thereof (the manner plantation) to my
              loving wife SARAH LANGLEY during her natural life......

19 Dec 1752   - On motion of SAMUEL SMITH its ordered that PETER HARBERT
6 MB 342 PAc deliver to him his part of his fathers estate in his
              hands likewise that the clerk deliver to him his part of
his fathers Estate in the office.

19 Dec 1752 - REDOLPHUS MALLBONE agst JONATHAN JACKSON an infant by
 6 MB 344 PAc WILLIAM CORNICK his guardian. The last will of JOHN
               RICHASONS decd dated 29 Aug 1714 with the following
devises: unto my gr-son JNO: RICHASON the son of THO: RICHASON the
Plantation whereon I now live.....in case my gr-son should die to the
next lawful heirs of my son THOMAS RICHASON & also negroes...........
will proved 4 Oct 1714. JOHN RICHASON the devisee died about 14 years
of age without issue.....THO: RICHASON, JOHNS father died & left issue
only two daughters MARY & ANNE & a son JOHN the devisee. The dau MARY
intermarried with REDOL: MALBONE.....the other daugher ANNE -(bottom
of page is badly torn)- ....(this is a long item about slaves
and their ownership) JOHN RICHASON died under age intestate leaving
no brothers or sisters of the whole blood, but only two sisters of the
half blood MARY & ANNE and that ANNE JACKSON grandmother of the said
defendant was the only sister of the whole blood to THOS: RICHASON
father of the said JOHN.............. we find that the DEFT: is eldest
son and heir at law of the said   JOHN JACKSON his father.............
........(there is more to this item)

17 Jan 1753 - The Court having viewed the New Prison in Newtown &
 6 MB 352 PAc being of Opinion the same is sufficient & therefore
               ordered that for the future the said prison be made use
of as the Common Goal of this County....Bounds to take in the 1/2 acre
Lott where the sd goal & Courthouse stands.

END OF 6 MINUTE BOOK EXCERPTS - PRINCESS ANNE COUNTY, VA.

DEED BOOK 7 PRINCESS ANNE COUNTY, VIRGINIA

1747 - 1755

++

Abstracts of all the genealogical data and of
all of the wills contained in the 714 pages of this
massive volume of Court Records.

15 Mar 1747   JONATHAN (M) MARTIN
7 DB 3 PAc   wd 1 Jun 1747 wp 15 Mar 1747 (Inventory p 9)
               wife ELIZABETH Exix., son PRESON MARTIN, dau KEZZIA MARTIN
Wit: HENRY JAMISON, JONATHAN MARTIN & THOMAS (X) OWENS.

19 Apr 1748
7 DB 7 PAc   THOS: WALKE to JOSHUA NICHOLSON 2 lots & houses thereon
               in Newtown joyning Sly on the Eastern Branch Wly on the
Street that leads from the gate to the old Catch Landing Nly on MR.
EDWARD HACK MOSELEYS land & Ely on a Branch that makes out of the
Eastern Branch.

17 May 1748 Dated 6 Apr 1748 - FRANCES MOSELEY wido & WILLIAM LAND &
7 DB 15 PAc MARY his wife selling to WM: GUY of Elizabeth River Parish
             Shipwright....50 acres - one tract of land at the head of
Broad Creek begin: at a gum at Logg Trap Dam Branch & running by mkd
trees NEly 39° 82 poles &c..

17 May 1748 EDWARD KEELING
7 DB 16 PAc wd 20 Dec 1747 wp 17 May 1748 Exor: brother WILLIAM
             To my brother WILLIAM KEELING my hole & sole estate.
Wit: JOHN GILES, WM: COX, WM: CROMPTON.

20 Dec 1748 THOMAS HUDDLESTONE
7 DB 59 PAc wd 14 Nov 1748 wp 20 Dec 1748 Inventory p 113
             Daus: AMY CANNON, DIRNA HUDDLESTON, BARBARA CAVENDER,
ELIZA: RANEY & MARY JONES. Sons: JOHN HUDDLESTONE & THOS: HUDDLESTONE
EXOR.

20 Dec 1748 JOEL SIMMONS witnessed a Deed 20 Oct 1748 but did not prove
7 DB 61 PAc it 20 Dec 1748 when it was recorded.

20 Dec 1748 Dated 14 Dec 1748 - SOLOMON EDEY & HANNAH his wife & one
7 DB 63 PAc of the sisters & co-heirs of THO: IVY decd who was son &
             heir of CAPT: JOHN IVY of Princess Anne County also decd
& one of the sisters & co-heirs of ALIFF late the wife of CAPT: MATTHAIS
MILLER or Norfolk County selling to ARTHUR SAYER 1/2 part of all that
tract lying in the Parish of Linhaven, 100 acres in two parts to be
divided whereon JOHN IVY father of sd HANNAH lately lived & was seized
in fee thereof including that part where WM: McCLANEY lived.

17 Jan 1748 THOMAS LANGLEY Deed of Gift to his wife BRIDGET a cow
7 DB 74 PAc calfe and other things. Dated 25 Nov 1746. Witnessed
             by WM: WHITEHURST & JNO: SNALE.

17 Jan 1748/9 WILLIS WHITEHURST
& DB 74 PAC   wd 22 Jul 1748 wp 17 Jan 1748/9 by JAMES SMYTH & MARY BOUSH
                                                        the witnesses.
              He named 2 brothers: ARTHUR & CHARLES WHITEHURST.

72

17 Nov 1748   WILLIAM PORTLOCK & MARKHAM HERBERT Gents. (took the oath
7 DB 83 PAc   of JANE CORBETTS) send Greeting. Whereas RICHARD CORBETTS
of Norfolk County has certain Indentures of Lease & Release dated 21
October 1745 did convey unto CAPT: JOHN HUTCHINGS of Norfolk County the
fee simple of 130 acres in Princess Anne County & it appears to us that
JANE wife of RICH: CORBETTS is sickly & impotent she cannot travel to
Princess Anne County Court.

21 Mar 1748   MARY BOUSH, sister of WM: COX, BENJA: COX & JNO: COX &
7 DB 96 PAc   sister of JOHN MOORE whose will dated 20 Dec 1748 names
              their mother, ANNE COX and these sister & brothers.

16 May 1749   MARY WHITEHURST of Lynhaven Parish
7 DB 104 PAc wd 23 Sep 1748 wp 16 May 1749 by the witnesses JOHN
              CUMBERFOOT and CASON MOORE JUNR: The witness MARY CUMBER -
FOOT did not prove the will.
Executor son, THOMAS WHITEHURST   Sons: THOMAS, ANTHONY & SOLOMON
Gr-sons: JOHN son of JAMES WHITEHURST, WM: son of ANTHONY WHITEHURST,
         MICHAEL? and JAMES EATON, GODFREY son of THOS: WHITEHURST,
         JAMES son of JAMES WHITEHURST, JOHN son of WM: WHITEHURST
Daus: ELIS: EATON, DINA CAPPS & SARAH HENLEY.   These last two daughters
      received the residue of estate.

16 May 1749   MARGARETT MALBONE's Deed of Gift to "my grandchildren, or
7 DB 105 PAc the son and daughter of (ISAK?) & URSULA MALBONE namely:
              GODFREY, JOHN, ALIF & MARGARETTE MALBONE." Dated 4 Apr 1749.

16 May 1749   HENRY SPRATT
7 DB 105 PAc wd 13 Mar 1748/9 wp 16 May 1749 by JNO: RUSSEL & WILLIAM
              OAKHAM witnesses thereto. Anoth witness was THOMAS GIBBS.
brother: JAMES SPRATT brother: PATRICK WHITE executor
cossen: FRANCES WHITE & her sister MARY WHITE, their younger sister
         BETTY WHITE. unto JOHN GREEN a young cow that has lost its calf.

16 May 1749   THOMAS GRANT (or GRANTE)
7 DB 106 PAc wd 21 Jan 1748/9 wp 16 May 1749 by HENRY JAMESON & THOMAS
              OWENS. ALEX: JAMESON was a witness.
wife: MARY GRANT exix: daughter: ONNER GRANT (her name is clearly
to JAMES EASTER & TO MARY EASTER   written)

20 Jun 1749   BARTHO: WILLIAMSON
7 DB 109 PAc wd 12 Apr 1749 wp 20 Jun 1749
              wife DINAH   sons: JAMES land joining on JOHN MATTHIAS
                              and JOHN DAVIS
daus: PRUDENCE, MARY & DINAH   ROBERT
                                  JOSHUA

17 Jul 1749   JAMES NIMMO witnessed a deed 17 Jul 1749
7 DB 116 PAc

19 Janry 1747 (this date is out of place in the book) Recorded again
15 Aug 1749 - Dated 6 Apr 1747 : THOMAS CORNISH Planter of Knots
7 DB 126 PAc Island in Parish of Coratuck....to his son, ELIAS CORNISH
              200 acres in the Northern branches of Coratoke.........

19 Sep 1749   JOHN THOROWGOOD son of FRANCIS to JOEL SIMMONS for Ŀ 12
7 DB 128 PAc   a tract of land on the Eastward side of Broad Creek and
              is the same land that FRANCIS THOROWGOOD father of the
said JOHN purchased from FRANCIS CARY? ..... 28 acres as by release
dated 13 Aug 1740.   Dated 19 Sep 1749 & Recorded same day. The
bounds of the land are not given.   (The date 13 Aug 1740 may not be
right but the date is definitely .....teenth Aug 1740)

7 DB 131 - same date as above: JOEL SIMMONS Boatwright to JOHN THOROW-
              GOOD son of FRANCIS & AMY THOROWGOOD, Mariner all of
Princess Anne County......JOEL is releasing any right and title to all
that tract or plantation that FRANCIS THOROWGOOD father of said JOHN
purchased from MATHEW PALLETT on the Eastern Shore containing 42 acres.

19 Sep 1749   JOHN AVIS
7 DB 132 PAc   wd 15 Sep 1748 wp 19 Sep 1749
              Witnesses: JOHN HANY, THO: (T) WHITEHURST & CASON MOORE
                         Junr.
son: WILLABY AVIS the old Plantation
son: JOHN AVIES
wife: RUTH   4 daus: ELIZABETH, RUTH, MARY & MARTHA
to JOHN RANEY 30 acres of land
Exors: wife and friend JOHN BONNEY

21 Nov 1749   WILLIAM DYER of Lynhaven Parish (he made his mark)
7 DB 140 PAc   wd 24 Sep 1747 wp 21 Nov 1749
              Wit: JNO: WMSON:, THO: WMSON:, CASON MOORE JUNR.
son: WILLIAM DYER plantation I now live on ...94 acres according to
        the direction of the pattern ....reversion
to son: HEZEKIAH.........reversion to dau: ELIZABETH.
wife: ELIZABETH DYER   daus: MARY & SARAH He also left other
land known as SHIPS.

21 Nov 1749   THOMAS TURNER & MARK ROBERTS made oath that on 31 Oct
7 DB 141 PAc   last they heard DINAH SULLIVANT a wid° decd say that it
              was her desire that her son MANNUEL BUTT should have his
young horse 7c....her 2 sons JOHN & MORRIS SULLIVANT cows &c..........
(The name may be Mannel and not Mannuel?)

21 Nov 1749   RUTH AVIS signed the Inventory of JOHN AVIS.

16 Jan 1749/50 SUSANNAH CHESHIRE of Lynhaven Parish
7 DB 145 PAc   wd 30 May 1746 wp 16 Jan 1749 by ANTHONY WALKE JUNR.,
              ANTHONY WALKE SENR: GENT & MRS. MONICA CONNER. Another
              witness was THOS: WALKE.
Son: JOHN THOROWGOOD
dau: PEMBROKE WRIGHT wife of CAPT: STEPHEN WRIGHT of Norfolk County
dau: ELIZABETH CHESHIRE the residue
Exors: CAPT: STEPHEN WRIGHT, CAPT. ARTHUR SAYER & daughter ELIZA: CHES-
      HIRE.

74

20 Mar 1749/50   RICHD: DROUGHT of Princess Anne County
7 DB 153 PAc   wd 1 Oct 1749 wp 20 Mar 1749/50 by both witnesses.
                 Wit: GEORGE WISHART & ROBT: MOSELEY
Mother: MARY LESTER exix.
sister-in-law: AMY LESTER
Reversion to be equally divided between REBECKA MOSELEY daughter of
ROBERT & AMY MOSELEY & MARY WISHART daughter of GEORGE & MARY WISHART.

20 Mar 1749/50   CHARLES SMYTH of Newtown, Merchant
7 DB 161 PAc   wd 2 Nov 1749 wp 20 Mar 1749/50 by all the witnesses.
                 Wit:THO: GRAINGER & GEORGE WEBLIN
wife: MARGT: all lands in town & Country for natural life.
son: TULLY SMYTH (after decease of wife) my plantation lying on the
       North Landing & 1 lott in Newtown purchased from ARTHUR SAYER.
son: PERRIN SMYTH... plantation in Little Creek
daus: BETTY, MARGARETT & ANNE ....3 lotts whereon I now live with houses
       &c .... 1 doz. silver spoons to be divided.......
To dau: BETTY a silver slasped Bible &c......books....................
Wife & friend CAPT: ARTHUR SAYER Exors.

20 Mar 1749/50   ROBERT WHITEHURST (he made his mark)
7 DB 166 PAc   wd   no date   wp by ANTHONY BURROUGHS & CHRIST: MOSELEY
                 Another witness was: ANTHY: WHITEHURST
wife: FLORENCE ..whole use of Plantation during her widowhood and
       afterward to
son: ANTHONY WHITEHURST
dau: MARY WHITEHURST
"the rest of my children" (not named)

20 Mar 1749/50   MARGARET JOHNSON of Princess Anne County (she made her
7 DB 167 PAc   wd 10 Mar 1749/50 wp 20 Mar 1749/50 by   mark)
                 all the witnesses: ARTH: SAYER, JOHN HARPER, THOS: HARVEY
dau: MARY NIMMO wife of CAPT: JAMES NIMMO
dau: JACOMINE HUNTER wife of MR. JOHN HUNTER
ge-son: JACOB HUNTER
two sons-in-law: JAMES NIMMO & JOHN HUNTER Exors.

20 Mar 1749/50   MARLING CUMMINGS
7 DB 167 PAc   wd 29 Dec 1749 wp 20 Mar 1749/50 (can't read the names
                 of the witnesses.
brother: JOSHUA CUMMINGS
Younger brother: CAILEB CUMMINGS
brother: BENJA: CUMMINGS
"My Mother, ELIZABETH CUMMINGS Exix."

20 Mar 1749/50   JOHN DYER of Lynhaven Parish (he made his mark)
7 DB 168 PAc   wd 6 Jan 1749/50 wp 20 Mar 1749/50 by SOLO: & SARAH
                 WHITEHURST witnesses thereto. Other wit: CASON MOORE JR:
wons: WILLIAM DYER 40 acres   & JNO: DYER 50 acres whereon I now
residue to wife: SARAH   live & 30 acres of swamp bought of
                                   JAMES MOORE.
My five children: JNO:, JAMES, SARAH & LYDIA & JEMIMA DYER

15 May 1750   JOHN TURNER of Princess Anne County
7 DB 168 PAc wd 6 Apr 1750 wp 15 May 1750 by all the witnesses
                Wit: ROBT: BURROUGHS, JAMES CARTWRIGHT & MARY CARTWRIGHT
to LEM'L: CARTWRIGHT my Plantation (with reversion to THO: TURNER) and
    things in the hands of ELIZA: NICHOLSON.
to THO: TURNER..negro, 52 shillings in the hands of ADAM LOVETT.......
to WM: SALMONS... negro....hoggs at ANNE NORRIS....40/ in the hands of
    THOMAS LANGLEY
to LEWIS PAIN? one cow....hogg.....Ł 3 cash
to JOB GASKING JUNR: 2 cows... 23/ in the hands of ANDREW SMAW?.......
    hogg at JOHN BIDDLES
to JOHN WILLIAMSON son of TULLY
to THOS: "   "   "
to FRA: "   "   "
to TULLY   "   "   "
to MARY   "   dau   "
to HENRY   "   brother of MARY(above)
to SARAH CARTWRIGHT dau of MARY BASSET
to ANTHONY WMSON: Ł 4 cash
                A bond of JAMES SMITH's with the interest thereon to be
equally divided among the above said WILLIAMSONS as they shall come to
age.
                To the child that ELIZA: PRICE now goes with 34 acres of
land belonging to the tract LEWIS PRICE now lives on but if it is a daughter to be equally divided between that & ANNE PRICE.
to MARY BASSET........
Residue to be equally divided between WM: SALMONS, THO: TURNER, JOB
GASKING JUNR., LEMUEL CARTWRIGHT & his sister SARAH CARTWRIGHT.
Exors: JOB GASKING JUNR: & LEMUEL CARTWRIGHT

15 May 1750   WILLIAM DALE of Princess Anne County being very sick & weak
7 DB 169 PAc wd 8 Dec 1749 wp 15 May 1750 by MARY ANNE DALE & JACOB
                ELLEGOOD. Other witness was JNO: KEELING
Wife: ELIZABETH....use of negroes during her natural life & after
        to
dau: BETTY DALE...all my land and marsh to sd dau & also my negroes
        Old Cale, Dick & Sary.
to MARY DALE alias McBRIDE, daughter of RUTH McBRIDE, but in case daughter
        BETTY DALE die without issue then the whole of my estate given to
        her to be equally divided between MARY ANNE & RACHEL DALE & the
        above MARY McBRIDE.....residue to wife & daughter BETTY DALE.

15 May 1750   Memorandum: Dated 17 Apr Apr 1750 Recorded 15 May 1750
7 DB 176 PAc That PATIENCE BURROUGHS late of Princess Anne County decd.
                about 4 days before her death made her nuncupative will in
these words: her son ARGALL THOROWGOOD to have her estate excepting a
small matter to her son ADAM THOROWGOOD as a token of her affection, in
particular all her wareing clothes to be given to BETTY THOROWGOOD dau.
of said ADAM excepting the choice of her suit of clothes to her sister
ABIGAIL WHIDDON & that she desired to see MAJ: NATHANIEL NEWTON to get
him to draw her will.....she said PATIENCE BURROUGH decd. declared &
published in the presence of the severall witnesses.
Wit: NATHA: NEWTON   signed: ANNE (X) RICE, BARBARA (X) MIMS?
                                    ELIZABETH (X) PAICKET

17 Jul 1750 - JOHN WILLIAMS SENR: of Princess Anne County
7 DB 192 PAc   wd 2 Jul 1750 wp 17 Jul 1750 by MARY WILLIAMS & CASON
              3rd wit: DENNIS DAWLEY   MOORE
wife: ELIZA: cow calfe &c...
son JNO WILLIAMS...cows &c..
my wife's son JOHN CAPPS..
Exors: wife & son Jno: signed: JOHN (‡) WILLIAMS Senr.
I add that whereas my son THO: WILLIAMS & dau MARY CARREL have been
marryed from me for some years past have received their portions of
my estate.......they are not to claim any part of my estate.

24 Aug 1750 - WILLIAM WIGGIN
7 DB 196 PAc   wd 29 Dec 1749 wp 24 Aug 1750 by both the witnesses
              Wit: JNO: (X) MONGOMERE & ROBT: MOSELEY
to my son-in-law EDWARD MOSELEY all my glasses?, tubs? to him.......
to my son FRANCIS WIGGIN my gun......................................
Residue to my wife during her life and then to be divided between
bouth my children.   wife EASTER exix.

12 Oct 1750 - FAIRFIELD - Eastern Branch of Elizabeth. COL: ANTHONY
7 DB 204PAc   WALKE, GENT: to CAPT: GEO: WISHART for 20 pistols of
money .... one lott & 1/2 acre of land near WAREHOUSE LANDING at
the head of the EASTERN BRANCH of Elizabeth River known by the name
of FAIRFIELDS. (This is a long deed)......Recorded 16 Oct 1750.

19 Dec 1750 - ABIA COX selling land that she bought of ROBERT HOLMES
7 DB 211 PAc   & JACOB TAYLOR, being the same place MR. ADAM HAYES
              gave to his daughter SARAH HAYES known by the name of
HAWKINS whereon said ABIA COX now livath.. to ROBERT CARTWRIGHT
                                        Rec. 19 Dec 1750

18 Dec 1750 - JAMES GISBORN (GISBOURN in signature)
7 DB 214 PAc   wd 22 Mar 1749/50 wp 18 Dec 1750 by AUGUSTUS LANE &
              EXIX: wife ELIZABETH   THO: (T) GISBORN
to son JOⁿ: my plantation..
              with reversion to younger son SOLOMON.................
Residue to wife ELIZABETH......... daughter SARAH...................
Witnesses who did not prove will were JNO: GISBORN & ? ETHERIDGE.

18 Dec 1750 - ELENOR (X) JONES of Princess Anne County
7 DB 214 PAc   Wd xxxxxx wp 18 Dec 1750 by both the witnesses: BATSON
              WHITEHURST SEN: & BATSON WHITEHURST JUNR:
Exor: HENRY BURGESS
Unto ANNE BURGESS dau of HENRY 1/2 of my estate to be put in custody
of her father until she comes of age or marrys.
Unto HENRY BURGESS the other 1/2 of my estate.....................

15 Jan 1750/1- WILLIAM PURDY
7 DB 221 PAc   wd 13 Nov 1750 wp 15 Jan 1750/1 by all the witnesses
              Wit: JOHN SENICA, JAS: (4·1) SENICA
son EVAN PURDY the manner plantation & 100 acres of land belonging to
it.......son HUGH PURDY 100 acres buond? (beyond?) where HORSKINS (HOS-
KINS) did live...3 sons HUGH, WILLIAM & EVAN 200 acs upon JONES ISLAND
2 daus DINAH WARD & MARGᵀ:

19 Feb 1750/1 - Dated 19 Sep 1749 - THOMAS LANGLEY'S Deed of Gift to
7 DB 229 PAc   his wife, BRIDGET ... 2 beds &c ... use of half the
                land whereon said THO: lives & other things, all the
Pewter she had before intermarriage with THO: LANGLEY .... household
goods ... negroes ...   Witnesses; CAPT; JNO: WHITEHURST & THO: CASON

19 Feb 1750/1 - JOHN KEY of Princess Anne County
7 DB 231 PAc   wd 27 Oct 1748 wp 19 Feb 1750/1 by ROBERT BURROUGHS
                Exor: son JNO:
son Jno: KEY the plantation .... my handmill ....
son JAS: KEY all my Smiths tools also one good feather bed &c .....
dau SARAH KEY.... sons JOSEPH, JOSHUA & JONATHAN ... dau ANNE BATSON

19 Feb 1750/1 - ROGER (T) WILLIAMSON SENR: of Princess Anne County
7 DB 236 PAc   wd 4 Jan 1750/1 wp 19 Feb 1750/1 by JNO: WMSON:
                & THO: GRAINGER. 3rd wit MAXIMILIAN BOUSH.
son: TULLY WMSON: son: SAM$^{\perp}$: WMSON, negro girl Aliph
son: JAS: bed, pott &c ....
son SOLOMON negro wench Nann, one pair milstones, pewter plates.....
dau: ELIZA: COOPER, negro child Mathew son: ROGER (spelled also
RODGER) ......son ANTHONY .... Exors: ROGER & SOLOMON

18 Feb 1751   - GEORGE CAPPS selling to SOLOMON WHITEHURST a parcel
7 DB 240 PAc   of Marsh at a place called CAPE PORPSES MARSHES, 25
                acres bounding on PETERS COVE CREEK on the West side
of the GREAT ISLAND.

19 Mar 1750/1 - SMITH (X) SHEPARD of Princess Anne County
7 DB 245 PAc   wd 16 Jan 1750/1 wp 19 Mar 1750/1 by LEML: CORNICK
                The other witness was ADAM DALE
wife FRANCES .... 4 children ......daus FRANCES, ELIZA: ....
son SMITH SHEPHERD the plantation..................................
son WM: SHEPARD plantation whereon JOHN BROWN Lives................
to two sons Swamp land ....

19 Mar 1750/1 - THOMAS (T) FRANKLIN
7 DB 247 PAc   wd 31 Jul 1747 wp 19 Mar 1750/1 by DINAH WARD
                Other wit: ELIZA: (X) SPANN, et als
son - DANNIEL FRANKLIN ... plantation whereon WILLIAM DAVIS lately
lived....150 acres ....
son THOMAS ... plantation whereon I live ... 74 acres ....
dau MARY FRANKLIN 50 acres I bought of WM: CREED ... wife SARAH.

16 Apr 1751   - SAMUEL POWER
7 DB 250 PAc   wd 7 Nov 1750 wp 16 Apr 1751 by THO: OWENS & JAMES
                ASHBY.
wife MARY ... six children I had by her ....
wife MARY the plantation ....to revert to son SAMPSON......
son SAM$^{\perp}$: 1/ ....son JOSEPH 1/ ....dau AMY Ⱶ 10 ....
residue to wife except negro Hannah to son LOWERY POWERS as soon as
he comes to age of 21 years .... if he dies .... to my four daus:
ELIZABETH, MARY & 2 youngest not yet baptised.

20 May 1751   - COL: MAXIMILIAN BOUSH the Elder, father to SAM'L: BOUSH
7 DB 260 PAc   & gr-father of LEMUEL BOUSH. There are other names in
               this deed...

15 Oct 1751   - ELINOR BUCHANAN OF Princess Anne County
7 DB 270 PAc   wd 2 Oct 1751 wp 15 Oct 1751   by ANNE NORRIS & SARAH
Other wit: SUSANNAH MOORE &   SNAILE
            JNO: HARPER   Exor: CHRISTOPHER WRIGHT
.....all of my estate (after debts are payd) to be equally divided between my children. (not named) No inventory of appraisement to be
made.

5 Aug 1751   - THO: WILES father of SAMUEL WILES
7 DB 275 PAc

29 Nov 1751   - RICHARD GARNER of Princess Anne County
7 DB 278 PAc wd 16 Feb 1750/1 wp 29 Nov 1751 by HENRY BURGESS
               The other wit: FRANCIS RUSSELL
wife: ELIZA: GARNER   dau: ANNE CONSAUL son: ADAM GARNER
wife and three children..... son-in-law WILLIAM CONSAUL & wife Exors.

18 Nov 1751   - CORNELIUS CALVERT, Mariner & ELIZABETH, his wife (one
7 DB 279 PAc   of the daughters   & co-heirs of JOHN THOROWGOOD SENR:
                 late of Princess Anne County of the one part selling
for the sum of ₤340 to CHRISTOPHER WRIGHT, Practitioner of Physick &
Chirurgery of Princess Anne of the other part.....one half part of
that tract or plantation of land in the Parish of Linhaven..........
705 acres in two parts divided whereon JOHN THOROWGOOD SENR: lived
.......which was set aside & assigned to said ELIZA: when sale ` by
ANTHY: MOSELEY & JAS: CONDON who were appointed by virtue of a Bill
of Chancery....exhibited in Court by WILLIAM KEELING JUNR: & MARY his
wife (the other daughter & co-heir of said JOHN THOROWGOOD SENR: decd)
plts agst SARAH THOROWGOOD & the said ELIZABETH then ELIZABETH THORO-
GOOD defts: together with JAMES KEMPE & WILLIAM COX that they or any
2 of them make partition & division of the sd lands whereof said JOHN
THOROWGOOD SENR: was seised in..........the said decree & return of
the said ANTHY: MOSELEY & JAS: CONDON remaining of record among the
records of Princess Anne Court may appeare .... which moiety or
one half part of said land is bounded by the GLEBE LAND, by the lands
of MR: WM: ROBINSON, by the land of the REV. HENRY BARLOW & by the
landMR. JOHN & MR. RICHD: DUDLEY together with all houses &c........
(This is a very long deed)   signed: CORNELIUS CALVERT
 Recorded 18 Nov 1751   ELIZABETH CALVERT

19 Nov 1751   - GERSHOM NIMMO witnessed deed 19 Nov 1751 between
7 DB 283 PAc   THOROWGOOD SPRATT to JAMES NIMMO - 100 acres in NANNYS
               CREEK.

17 Dec 1751 - Dated and Recorded the same day: - DAVID VALLENTINE
7 DB 290 PAc   and FRANCES, his wife, one of the sisters & co-heirs
                of THO: COCKROFT whose plantation descended unto
MARY, SARAH, ANNE ELIZA: & FRA: COCKROFT sisters & co-heirs of THO:
COCKROFT decd. DAVID & FRANCES VALLENTINE selling their 1/5 part
of the plantation unto WM: TAYLOR.

18 Feb 1752 - LANCASTER LOVETT SENR: of Princess Anne County
7 DB 303 PAc   wd 21 Jan 1751/2 wp 18 Feb 1752 by WILLIAM KEELING
                 Senr; & WILLIAM WOODHOUSE
.....being very sick and weak.......... to son JOHN LOVETT all my
plantation & land whereon I live & STRATTON ISLAND 100 acres lying in
the Western Swamp which fell to me by the death of my brother WILLIAM
LOVETT to be sold by my Exor: to pay my debts, ...a large looking glass.
to my wife ALIFF LOVETT use of half of my negroes during her natural
life & after her decease to fall to my son JOHN. To son JOHN the
other half of my negroes.....Residue of estate to be divided between
my wife and my son JOHN. I appoint WILLIAM KEELING son of WILLIAM
KEELING my whole and sole Exor.

18 Feb 1752 - WILLIAM MALBONE of Princess Anne County
7 DB 305 PAc   wd 3 Feb 1752 wp 18 Feb 1752 by COL: JACOB ELLEGOOD
                 & MARY RICE. Exors: FRANCIS LAND & my cozen WM:
MOSELEY. .... My plantation where I now live to my cozen
WILLIAM MOSELEY son of MAJOR FRANCIS MOSELEY........ my riding horse
Esquire to my friend FRANCIS LAND. Residue of my estate to be div-
ided between all the children of my uncle MAJOR FRANCIS MOSELEY.....

29 Feb 1752 - ROBERT BURLEY of Princess Anne County
7 DB 307 PAc   wd 24 Jul 1749 wp 29 Feb 1752 by WILLIAM GODFREY
                 to wife MARTHA (her name is in the probate) a hoss
named Prince, a chest: to daughter SUSANNAH my chest & one feder bed
& puter plaits &c.....to my bro-in-law LAM: WHITEHURST bottles,
all my towls that I work wood.......... to wife all my cattle &
household stuff after her decease to be sold and divided between my
children.

17 Mar 1752 Recorded - Dated 6 Feb 1752: - JOHN THOROWGOOD decd.,
7 DB 309 PAc   father of MARY wife of WILLIAM KEELING JR. & of ELIZA-
                 BETH wife of CORNELIUS CALVERT of Norfolk County,
Mariner selling to LEMUEL CARTWRIGHT 50 acres......................

12 Mar 1752 - PETER MALBONE
7 DB 314 PAc   wd 3 Oct 1749 wp 12 Mar 1752 by CORNELIUS HENDLEY &
Exor: wife and son JAMES   EDWARD (B) BONNEY.
to son JAMES MALBONE the plantation I now live on to a division already made between him & his brother PHILLIP containing 180 acres.
100 acres in CARVERS WOODS to son JOHNATHAN at JNO:'S cost otherwise
JAMES to have it & JNO: to have the land I live on.   son PETER,
son PHILLIP, ...all my sons JAMES, PHILLIP, JOHNATHAN, PETER,
MALICHA, SOLOMON & JOHN.   WIFE - MARY use of estate.............

5 Mar 1752 Recorded 17 Mar 1752 - WALTER SCOTT of Princess Anne County
7 DB 318 PAc   Shipwright to JONAS CAWSON of PAco, Shipwright a tract
                 of land on the South side of the Eastern Branch of Eliz:
River in the said county of Princess Anne containing 62 ½ acres and is
the same land said WALTER SCOTT bought of THOMAS MOORE...............
Wit: WM: PORTLOCK, JNO: WHIDDON, CHRISTOPHER CAWSON

17 Mar 1752 Recorded - Dated 17 Mar 1752: - JOHN WHIDDON of Norfolk
7 DB 319 PAc   County - deed of gift to his godson JOHN CAWSON, son
                of JONAS CAWSON of Princess Anne County a negro girl
named Pleasant. JONAS CAWSON to have use of negro until said JOHN
CAWSON attains to the age of 21 years.

21 Apr 1752 Recorded - Dated 23 Mar 1752: - ANNE HAYNES deed to
7 DB 321 PAc   ANDREW STEWART of 1/3 of the plantation her dower
                from her former husband RICHD: POOLE decd.

20 May 1752 Recorded - Dated 14 May 1752: - RICHARD DUDLEY & MARY his
7 DB 324 PAc   wife, daughter of CAPT: TULLY SMYTH decd of Princess
                Anne County to JOHN DUDLEY a plantation of 140 acres
the same place that RICHARD DUDLEY the Elder decd father of aforesd:.
RICHARD DUDLEY had in exchange of MR. CHARLES SMYTH decd...........
being on the Western side of Lynhaven............................

19 May 1752 Recorded - Dated 16 Mar 1752: - MR. SAM: SMITH GENT: atty
7 DB 325 PAc   of CAPT: THO: QUAY Exex & Adm of the County of Norfolk
                selling to TULLEY MOSELEY of Princess Anne County for
Ŀ6 a tract of land known by the name of EDMONDS his new survey containing 50 acres and is the same land that MR: TULLY EMPEROR gr-father to
the present TULLY MOSELEY in his last will gave unto his gr-son
THOMAS MOSELEY and by right of kniship invested with GEORGE MOSELEY
who sold said land unto the aforesd THO: QUAY, GENT: said land lying
on the Wward end of the aforesd TULLY MOSELEY & adjoyning land whereon
he now liveth...

16 Jun 1752 -   WILLIAM FENTRISS SENR: of Princess Anne County
7 DB 330 PAc   wd 28 Apr 1752 wp 16 Jun 1752 by ABRAM WILLEROY &
                 JEREMIAH FENTRESS. Exor: son ANTHONY FENTRISS
wife MARY all the land during her natural life..................
daughter MARTHA her lifetime in my new Dwelling House................
son SAMUEL FENTRISS 100 acres .... son WM: after Mothers decease 100
acres I bought of THOMAS SCOTT....... son THOMAS 100 acres.........
son ANTHONY 150 acres over the road the land I bought of CORNAL (COL)
SAMUEL BUSH (BOUSH) & 50 acres at the Dams I bought of THOMAS SCOTT...
daus: ANN BALLINTIN 5/....gr-son WILLIAM VILLARY 50 acres...........
dau LIDDY cow and calf.....dau MARY 5/.....gr-dau MARY VILLARY a heaffer
....dau MARTHA after wife's decease residue of estate................
(name Villary spelled in this will Villarry, but so many other words are
misspelled too.)

21 Jul 1752 Recorded - Dated 7 Jul 1752: - THOMAS BOLITHO and TREPHANA
7 DB 335 PAc   his wife to BENJAMIN DINGLEY GREY of Northampton
                           County. 313 acres in Princess Anne County begin
at a Red Oak .... land of JONAS COSTEN (CAWSON?)................
COSTEN & SCOTTS line to the main road.....binding upon said road down
to McCOYS BRANCH then binding upon the mouth thereof then binding
upon the River by .... to the mouth of NOTTS BRANCH......
(these bounds are not very clear and hard to read - see what follows)

21 Jul 1752 Recorded - Dated 1 Jul 1752: - THOMAS BOLITHO of Princess
7 DB 336 PAc   to BENJAMIN DINGLEY GREY late of the County of North-
                hampton 102½ acres in the Parish of Lynhaven, PAco &
is part of the same land conveyed from JAMES McCOY to JOHN BOLITHO by
way of lease & release dated 15 & 20 of Nov. 1707......215 acres the
102½ acres is contained in a Pattent granted to Michael McCOY for
115 acres dated 20 Apr 1683 (or 1688?) but only 102½ acres.

22 Jul 1752 Recorded - Dated 1 Jul 1752: - WILLIAM TAYLOR of Princess
7 DB 338 PAc   Anne County to WILLIAM HARPER ..... all that part of
                a certain tract which JOHN COCKROFT decd gr-father to
said WM: TAYLOR on the mothers side by deed of lease & release 3 & 4
Jun 1718 purchased of JOHN THOROWGOOD & PEMBROKE his wife lying in
LITTLE CREEK, PAco. on the N. side of the Main Road that leads to
NEWTOWN containing 60 acres & all houses &c......................

26 Sep 1752 Recorded - Dated 20 Sep 1752: - WILLIAM STIBBINS & wife
7 DB 343 PAc   ELIZA: selling land which is part of a larger tract
                given by will of ADAM KEELING decd father of said
ELIZABETH ....selling to JOHN CANN..........................

26 Sep 1752 Recorded - Dated 2 Sep 1752: - MR. WILLIAM LANGLEY of
7 DB 347 PAc   Norfolk County to CAPT: JAMES IVY of Norfolk County
                250 acres on Eward side of Lynhaven River in Princess
Anne County......also a tract of 50 acres lying in the Swamp near
BUSKEYS....Release signed WILLIAM LANGLEY & ELIZA: (X) LANGLEY wife
having been privily examined.

26 Sep 1752 - In a deed of this date THOMAS CANNON'S wifes name is
7 DB 356 PAc   given as AMY.

26 Sep 1752 Recorded & dated same day - (see lease & release pp 357, 358)
7 DB 346 PAc   THOMAS LANGLEY sold to THO: CANNON 155 acres in fee
                simple by lease & release it is the same land & marsh
formerly granted by pattent to CHRISTOP: COCKE decd 28 Apr 1711 lying
in the Parish of Lynhaven in Princess Anne County by him conveyed to
ROGER FOUNTAIN & by him conveyed to JOHN CORNICK & by him conveyed to
JOHN HENLEY & by him conveyed to LEMUEL LANGLEY decd father to the above
named THO: LANGLEY.

26 Sep 1752 - JAMES LANGLEY
7 DB 367   wd 5 Dec 1751 wp 26 Sep 1752 by all the witnesses.
                Wit: WILL: NIMMO, JAMES ASHBY & ANNE (+) POWER
wife SARAH - use of 2 negroe men during her natural life & other negroes
(they are named) to be equally divided between my 2 daughters.
daus: ANNA now wife of DR. GEORGE ROVIERE and FRANCES LANGLEY.
to dau: ANNA ROVIERE the plantation I purchased of GEORGE COLLINS &
use of my Manor Plantation reserving the use thereof to my wife
during her natural life. Also to dau: ANNA my plantation called
BROWNS being 100 acres - also slaves, 8 in all, to ANNA.
to dau: FRANCES LANGLEY the Plantation which I purchased of MR: -(Blank)-
IVY, also the plantation I bought of CHARLES GRIFFIN and 8 slaves (they
are named) & 2 silver spoons with the trimmer and tongs & one bed &

furniture.
to son-in-law GEORGE ROUVIERE my silver hilted sword & cane.........
Lands and marshes not heretofore mentioned to be divided between my
two daughters. Residue to be divided between my wife & daughters.
I desire no Inventory or Appraisal to be taken.....................
my wife, SARAH to be executrix....

26 Sep 1752 Recorded - Dated 4 Jul 1752; - SAMUEL SMITH admr: of est-
7 DB 364 PAc   ate of CAPT: THOMAS QUAY decd to GEORGE WISHART of
                PAc. 50 acres adjoining land of COL: WILLIAM CRAWFORD
in Princess Anne County as part of the estate of the said THO: QUAY
which SMYTH was empowered to sell by the heirs of THO: QUAY decd.

14 Oct 1752 - THURMER HOGWOOD, JAMES ASHBY & THO: WISHASH (WISHART?)
7 DB 371 PAc   signed the audit of the estate of JAMES JONES decd.
                (This is the first time THURMER HOGGARD has appeared
in this book although he was in Princess Anne County at an earlier date)

22 Nov 1752 Recorded - Dated 30 Oct 1752; - BENJAMIN DINGLEY GRAY of
7 DB 373 PAc   Princess Anne County to WILLIAM HANCOCK of Princess
                Anne County 102½ acres of land adjoining to the land
of said HANCOCK begin: at a branch called McCOYS BRANCH in the road
thence along said road SW 41° 16 poles th SW 52° 20 po th SW 75° 16
po th SW 27° 14 po th SW 59° 30 in 12 po...(this goes on and on with
degrees on every measurement)..................................

11 Dec 1752 - SUSANAH wife of BENJAMIN DINGLEY GRAY is ao sickly and
7 DB 375 PAc   impotent that she cannot travel to the Court of our
                County. EDWARD HACK MOSELEY & NATHANIEL McCLANAHAN
in pursuance of the Commission have privily examined her. (See above
deed 7 DB 373)

21 Nov 1752 - MARY wife of JOHN LOVETT privily examined for deed of
7 DB 381 PAc   JOHN LOVETT to EDWARD PETTY.........................

21 Nov 1752 - JOHN MUNDEN the Elder of Princess Anne County
7 DB 391 PAc   wd 19 Oct 1752 wp 21 Nov 1752 by the witnesses
                Wit: JOEL CORNICK, ROBERT HOLMES, MARY (X) WHICHARD
Exor: JOHN MUNDEN
to son JOHN my plantation whereon I now live, all my working tools,
my hand mill & my great Bible.....to son AQUILLA MUNDEN 50 acres I
bought of JOHN LAMOUNT, one bed & furniture & his bedstead..........
to son STEPHEN negro boy Will, one bed &c.........to MARY WHICHARD
one low bed & furniture &c......Residue to be divided among all of
my surviving children. unto my daughter JANIE LEGGET to him and his
heirs one cow & calf....unto my granson JNO: BROCK one cow & calf...

19 Dec 1752 - JOHN DORY
7 DB 401 PAc   wd 17 Nov 1752 wp 19 Dec 1752 by all the witnesses
                Wit: THO: WALKE, WM: JACOB, ADAM LOVETT
Exor: wife & CAPT: ARTHUR SAYER...... (see Deed 7 DB 406 dated 16 Jan
1753 PEGGE DORY wid^{o} of JOHN DOREY decd sells land to FRANCIS CLARK..
at the North Landing......75 acres...............................

26 Oct 1752   -   MARGARET WHITEHURST in a Deed of Gift to her son EDWARD
7 DB 408 PAc   BONNEY states that she was relict (previously) of
                  RICHARD BONNEY.....this is concerning land whereon
WILLIAM BONNEY formerly lived and EDWARD BONNEY my son now liveth...

17 Jan 1753 -   SAMUEL HOLMES of Princess Anne County
7 DB 409 PAc   wd 4 Oct 1752 wp 17 Jan 1753 by HENRY & JAMES HOLMES
                3rd witness: THOMAS CONE   Exor: wife SARAH & son JOHN
son JOHN, wife SARAH, son SAMUEL.
Three are to divide Increase of a slave son SAMUEL, ELIZABETH HOLMES
and FRANCIS HOLMES. The last two are not called son or dau.
dau DINAH JONES.

20 Mar 1753 Recorded - Dated 1 Feb 1753: - WILLIAM GUY of Norfolk Coun-
7 DB 422 PAc   ty to GEORGE LAMNSON? of Princess Anne County......
                50 acres near the head of a Branch of BROAD CREEK and
is the same land MR. THOMAS LAWSON formerly conveyed unto ANTHONY
MOSELEY son of WILLIAM MOSELEY being in the Parish of Lynhaven, PAc
& adjoining lands of MR. TULLY SMYTH & MR. THOMAS LAWSON...........
(The bounds are not given)

10 Jan 1753 - MOSES FENTRIS is father of LEM: & AARON FENTRISS
7 DB 425 PAc

20 Mar 1753 Recorded - Dated 20 Mar 1753: - MARY WARD relinquishing
7 DB 428 PAc   her right of dower to a tract of land where LANCASTER
                LOVETT lately the husband of the said MARY WARD decd
was seized for Ⱡ 2.5/.......300 acres and is the land whereon LAN-
CASTER LOVETT, party hereto liveth & he not to be molested &c.......
(It would seem from this that Mary was not the mother, probably step
mother of this Lancaster Lovett?)

20 Mar 1753 - WILLIAM KEELING the Elder of Princess Anne County
7 DB 430 PAc   wd 3 Mar 1753 wp 20 Mar 1753 by WILL^m: CRUMPTON, WM:
                COX. 3rd witness was ALEXANDER KEELING.
Exor: son WILLIAM.......son WILLIAM negro man Jack & bed and Furniture
table, my sword & great glass, my plantation and houses thereon I now
live & 50 acres lying in the HUTTLEBERRY SWAMP (HUCKLEBERRY?)
son JOHN one negro Frances, also powel & bed & furniture, my pistols
& holsters.........dau FRANCES SMITH one negro woman Cate & her increase, bed & furniture...........dau ELIZABETH THOROWGOOD one negro
Sarah & increase, bed & furniture.........dau MARY one negro garle
Fillis & increase& my best oval table & a small looking glass & a feather bed and furniture & a ewe lamb.....son HENRY one negro boy Frank
& my new desk & gun & a feather bed & furniture & 50 acres of land
lying in the Swamp near the Broad Run.....dau MARGARET one negro boy
Hulen & a negro girl Nan & her increase & a cow & calf.............
dau ANNA one negro boy Nicholas & one negro girl Lidda & her increase
& a cow & calf.....to my 3 sons WM:, JOHN & HENRY all my Carolina
Possessions to be equally divided ....to my 2 gr-children WILL-
IAM & ARGYL THOROWGOOD one negro garle Jane & also one bed & some
furniture which the said JOHN THOROWGOOD has got in possession already
...to wife AMY one negro man Harry, wench Rose, residue during her
natural life and after to be divided among all my children.

20 Mar 1753 - ROBERT MARTINDALE of Princess Anne County
7 DB 431 PAc   wd 17 Jan 1753 wp 20 Mar 1753 by all the witnesses
                Wit: ROBERT DICKSON, WM: HANCOCK, ANTHONY LAWSON.
Exor: EDWARD HACK MOSELEY...........all lands lying in Yorktown being
one acre which I bought of GAVIN REED with the appurtenances be sold
by my executors and also what goods and effects I die possessed of for
the most that can be had in money........to MR. JAMES PASTEUR of Norfolk County whatsoever may be due him from me........to my brothers
and sisters: JOHN MARTINDALE of Wilmington at Cape Fare in N. C.,
WILLIAM MARTINDALE, ELIZABETH TODD, JEANE BARNS and MARY SAUL of
Cumberland in the Kingdom of Great Britain after debts are paid that
money which the lands & appurtenances goods & effects shall be sold
for & residue of any other estate to be equally divided.............

20 Mar 1753 - ELIZABETH (E) GISBORN of Princess Anne County
7 DB 432 PAc   wd 2 Feb 1753 wp 20 Mar 1753 by BENJAMIN CUMMINGS &
                JAMES TOOLEY. The other witness was ELIZA: CUMINGS
Exor: son JOSEPH CORBEL......to dau PRUDENCE LEGET bed & furniture
& bedsteed.........son JAMES SIMMONS bed & bolster, blue rug, 1
blanket & 2 sheets, a bedstead, mat & cord & if he be dead I cut him
off with 1 shilling........to PRUDENCE SIMMONS one cow &c........son
JOHN SIMMONS 20/ with what he has received already being his part...
...to daus ANN MILLER & ELIZABETH LEGGET and PRUDENCE LEGGET my waring
close (clothes) to be equally divided.....to son JOSEPH CORBEL 1 barel
of Port & 4 barrels of corn & 8 sows & 18 piggs & my patch of wheat
that is growing. (there is a scratched out line - to grandson JAMES
SIMMONS 1 feather bed & bolster -) Residue to be divided between
dau ANN MILLER, ELIZABETH LEGET, son JOSEPH CORBEL, & PROVIDENCE LEGET
......to PROVIDENCE SIMMONS 25 yds of cloth some whaling & lyning.

20 Mar 1753 - EVE (X) ETHERIDGE
7 DB 433 PAc   wd 6 Feb 1753 wp 20 Mar 1753 by all the witnesses
                Wit: HENRY JAMESON, ANNE BALL, ANN ETHERIDGE
Exor: son ANTHONY ETHERIDGE.......son DAVID ETHERIDGE my land in
during his natural life not debarring of my grandson RICHARD ETHERIDGE
of building & the use of some part of my land.....to dau-in-law MARY
ETHERIDGE her thirds in the land in during xxxxxxxx her widdohood
....my lands after DAVID;s decease to RICHARD ETHERIDGE....to my dau
AMY BALLONS (BALLANCE?) 2 cows & calf......to my gr-dau ELIZABETH
ETHERIDGE......Residue to Executor ANTHO: ETHERIDGE................

20 Mar 1753 - FRANCIS SOREY (this name may be IVEY, but I doubt it.)
7 DB 433 PAc   wd 1 Apr 1747 wp 20 Mar 1753 by JACOB BARBER & JAMES
                ETHERIDGE.   Exor: wife ANN & son ANDREW
son ANDREW my plantation whereon he now liveth.......dau SEDEY my
plantation whereon she liveth.....dau DINA my manner plantation
whereon I now live &c........to wife ANN all my worldly goods to do
with as she will see fit.

20 Mar 1753 - JAMES HAYNES of Princess Anne County
7 DB 435 PAc   wd 26 Jan 1753 wp 20 Mar 1753 by all the witnesses
                wit: LEMUEL CORNICK, ERASMUS HAYNES & WILLIAM SULLIVAN
Exor: wife - all my estate to be divided between my wife & 2 children.

12 Mar 1753 - ELIZABETH MONGOMEE (MONTGOMERY?)
7 DB 436 PAc   Nun. wd 8 Mar 1753 wp 12 Mar 1753 by ELIZABETH (X)
                WIGGINS & BURROUGHS MOSELEY
to my son JOHN MONGOMEY the fole that my mare is big with..........
&.......to my son JOHN MONGOMRY my shep (sheep) because thay are my
ow(n) property..

20 Mar 1753 - HENRY HOLMES
7 DB 436 PAc   wd 24 Jan 1753 wp 20 Mar 1753 by THOMAS CONE & JOHN
                CHAPMEN. 3rd wit: JAMES HOLMES.
Exors: brother JAMES HOLMES & JOHN CHAPMAN
to brother JAMES HOLMES my Plantation which I now live upon & all the
land pertaining to it provided he pays unto my daughters: ELIZABETH
HOLMES Ŀ 20 at age of 21;& negroes....dau TAMER HOLMES Ŀ20 & negroes
.....brother JOHN HOLMES all my wairing clothes....... this will
gives cattle &c to each but the bulk of the estate is left to JAMES.

17 Apr 1753 Recorded - Dated 4 Dec 1752: - EDWARD ATWOOD of Princess
7 DB 438 PAc   Anne County selling to JOHN HENLEY SR: 20 acres in
                PAc beginning on the South side of EDWARD ATWOOD's
line of marked trees....................(full bounds are given.)

16 Apr 1753 - HENRY BARLOW, Clark & his wife SUSANNAH of Northampton
7 DB 442 PAc   selling to CHRISTOPHER WRIGHT practitioner of Physick
                & surgery of Princess Anne County a tract of 50 acres
of land which HENRY BARLOW purchased of MARK POWEL (looks like Plowel)
bounded by a ditch, a line of mkd trees on THOROWGOODS LANE, now the
said WRIGHTS, & a line of mkd trees on RICH: DUDLEYS, now heir of
JOHN DUDLEY decd, GEORGE WEBLIN & MARK POWELS, now WILLIAM ROBINSONS
land.

17 Apr 1753 - JACOB ELLEGOOD of Princess Anne County
7 DB 447 PAc   wd 22 Mar 1753 wp 17 Apr 1753 by WILLIAM KEELING &
                JOB GASKINGS. 3rd wit: SOLOMON WILKINS
Exor: wife ANN & son-in-law WILLIAM ATCHESON ....
My 3 plantations that I bought of JM: CONDONS heirs, my FERRY PLANTA-
TION & my Plantation in Carolina known by the name of MORSES POINT te
be sold and the money to be equally divided between my 3 daughters or
the survivor of them......to WILLIAM ATCHESON & REBEC^a: his wife negroes......to son JACOB the Plantation whereon I now live and all my
swampland......to wife the the use and benefits of the Plantation
whereon I now live & my Swampland to my loving wife during her natural
life......If JACOB should die the said Plantation to WM: ATCHESON &
REB^n: his wife & the Swampland to be divided between my 2 daughters
ANN & MARGRIT ELLEGOOD.....tract of land bought of ISAAC WHITE to his
two daughters SARAH & ELIZABETH....residue to wife and children.

17 Apr 1753 - CAPT: JAMES NIMMO
7 DB 448 PAc   wd 19 Mar 1753 wp 17 Apr 1753 by GEOR: ROUVIERE,
                JACOB HUNTER, JOHN HARPER. Exors: sons GERSHOM & WM:
....use of negroes Windsor, Nan, Rose, Sarah, Dinah, Cherry & Essex
to my wife MARY during her natural life.........son WILLIAM negroes
Bob, Harry & Jone......son GERSHOM negroes Little Moody, Regall,
Savinah & Plantation I bought of JA^s: FENTRESS...... son JACOB all

all my land & marsh at NANNYS CREEK......son JAMES negroes Hale, Great
Mudy & Pleasant, also to JAMES all my lotts or pieces of lotts in
NEWTOWN.....daughter JENNET NIMMO negroes Hannah, Jack & Moll.........
All the negroes my said wife has the use of for life together with all
my other negroes not before devised to be equally divided between all
my children to make the rest of my childrens negroes equal to those of
my sons WM:, GERSHOM & JAMES........Residue to be divided between wife
and children.

17 Apr 1753   -   JOHN HUNTER of Princess Anne County
7 DB 449 PAc   wd 28 Feb 1753 wp 17 Apr 1753 by AMY BARROT & ARTHUR
                 SAYER. 3rd wit: DINAH WILLIAMSON made her mark X
Exor: wife JACOMINE........wife JACOMINE use of all my lands Plantations
& houses during her natural life..........son JACOB HUNTER the Plantation whereon I now live.......daughter MARGARET HARPER a negro girl
Sue.....daughter MARY CARTWRIGHT negro girl Jona.....daughter JACOMINE
HUNTER a negro girl Sarah.....son JOHN a negro boy Bobb......son THO:
a negro boy George....son JAMES negro boy Ishmael.......daughter
ELIZABETH HUNTER a negro boy Mingo.....daughter PEMMY HUNTER a negro
girl Sue...daughter JOYCE a negro boy Mexico.....to wife JACOMINE HUNTER
the use and labor of the following negroes: Phillis, Magg, Rachel, Sam,
Robin, Beaver & Benk.....I give negroes Phillis, Magg, Rachel, Sam,
Robin, Craver & Ben with theire increase together with what of my per-
sonal estate shall be left to be divided between my 9 children: MARG-
ARET HARPER, MARY CARTWRIGHT, JACOMINE HUNTER, JOHN HUNTER, THO:, JAMES,
ELIZABETH, PEMMY & JOYA..

17 Apr 1753   -   JOHN BATTIN (made his mark G)
7 DB 450 PAc   wd 6 Mar 1753 wp 17 Apr 1753 by TULLY WILLIAMSON &
                 JOHN (‡) HOLTH.   EXOR: son GEORGE & dau DINAH MASON
unto MR. JOHN BONNEY SENR: 100 acres which said land I bogt of JOSEPH
COOPER And adjoins said BONNEY land he now lives on.................
Daughter DINAH MASON 100 acres which is the land WILLIAM BATTIN formerly lived on.......joyning upon TULLY WILLIAMS land & one calfe......
son GEORGE BATTEN my Plantation I now live on, my carpenters tools,
one great pot after his Mothers decease...if he die without heirs then
my will is that my 2 daughters MARY BATTIN & SARAH BATTIN should have
the said land equally divided.....I give the whole proper use of the
said plantation to my loveing wife MARY BATTIN during her widowhood.

17 Apr 1753   -   WILLIAM MORRIS of Lynhaven Parish, Princess Anne County
7 DB 451 PAc   wd 3 Mar 1752 he made his mark (M) wp 17 Apr 1753 by
                 JOSIAS MORRIS. Other witnesses JAMES NIMMO & JAMES(X)
ALDERSON.   Exor: wife ELIZABETH & sons WILLIAM & THOMAS.............
son WILLIAM the land & plantation whereon he liveth & other things....
wife ELIZABETH.....son THOMAS the plantation whereon I now live with
reversion to son JOSIAH with reversion to FRANCIS MORRIS.............
son ARTHUR 150 acres first laid off out of 300 acres bought of my brother JOSIAH MORRIS known by the name of Soppond Clearing............
son JOSIAH 150 acres of the 300 acres above mentioned which I bought
of my brother JOSIAH MORRIS known by the name of Longridge...........
son FRANCIS all the lands & Marshes belonging to me known as Hickory
Ridge & gun I bought of FREDERICK GREGORY & other things...........

17 Apr 1753 - WILLIAM (✓X\) OAKHAM
7 DB 452 PAc   wd 15 Feb 1753 wp 17 Apr 1753 by WILLIAM SENECA &
                GEORGE BOOTH. Other wit: JOHN BATTEN.
 Exor: wife SARAH.....son WILLIAM OAKHAM 100 acres Eward side of the
Branch. (Bounds partially given).....son JOHN the Plantation where I
now live with 120 acres......& 50/.......If either son WM: or JOHN
die revision of their land to son WILLABY OAKHAM & ₺5 in hands of
ROBT: LAND..........dau ISABELL RUSSEL.....wife SARAH......dau MARY
OAKHAM.

17 Apr 1753 - ERASMUS HAYNES
7 DB 453 PAc   wd 5 Mar 1753 wp 17 Apr 1753 by FRANCIS CORNICK &
                JOHN BONNEY SR:. The other wit: JOHN WHITEHEAD SR.
Exor: son ERASMUS........my live stock to be equally divided amongst
all my children and my son JAMES son to have an equal share........
son ERASAMUS HAINES the plantation I live on......son JOEL the plan-
tation I bought of WALLSTONE......son JOSHUA all the land I bought of
GEORGE BOOTH & THO: JONES.........son THOS: a negro............son
WILLIAM a negro........four young sons..... son FRANCIS.......SON
HENRY.........sons ERASAMUS, JOEL & JOSHUA 100 acres of Marsh by the
North River.

17 Apr 1753 -   JOHN (I) GRIFFIN
7 DB 454 PAc   wd 2 Apr 1753 wp 17 Apr 1753 by all the witnesses
                Wit: THO: (T) WHITEHURST & JOHN POWER
Exor: wife and son JOHN...
son JOHN all my whole possessions of land and marsh containing 365
acres.......dau: ELIZABETH GRIFFIN......dau: RUTH BROWN............
gr-son MOSES BROWN......Residue to be divided between wife & dau:
ELIZABETH & my daus: NANY & FRANCES & SARAH....(wife not named)

17 Apr 1753 - JOHN DUDLEY
7 DB 455 PAc   wd 8 Apr 1753 wp 17 Apr 1753 by all the witnesses
                Wit: JOHN FLINCH, DANEL DUDLEY, ROBT: BURROUGH
Exor: father-in-law WILLIAM CARTWRIGHT.............................
son RICHARD DUDLEY THE PLANTATION WHEREON I now live excepting 50 acs.
adjoining to DR: CHRISTOPHER WRIGHT his land...revision to my brother
DANIEL DUDLEY...... father-in-law WILLIAM CARTWRIGHT the above said
50 acres.....residue to wife MARGARET DUDLEY.

15 May 1753 Recorded - Dated 25 Jan 1753 ; - JOHN LAMOUNT to ROBERT
7 DB 457 PAc   DICKSON for ₺ 40. 150 acres, the same Plantation where
                said JOHN LAMOUNT bought of ROBERT PATTERSON & wife
SARAH being the land whereon the sd LAMOUNTS Family now lives with all
Houses &c.......& a negro woman Grace & her son Charles. ₺ 40. to be
paid 5 Jan 1755.
Wit: ROBERT & SARAH PATTERSON, EDWARD CANNON, ELIZA: CANNON, JACOB
ELLEGOOD, LEM: CORNICK, NATH'L: NEWTON.

7 DB 462 PAc - JOEL CORNICK to ALEXANDER LEGGETT - this book is full
                of Deeds in which JOEL CORNICK is one of the partys.

15 May 1753 - ANN (A) BLAIR of Princess Anne County
7 DB 467 PAc   wd .... wp 15 May 1753 by MARY HEWITT & HILLARY
                 KEATON. Other wit: GEORGE HEWITT, ANDREW BRAN
Exor: MR. ADAM TOOLY & MR. SOUTHWOOD SIMMONS........................
son JOHN SIMMONS ....dau BETTY HERBERT all my land lying and being
in Princess Anne County at the head of Blackwater River.......355
acres......youngest son WILLIAM SIMMONS the plantation whereon I
live 255 acres...........   COUSINS: THOMAS HERBERT & JOHN HERBERT
Ŀ 4 for the education of the 2 aforesaid.,....If said dau BETTY
HERBERT & JOHN SIMMONS should die without heirs then land shall
return to sd THOMAS & JOHN HERBERT.....if son WILLIAM SIMMONS should
die without heirs land shall return to son JOHN SIMMONS & BETTY HERB-
ERT if they die land to revert to poor of the parrish...............
my 3 children JOHN & WILLIAM SIMMONS & BETTY HERBERT...............
2 sons to be boarded out to educate them.

19 Jun 1753 Recorded and Dated the same day - WILLIAM NICHOLSON by his
7 DB 473 PAc   last will and testament bequeathed to his two sons
                 GEORGE NICHOLSON & LEMUEL NICHOLSON and the same land
that WILLIAM NICHOLSON (son to the aforesd WM: NICHOLSON) and father
to MALACHI NICHOLSON purchased of the aforesd GEORGE NICHOLSON his
brother.

17 Jun 1753 - WILLIAM CARTWRIGHT of Princess Anne County
7 DB 474 PAc   wd 20 May 1753 wp 17 Jun 1753 by the witnesses
                 Wit: JAMES CARRAWAY, LEWIS PRICE & WILLIAM (+) HOLMES
Exor: wife MARY & son ROBERT...........wife use of the plantation
during her widowhood......son ROBERT plantation whereon I now live..
.... gr-son WILLIAM CARTWRIGHT plantation whereon sd son ROBERT now
livethwith reversion to son ROBERT.....daus ELIZABETH HARPER, MARGARET
DUDLEY, MARTHA CAROWAY, FRANCES, ANNE, SARAH, AMY..................
educating & bringing up my 3 children ANNE, SARAH & AMY............

19 Jun 1753 - GEORGE (G) BEARRY (BEARY in signature)(BERRY in Probate)
7 DB 475 PAc   wd 27 Dec 1752 wp 19 Jun 1753 by the witnesses
                 Wit: JOHN RUSSEL, JOHN COATES & EDW: CAPPS
Exor: sons THOMAS & JOHN BARY......son JOHN BARY the Manner Plantation
70 acres.....son THOS: BARY the plantation where his brother GEORGE did
live 70 acres.....son RICHARD bed & furniture &c.... son GEORGE.......
unto ROSAMON MORSE a heifer & ewe &c.....Residue to wife SARAH BERRY.

19 Jun 1753 - WILLIAM BENSON of Princess Anne County
7 DB 476 PAc   wd 19 Dec 1751 wp 19 Jun 1753 by LEMUEL & FRANCIS COR-
                 NICK. Other wit: THO: (+) KEELING JR.
Exor: ELIZABETH DALE........to BETTY DALE my plantation whereon I now
live.....the plantation whereon JOHN KEELING now lives to MARIAN KEEl-
ING wife to said JOHN KEELING & my swamp land and my part of Marsh at
the OLD INLET & .....a pot that was her fathers........unto RACHEL DALE
4 negroes to her & her children..........my sister ELIZABETH DALE......
negro man Cesar and all the rest of my estate......................

19 Jun 1753 - ROBERT (R) MASON
7 DB 477 PAc   wd 22 Feb 1753 wp 19 Jun 1753 by all the witnesses
                Wit: JOHN RUSSELL, JOHN (X) BATTEN, FRANCIS SHIP (X)
Exor: wife MARY & son JAMES.......son JAMES MASON all my land and
plantation after his mothers decease......dau BETTY MASON a bed &
furniture &c.....Residue to dau BETTY MASON after wifes decease.....

19 Jun 1753 - WILLIAM (W) CORNICK
7 DB 477 PAc   wd 11 Apr 1753 wp 19 Jun 1753 by JOHN RUSSELL & JOHN
                MORSE. 3rd wit: JOHN WHITEHEAD SR.
Exor: wife BETTY........son JOHN CORNICK all my land at NANCE CREEK
....unto my 3 children JOHN, NATHAN & ELIZABETH all my negroes at
NANES CREEK .....son underage,...Residue to be divided between wife
BETTY & 3 children, between their Mother & them....................

19 Jun 1753 - JOHN CAPPS (‡)
7 DB 478 PAc   wd 10 Oct 1752 wp 19 Jun 1753 by all the witnesses
                Wit:CHARLES (+) HARTLY & CASON MOORE
Exor: wife DINA & friend SOLOMON WHITEHURST.........................
son JAMES CAPPS the land that belonged to EDWARD CANNON.............
son HILLARY land that was DENNIS CANNONS....son JOHN all the remainder
of my high land, Marsh land to be equally divided..................
dau MARGARET...my 4 children JOHN, SOLOMON, CHARLES & AMY all the
remainderwife DINA to have the use during widdowhood.

19 Jun 1753 - CORNELIUS (H) HENLEY
7 DB 479 PAc   wd 25 Dec 1752 wp 19 Jun 1753 by JOHN (X) FENTROUS &
                MOSES MEDALIN. EXOR: "wife now DINNA HENLEY"& son-
in-law CASON MOORE.........son JAMES HENLEY the plantation whereon I
now live & the 1/3 part of an Island of Marsh called GREAT FRESH POND
...he to let his sister KEZIA have a small ridge of land on the South
Side of the Manner Plantation & is divided from said Plantation by a
low slash or Valley that runneth Ely to PETER MALBONES line, his sister
to live on the sd land all the dayes of her natural life to enjoy the
ridge known as DOGWOOD RIDGE...dau KEZIA MOORE, dau MARY HENLEY, dau
ELIZABETH HENLEY.......residue to wife NOW DINNA HENLEY during her
natural life forbidding her so sell anything after her death to be
divided between my three daughters.

19 Jun 1753 - SOLOMON CEEATON (Could this name be Seaton?)
7 DB 480 PAc   wd 10 Mar 1753 wp 19 Jun 1753 by FRANCES ETHERIDGE &
                EDMOND CREEKMOORE
Exor: sons JOHN CEEATON & HILLARY CATON   (note difference in name)
son JAMES THE Manna plantation whereon I now live bound upon a Valle
joyne upon his brother JOHN'S feald running up to the Hickory Branch
joyen to ANDREW ETHERIDGE......son JOHN the land where he now dwells
....son HILLARY the plantation joyin upon HAGETS RUN and so running
up the HERRING RUN .... son THOMAS 50 acres of land in the new survey
joyen to his brother JOHN....dau SARAH CEEATON a feather bed &c.......
to HOPE GLASCO one 2 year old heifer....Residue to be divided between
all my children.

20 Jun 1753 Recorded - Dated 2 Jun 1753: - THOMAS LAWSON - Appraisal
7 DB 483 PAc   of his estate totalled Ŀ 290.00

9 Jul 1753   -   ROBERT CARTWRIGHT of Princess Anne County oldest son
7 DB 485 PAc   & heir at law of WILLM: CARTWRIGHT late of Princess
                 Anne decd & one of the executors of WILLM: CARTWRIGHT
decd & MARY CARTWRIGHT the other exor: of WILLM: CARTWRIGHT decd
which sd WILLM: CARTWRIGHT decd was Exor: to JOHN DUDLEY decd and
which sd ROBERT CARTWRIGHT & MARY CARTWRIGHT are also exors: to sd
JOHN DUDLEY decd of the first part & the REV. MR. ROBT: DICKSON and
ANTHONY WALKE the Elder, CAPT: JAMES KEMPE, MAJ: NATT: NEWTON, MR.
EDWARD HACK MOSELEY, MAJOR THOMAS WALKE, CAPT. ANTHO: MOSELEY, CAPT:
GEORGE WISHART, CAPT: JOHN WHITEHURST, MR. JOHN BONNEY SENR:, MR.
JOHN WHITEHEAD & MR. ADAM TOOLEY GENT: Vestrymen of Lynhaven Parish
of the other part. (This is an interesting deed about 50 acres of land
sold to the Vestry which had been left to WILLIAM CARTWRIGHT by JOHN
DUDLEY. AGW)

17 Jul 1753   -   TULLY ROBINSON SMYTH of Princess Anne County
7 DB 490 PAc   wd 3 May 1753 wp 17 Jul 1753 by GEO: ROUVIERE &
                 WILLIAM KEELING.
Exor: wife FRANCES & WILLIAM KEELING.............3 daughters ELIZABETH,
FRANCES & SUSANNAH SMYTH 6 silver spoons that was my own purchase & all
my part of the silver spoons that was my fathers & negroes Cate & Harry,
and their increase.....all to be equally divided.........to my mother
a bay horse.....to wife FRANCIS all my part of my fathers estate not
given before during her widowhood &c.................................

17 Jul 1753   -   KITELY ROE
7 DB 492 PAc   wd 26 Mar 1753 wp 17 Jul 1753 by JOHN CARTER, WM:
                 WILLIAMS, & MICHAEL FLING.
Exor: wife MARY.......to wife MARY hogs in Blackwater & furniture there
.....dau ELEANOR PHILLIPS Plantation I bought of ISRAEL SLAUGHTER .....
ELEANOR is under twenty-one years.....brother ROBT: ROE land that
formerly belonged to RICHARD MOY........to SARAH CUMMING wife of BENJA-
MIN CUMMINGS one bay mare, bed & furniture which SARAH now has in her
possession & 5 acres Swampland....to JOHN FENTRIS son of SOPHIA FENTRIS
land, gun..........to JAMES FENTRIS son of SOPHIA FENTRIS underage land
&c....to WILLIAM FENTRIS son of SOPHIA land, he is also underage, & ....
If JOHN, JAMES & WM: FENTRIS Should die reversion of their land to go
no further in the FENTRIS name but to return to KITELY ROE son of
ROBERT ROE......to SOPHIA FENTRIS use of profits of all my stock, all
my household goods the time during the time she lives single..........
Residue to be sold to pay debts & remainder part of money to be equally
divided between FANNY, JAMES & WILLIAMS sons & dau of SOPHIA FENTRESS....
wife Executor....17 Jul 1753 will presented in Court by ALEX^r: ROSE
appointed by the Court who made oath .

Aug 1753 - & DB 502 PAc - THOMAS GARDNER & MARGARET his wife........

21 Aug 1753 Recorded - Dated 17 Jul 1753: - JOHN ELLEGOOD decd, father
7 DB 502 PAc   of WILLIAM ELLEGOOD and by him (John) in his will dated
                 30 Sep 1740 recorded in Norfolk County devised to his
son MASON ELLEGOOD & heirs of his body who died in his minority without
issue.

21 Aug 1753 Recorded - Dated 1 Aug 1753; - WILLIAM NIMMO JUNR: of Prin-
7 DB 504 PAc   cess Anne County eldest son & heir at law of JAMES NIMMO
               late of Princess Anne County decd. selling to COL: EDWD:
HACK MOSELEY for ₤ 6/9 ... half of a lott of land in Newtown whereon
the New Courthouse now stands.

21 Aug 1753 Recorded - Dated 17 Aug 1753: - JOHN WILLOUGHBY of North
7 DB 504 PAc   Carolina selling to JAMES FENTRIS of Princess Anne Co.
               50 acres in Black Water precinct begin: at a pine by
the Swamp side joining on the NW side of JOHN GISBURNS line.

1 Aug 1753 Recorded - Dated 31 Jul 1753: - JOHN KNOWIS (as hard as your
7 DB 506 PAc   editor tried to make this name Harris I am still convinced
that it is Knowis) of North Carolina to JAMES FENTRIS of Princess Anne
County 263 acres....bounds are given.....a corner tree of sd SIMMONS
and GRISBOURNES......Ely to JASPER LANES corner holly..............

22 Aug 1753 - Recorded & dated the same day: - JOSIAH MORRIS SENR: of
7 DB 507 PAc   Princess Anne Co. - Deed of Gift: 3 sons JOSIAH, WILLIS
               and WILLOUGHBY MORRIS......to JOSIAH 200 acres at NANNYS
CREEK (bounds are given)....to WILLIS 200 acres joining Wly on JOSIAH'S
beginning on the said creek.....to son WILLOUGHBY 200 acres joining
Wly on WILLIS beginning at the dams....on RICHARD LESTER'S LAND.

21 Aug 1753 Recorded - Dated same day - SARAH JACOB Deeds of gift to
7 DB 508 PAc   son ISAAC JACOB and to dau REBECA JACOB.

21 Aug 1753 - GEORGE CAPPS
7 DB 510 PAc   wd 8 Jan 1751 wp 21 Aug 1753 by all the witnesses
               Wit: SOLOMON (+) WILLIAMS & RICH: (R) CAPPS
Exor: wife SARAH CAPPS.....to son GEORGE CAPPS my manner Plantation
containing 20 acres if he dies underage to fall to my son WILLIAM CAPPS
.....I give to my son WILLIAM CAPPS my other plantation and land on
MUDDY CREEK joining upon JOHN SHEARWOOD 20 acres to my wife... 25 acres
of marsh lying upon CHARLES KELLEYS GREAT ISLAND....Residue to my wife
her widdowhood and soon after to be divided between my three children
GEORGE, WILLIAM & PEMBROOK CAPPS.

21 Aug 1753 - Inventory of MR. CORNELIUS HENLEY gives these relation-
7 DB 511 PAc   ships: son JAMES, dau KEZIA, dau MARY, dau ELIZABETH.

17 Sep 1753 Recorded - Dated 13 Sep 1753: - JOHN LAMOUNT, wife LIDIA
7 DB 516 PAc   had been privily examined, Deed of Gift: to my eldest
               son ARTHUR 1 year old heifer; to my son THOMAS my
Plantation lying on ROODED (RUDEE) CREEK which I bought of THOMAS HILL,
50 acres, 1 handmill.....; to my youngest son CORNELIUS my manner Plantation 150 acres which I bought of ROBERT PATTERSON & his wife.........
to dau ELIZABETH, to dau LYDIA........retaining the use of all land
and articles during the whole course of my life.

16 Oct 1753 - Dated 15 Oct 1753 INVENTORY of CAPT: WM: KEELING. The
7 DB 521 PAc   Estate totaled ₤248.00.2

16 Oct 1753 Recorded - JOHN (‡) PRESCOTE of Norfolk County for & in
7 DB 521 PAc   consideration of the good will & respect I bear unto
                my son-in-law ANTHONY ETHERIDGE ₤20., one negro woman
named Moll.

16 Oct 1753 Recorded - Dated 28 Aug 1753: - THURMER HOGGARD, WILLM:
7 DB 522 PAc   HUNTER & THO: WISHART appraised the estate of MR.
                HENRY HOLMES decd.

20 Nov 1753 Recorded - Dated 20 Nov 1753; - WILLIAM KEELING executor
7 DB 527 PAc   of the last will & testament of LANCASTER LOVETT decd
of Princess Anne County to DAVID McCLENEHAN of the same county for
₤ 13.10, 100 acres of swamp land in the Western Shore swamp is the
moity in 1/2 part of a tract of land called GOAT HERDS GROUNDE which
formerly belonged to JOHN LOVETT decd. father to the said LANCASTER
LOVETT which moiety 1/2 part was devised by JOHN LOVETT in his will
dated 12 Apr 1738 to his son WILLIAM LOVETT who is since dead without
issue & without will....sd land descended to sd LANCASTER LOVETT as
heir at law to sd WM: LOVETT & which sd LANCASTER LOVETT decd in his
will dated 21 Jan 1751 devised to be sold by WILLIAM KEELING his exor:
towards paying his debts.

20 Nov 1753 Recorded - Dated 14 Sep 1752:- Deed of JOSEPH WALSTONE
7 DB 529 PAc   & MARY his wife of Princess Anne County selling 50
                acres called CREEDLES to HENRY BURGESS.............
The same place which RICHARD GAINON gave to his dau MARY the wife of
said JOSEPH WALSTONE. ·

20 Nov 1753 Recorded - Dated 31 Oct 1753: - MAXIMILLIAN BOUSH - Deed
7 DB 531 PAc   to CAPT: WILLIAM KEELING for 50 acres on the Eastern
                Shore......The bounds are given.

20 Nov 1753 Recorded - Dated 17 Oct 1753: - GODFREY MALBONE of Newport
7 DB 532 PAc   in County of Newport in Colony of Rhode Island in New
                England.....in consideration of the affection I bear
unto my cousin FRANCIS MALBONE of Norfolk Borough & 5 shillings have
conveyed unto sd FRANCIS MALBONE a certain Plantation on the Eastern
Shore of Lynhaven River in Princess Anne County... 100 acres & is the
same land which I the said GODFREY MALBONE am possessed of as heir at
law to WILLIAM MALBONE late of Virginia, Planter decd.

21 Nov 1753 Recorded - Dated 25 May 1753: - MARY KNOWIS, wife of JOHN
7 DB 533 PAc   KNOWIS;her former husband.JOHN SMITH; ....
                To her son JAMES SMYTH...to dau MARY WHITEHURST.....
to dau AMY SMYTH....to dau ELIZABETH SMYTH....to dau KEZIAH SMYTH...
& to dau FRANCIS (last name not given)

20 Nov 1753 - JOB GASKING
7 DB 535 PAc   wd 8 Nov 1753 wp 20 Nov 1753 by MARTHA (X) KEELING
                & MARY WHITE & ADAM KEELING. Exor: sons JOB & CHARLES
to son JOB the Plantation whereon he now lives.....to sons: CHARLES,
LEM[1]:, HENRY; to daus: SARAH KEELING & the two youngest REBECCA &
son JACOB; son-in-law JOHN KEELING......"my seven children".

20 Nov 1753 - JOHN RAINEY
7 DB 536 PAc   wd 11 Mar 1752 wp 20 Nov 1753 by JOHN (H) DEARMOOD &
                CASON MOORE - 3rd wit: JEAN DEARMOOD
Exor: friend JOHN BONNEY JUNR: & MORRIS HILL
...to son JOHN RANY the Plantation 110 acres... to dau MARY RANY....
to son THOMAS RANY 50 acres Marshland at the SALT PONDS.............
residue to be sold & the money equally divided between my 4 children
namely: THOMAS, BETTY, AMY & ANNY RAINEY. Ordered by the Court to be
recorded for the Benefit of the Legatees. The Executors refused to
take on them the Burthen & the wido: renouncing the same.

18 Dec 1753 Recorded - Dated 17 Dec 1753: - THOMAS LESTER selling to
7 DB 537 PAc   ADAM THOROWGOOD 75 acres bounded on the one side by
               the land of MR. ADAM THOROWGOOD on the other side by
land of MR. THELABALL on the Eastermost & by the River & is the same
land that RICHARD HOSKINS devised to his sister MARY.

18 Dec 1753 Recorded - Dated 8 Dec 1753: - EPAPHRODITIS MUNDEN & MARY
7 DB 540 PAc   his wife (she made her mark X) selling to JNº: LOVETT
all of Princess Anne County for Ł 30 the said MARY'S right of dower
of all that tract of land whereon said JOHN LOVETT now lives & in the
same that LANC: LOVETT died possessed of & left the said MARY in possession of 1/3 thereof 850 acres....

18 Dec 1753 Recorded - Dated 22 Sep 1753: - JAMES HUNTER to SAMUEL
7 DB 541 PAc   TENANT, Merchant & ELIZ: his wife who is the eldest
               daughter of said JAMES HUNTER ... 400 acres which
JAMES HUNTER purchased of GEORGE SHIRLEY of Princess Anne County as
by Deeds dated 19 & 20 Sep 1748 on the S side of the E Branch of Eliza:
River & is part of a pattent granted to JOHN SHIRLEY 21 Apr 1690 for
450 acres bounded by lands of COL: ANTHONY WALKE, FRANCIS ACKISS &
GEORGE WILLIAMSON.

18 Dec 1753 - THOMAS (I) ELKS or ELLIS?
7 DB 544 PAc   wd 28 Oct 1749 wp 18 Dec 1753 by RICHARD TINTON & ROBT:
               READ. The other wit: EDMUND DOD & GEORGE HEWITT
Exor: wife ELIZABETH...to her disposall all my goods, chattells &c.

17 Dec 1753 Recorded - Dated 15 Nov 1753: - NATHANIEL NEWTON selling
7 DB 545 PAc   MR. JONATHAN SAUNDERS 260 acres in Princess Anne Co.
               and is the same land which the said NATH: NEWTON pur-
chased of GEORGE MOSELEY as by Deeds dated 27 & 28 Jan 1743/4. Bounds
are not given.

18 Dec 1753 - JAMES MOORE
7 DB 547 PAc   wd 11 May 1753 wp 18 Dec 1753 by THO: GRAINGER, JAMES
               GODFREY & JOHN CHAPMAN. Other wit: THOMAS BULLER
Exor: friend WILLIAM NIMMO & son JAMES MOORE.....dau: ANNE TATUM....
sons: JAMES MOORE all the Plantation I bought of FRANCIS SPRATT and
his brother THOROWGOOD SPRATT... son JOHN? (inkspot on name) 1/2 the
houses in Norfolk... son FRANCIS my dwelling house in Norfolk.......

15 Jan 1754 Rec. & Dated same day - DINAH (T) BONNEY Deed of Gift to
7 DB 553 PAc   daughter FRANKEY BONNEY.

18 Jan 1754   - CHARLES WHITEHURST
7 DB 554 PAc   wd 18 Nov 1753 wp 18 Jan 1754 by all the witnesses
                Wit: THOMAS (T) ROBINSON & DENNIS DAWLEY
Exor: CAPT: JOHN WHITEHURST & ARTHUR WHITEHURST........wife MARY...
sons WILLIAM & CHARLES.....daughter AMY..........................

15 Feb 1754 Recorded - SAMUEL WILES to MICHAEL FENTRIS a Plantation
7 DB 572 PAc   of land whereon MICHAEL FENTRIS now liveth 100 acres
                in Princess Anne County on the S side of the E. Branch
of the Elizabeth River.....it being the same land AUGUST DAMNUM conveyed to the said SAM[1]: WILES 21 Apr 1752.

16 Jan 1754   - THOMAS KEZON, Yeoman (spelled CASON in signature)
7 DB 573 PAc   deed to EDWARD FRIZZLE.............................

16 Apr 1754 Recorded - Dated 6 Sep 1753: - ANTHONY LAWSON & CHARLES
7 DB 580 PAc   both of Princess Anne County to ELIAS CORNISH of
                Curratuck County, N. C. ...for 5/ in hand paid......
a tract of land 150 acres in PAco. near a Bay called BACK BAY & is
part of a larger tract of land which THOMAS LAWSON, father to the
abovesd ANTHONY & CHARLES gave in his will to sd ANTHONY & CHARLES &
THOMAS LAWSON his sons, which sd son THOMAS is since dead whereby his
part descended to ANTHONY heir at law who hereby sells 2/3 & sd
CHARLES 1/3 of sd 150 acres....Bounds are given.

16 Apr 1754 ≡ ROBERT HUGGINS
7 DB 587 PAc   wd 21 Aug 1753 wp 16 Apr 1754 by JOHN SHIPP & THO:
                GRAINGER & DINAH)X(GRAINGER
Exor: wife MARY and son ROBT: HUGGINS
sons: ROBERT, NATT underage, MARKHAM; my father PHILIP formerly lived;
dau OLIVE (ALIFF?) gr-son WILLIAM CARTWRIGHT; dau ARGENT..............

16 Apr 1754   - JOHN (I) GORNTO
7 DB 589 PAc   wd 5 Oct 1752 wp 16 Apr 1754 by JOHN HAYNES & WILLIAM
                WOODHOUSE. 3rd wit: MARY HENLEY
Exor: sons JOHN & ARTHUR GORNTO........son ARTH UR land I bought of
JOHN WILLIS....& land I bought of ADAM HAIES...& land I bought of CAPT:
JAMES DAUGE........sons JOHN & ARTHUR all my marshes....4 daughters
FRANCES, ELIZABETH, AMY & LIDIA......to son JOHN plantation I now live
on 317 acres &50 acres of swamp I bought of MAJ: HENRY SPRATT.......
dau MARGARET HENDLEY.....(wife is not mentioned in this will)

16 Apr 1754 ≡ JOEL CORNICK
7 DB 590 PAc   wd 12 Jan 1754 wp 16 Apr 1754 by all the witnesses
                Wit: HENRY)X(CORNICK, ELIZABETH FONTAINE & MARGRIT
)X(BROCK.   Exor: wife & LEMUEL CORNICK.......son JOEL the plantation
whereon I now live with reversion to son WILLIAM...son HENRY land I
bought of LEMUEL CARTWRIGHT & land bgt of COCKROFT OLD, HENRY IS underage. to 3 sons JOEL, HENRY & WILLIAM 11 negroes to be equally divided
as they shall come to age....unto wife all the money & debts due me &
5 negroes. (It might be possible to clear up some of the confusion

in the several lines of the JOEL CORNICKS if the names of the slaves
are noted in later wills of these children: JOEL, HENRY & WILLIAM
received 11 slaves: Moll, Hannah, Sarah, Miriah, Dick, Kate, Rose,
Rachel, Joshua & Daniel & Rose. His wife (not named) received 5
negroes: Bob, Mingo, Ned, Sarah & Nan.

16 Apr 1754 - RICHARD SMITH of Princess Anne County
7 DB 591 PAc   wd 9 Jan 1752 wp 16 Apr 1754 by JOHN GISBURN. The
                other wit: JACOBUS HUTH (X).   EXOR: SOLOMON HEATH
....to HALSTEAD HOLEWELL 75 acres of my new survaid land joining on
AARON PRESCOTTS & JAMES LANGLEYS line.....sister SARAH KEETCH? my
Plantation at the head of the river allowing my Mother during her
widowhood Plantation at the head of a branch....to my cousin RICH:
HEATH....to sister LIDIA SMITH....to sister ELIZABETH SMITH.

16 Apr 1754 - CHRISTOPHER PHILPOT
7 DB 592 PAc   wd 6 Feb 1753 wp 16 Apr 1754 by GILBURT JAMES &
                ELIZABETH SMITH. 3rd wit: RICHD: SMYTH (he was decd,
his will pvd the same day)   EXOR: wife MARY
...dau ELISABETH, underage, all my lands with reversion to RACHEL
WEST....residue to wife MARY during her widowhood.

16 Apr 1754 - WORSELL ALDERSON
7 DB 592 PAc   wd 12 Aug 1752 wp 16 Apr 1754 by JOHN (‡) HAYES.
                The other wit: SARAH (X) HAYES.   EXOR: ARTH: SAYER
...son JOHN ALDERSON my spoon molds &c......residue to be divided
between my wife and all my children.................................

17 Apr 1754 - FRANCES (X) BROWN relict of EDW: BROWN decd........
7 DB 593 PAc   Deed of Gift to Daughter ELIZABETH HILL & her husband
                MORRIS HILL all my estate......Dated 1 Sep 1753.......

19 Feb 1754 Recorded - Dated 4 Feb 1754: - JOHN MERCER of Norfolk Co.
7 DB 594 PAc   Planter & MARTHA his wife & FRANCES CONDON of the
                Borough of Norfolk, Spinster, to WILLIAM AITCHISON,
Merchant.....Whereas CAPT: JAMES CONDON late of PAco. departed this
life intestate without issue ... died possessed of the Fee Simple
estate of 180 acres on the Eastern Shore of Princess Anne County where
he lived & dyed & one other tract 250 acres Swampland which lands descended to his five sisters ELIZABETH late wife of WILLIAM STEVENSON,
FRANCES CONDON party to these presents, MARTHA now the wife of JNO:
MERCER (and party to these presents) JANE who married ELIAS WILLS and
SARAH who married MR. JOHN GIMMETLAND and whereas sd JOHN MERCER &
his wife, ELIAS WILLS & JANE his wife & FRANCES CONDON did lately sell
the parts of the sd 2 tracts of land which descended to sd MARTHA, JANE,
& FRANCES to JACOB ELLIGOOD late of PAco. Gent, decd., & whereas sd
SARAH wife of JOHN GIMMELL died leaving JOHN her only son & FRANCES
her only daughter & son JOHN GIMMELL dying underage and without issue
his part descended to his sister sd FRANCES GIMMILL & she dying without
issue 1/5 part descended to ELIZA: wife of sd STEVENSON, MARTHA MERCER,
JANE WILLS & FRANCES CONDON. Now this Indenture witneseth that sd.
JOHN MERCER & MARTHA his wife and FRANCES CONDON for 5/ in hand paid
by sd WILLIAM AITCHINSON have sold all the parts of the 2 tracts of
land which descended to them..................................

22 May 1754 Recorded - Dated 10 Feb 1754: - JOSEPH BELL of North Caro-
7 DB 600 PAc   lina of the one part...and MARY FAZACKERLY of PAco....
                one RICHARD CORBETT late of PAco. decd grandfather to
said MARY FAZAKERLY in his will dated 12 Oct 1720 bequeathed a negro
woman PHILLIS & her increase except ....two of the first children
of hers to his daughter ABIGAIL CORBITT and the said Phillis to my
daughter MARY CORBETT in case my 2 daughters die then the other sister
shall have her part &c...... after RICHARD CORBETS decease his daughter
ABIGAIL married THOMAS FAZAKERLEY & since is dead leaving issue, the
abovesd. MARY FAZAKERLY & that sd. ABIGAIL together with the sd THOMAS
her husband possessed themselves with the first two children of sd.
negro...THOMAS FAZAKERLY father of sd. MARY only daughter of ABIGAIL.

21 May 1754 - MICHEL (M) FENTRIS of Princess Anne County
7 DB 612 PAc   wd 22 Apr 1754 wp 21 May 1754 by MATTHEW MATTHIAS &
                 NATH: NICHOLAS. 3rd wit: THO: GRAINGER
Exor: wife ELIZA: & kinsman MOSES FENTRISS son of MOSES FENTRISS
...dau KEZIAH FENTRIS 3 cows & yearlings &c....son JOHN FENTRIS 1/....
residue to be sold to the highest bidder if any money is left after
debts are paid to wife ELIZABETH during her natural life and after to
dau KEZIAH with reversion to gr-dau AMY WHITEHURST.

21 May 1754 - MALACAI (MALACHI?) NICHOLSON (NICHORSON in will)of Nco.
7 DB 603 PAc   wd 4 May 1754 wp 21 May 1754 by the witnesses.
                 Wit:EDW: LATIMER, JOSIAH WILSON, LEM[l]: LANGLEY
Exor: GEORGE OLDNER..........my land lying in Princess Anne County may
be sold at Public Saile & likewise my negro called Farmer all my stock
of household furniture to be sold at public saile & then collected with
my other just debts to be disposed of as follows: to my brother WILLIAM
NICHOLSON ₤ 5, to my sister PRUDENCE WILSON ₤ 5, residue to be equally
divided between DINAH OLDNER & ELIZA: THUCKAM? & ANN CHILLIS?

21 May 1754 - AND[w]: NICHOLAS
7 DB 615 PAc   wd 13 Dec 1742 wp 21 May 1754 - Will presented in
                 Court by ARCH[d]: WHITE appointed by the Court who made
oath and proved by the oaths of BLANDINAH JOLLEY. The other witness
was WM: WIGGING. EXOR: MR. ROBT: TODD.................unto my loving
wife all that I have in the world.....she not carrying it out of the
County and after.....to ROBT: TODD, March/ (Merchant?) in Newtown all
that I leave my wife in possession with.

18 Jun 1754 Recorded - Dated 12 Jun 1754: - ANTHONY LAWSON...Deed of
7 DB 625 PAc   Gift to my cousins ANNE NEWTON dau of COL: NATH: NEWTON
                 & CHARLES SAYER son of CAPT: ARTH: SAYER ...2 negroes.

18 Jun 1754 - WILLIAM (W) SALMONS of Princess Anne County
7 DB 627 PAc   wd 29 Apr 1754 wp 18 Jun 1754 by LEM[l]: STONE & JAMES
                 CASON. Other wit: DAVID FENTRISS. EXOR: None named
...son WILLOBY SALMON 65 acres lying upon the HORSE BRIDGE RUN called
the DOGWOOD RIDGE....son WILLIAM the rest of my land & Plantation whereon I now live after my wifes decease....to wife the residue her widdowhood after to be divided between all my children.

17 Jun 1754 Recorded - GERSHOM NIMMO surveyed land for the following:
7 DB 626 PAc   DENNIS DAULEY   150 acres in MUDDY CREEK Princess Anne Co.
                24 Nov 1750.
                ANNE GILES 111 acres which is her Dower upon the Eastern
Shore - 5 Feb 1750/1.
WIDDOW LOVETTS, LANCASTER LOVET, JOHN LOVET & WIDOW WARDEN 879 acres &
divided it on the Sea Side - 3 Apr 1751.
WM: JACOB 40 3/4 acres of CYPRUSS SWAMP near the North Landing 26 Aug 1751
PETER DALE 250 acres 3/4 in BROAD CREEK 15 Nov 1751.
CAPT: ANTHONY WALKE & CAPT: GEORGE WISHART 64 acres & 1/2 & divided, 21
Nov 1751.
LEM¹: FENTRISS, JAS: FENTRISS, JOHN FENTRISS & WILLIAM FENTRIS 263 acres
CYPRUS SWAMP 31 Dec 1751.
WILLIAM & JAMES RANDOLPH 211 acres & divided in BLACKWATER 22 Nov 1751.
ADAM TOOLEY 161 acres in BLACK WATER 6 Dec 1751
JOHN PHILPOTT 20 3/4 acres in BLACKWATER 13 Dec 1751
SOLOMON WOOD 50 acres   26 May 1752
BENJ: DINGLEY GRAY 313 acres of land & marsh opposite to NEWTOWN 2 Jul 1752
     "   "   "   102 1/2 acs of land   26 May 1752
THO: OLDS   37 1/2 & 49 3/4 acres of land in BLACK WATER 17 Oct 1752
RICH: WILLIAM SYLVESTER 389 1/2 acres in BLACK WATER 19 Oct 1752
WILLIAM WOOD   60 1/4 acres in BLACK WATER 25 Nov 1752
ROBT: REV. KITELEY & LARENCE DAWLEY & ROE? 448 acres in BLACK WATER
                                                        5 Dec 1751
CHAS: WHITEHEAD 125 1/2 acres in BLACK WATER 6 Oct 1752
RALPH CAPPS 89 1/2 acres of low land in MUDDY CREEK 2 Oct 1753
MICHAEL FENTRISS 115 1/2 acres 13 Apr 1754
JONATHAN SAUNDERS & GEORGE OLDNER 136 acres of Escheat land 20 May 1754
ROBERT MURDEN 100 1/2 acres in NORTH WOODS 29 May 1754
SIMON WHITEHURST 21 1/2 acres in the NORTH WOODS
Presented at Court 17 Jun 1754 and ordered to be Recorded.

16 Jul 1754 - ANTHONY ETHERIDGE in a deed to SIMON MATTHIAS ....
7 DB 632 PAc   his name is spelled ETHERIDGE in the deed but the
                signature gives the name as ETHERD .

20 Aug 1754 - ARTHUR WHITEHURST
7 DB 640 PAc   wd 5 Jun 1754 wp 20 Aug 1754 by all the witnesses.
                Wit: THO: WRIHT (sic) JOHN WHITEHURST & MARY WHITEHURST
Exor: wife MARGITT & THOMAS WARD & ROBERT WARD
son FRANCIS my Plantation with reversion to son ARTHUR................
all my childred when they come to age a parcel of land in the NEGRO
SWAMP.....son ODEN WHITEHURST.......son TULLY WHITEHURST..............

19 Aug 1748 Recorded - JAMES TOOLY & BETTY his wife of Princess Anne
7 DB 641 PAc   County to WILLIAM FENTRIS of the same county ...100
                acres and is the same land that JOHN HERBERT formerly
bequeathed in his will to his son THOMAS HARBERT dated 28 Apr 1728....
sd land lying upon BLACK CREEK and adjoining land of JOHN PHILPOT &
descended to the abovesd BETTY as being the daughter of the aforsd
THO: HERBERT.

19 Nov 1754 Recorded - Dated 18 Nov 1754: - EDWARD HACK MOSELEY to
7 DB 644 PAc   GERSHOM NIMMO all that tract of land containing part
               of an acre 5 1/4 chain from a chinkerpen stake along
the road that leads to PUNGO.......it being 1/2 acre EDW: HACK MOSELEY
bought of JAMES FENTRIS.

19 Nov 1754 Recorded - Dated 18 Nov 1754: - GERSHOM NIMMO to EDWARD
7 DB 646 PAc   HACK MOSELEY all that piece or parcel of land con-
               taining part of an acre.....stake that is opposet to
ABSOLAMS House running along the Road that leads to the NORTH LANDING
.....along the road that leads to PUNGO......which the sd GERSHOM
NIMMO & EDWARD HACK MOSELEY intend to have a new Road between their
lands which leads to PUNGO.

19 Nov 1754 Recorded - JAMES OAST and wife JOYCE selling to JAMES ASHLEY
7 DB 650 PAc   of Norfolk County a Plantation adjoining to Little
               Creek 100 acres formerly granted to RICHARD WILLIAMS
by Patent 29 Oct 1673...... WITNESSED BY: THURMER HOGGARD, ALEX:
POOLE & JOHN INCE. (THURMER SIGNS: THUR:)

19 Nov 1754 - MARGARET (M) SAYER of Princess Anne County, wid°
7 DB 661 PAc   wd 18 May 1754 wp 19 Nov 1754 by COL: ANTH°: WALKE,
                & ANNE MOSELEY. 3rd wit: ELIZ: (W) PURSLEY?
Exor: son ARTHUR SAYER.........dau FRANCES BOUSH....... gr-daus: MARG-
ARETT WALKE, FRANCES SAYER, MARGARET BOUSH & gr-daus: ANNE & MARGARET
NEWTON when of age of 18 years.......GR_-dau MARGARET MALBONE.........
gr-sons: JONATHAN SAUNDERS, ANTHONY LAWSON..............Residue unto
my son ARTHUR SAYER....my dau FRANCES BOUSH and the children of my dau
ELIZA: NEWTON decd....1/3 to ARTHUR ... 1/3 unto dau FRANCES & remaining
1/3 to the children of daughter ELIZABETH NEWTON, my gr-children as
before mentioned.

4 Sep 1754 - AUDIT of WILLIAM CARTWRIGHT to MARY & ROBT: CARTWRIGHT
7 DB 664 PAc Total cash ₤ 101.05.10. On list of names and amounts
              paid: Account of THOS: KEELING an Orphan in Rhode
Island ₤ 2.06.00.   Recorded 17 Dec 1754. Audit ordered 20 Aug 1754.

17 Dec 1754 - Appraisal of JOEL CORNICK ...... total ₤ 186.08.07.
7 DB 665 PAc

21 Jan 1755 - ROBERT BURFOOT & AMY his wife of PAco to WILLIAM HOLMES
7 DB 664 PAc   land on Eastern Shore of PAco and is the equal part or
               dower of the same land which WILLIAM CONSAUL decd died
possessed of & AMY his wife, now wife of sd BURFOOT.................

21 Jan 1755 Recorded - Dated 19 Dec 1754: - CHARLES EDWARDS Deed of
7 DB 669 PAc   Gift to his children: son WILLIAM the plantation 100
               acres........son CHARLES land over the run ....
son HENRY land I bgt of MICHAEL FENTRISS......dau ELIZABETH..........
wife SARAH......Residue to be divided between and among my 4 children
FRANCIS LAND, dau ELIZABETH & sons SOLOMON & OBEDIAH EDWARDS ....

21 Jan 1755 - AMBROSE BURFOOT
7 DB 670 PAc   wd 1 May 1754 wp 21 Jan 1755 by MARY (X) ELLIS &
                 ROBERT PATTERSON.   Exor: son ROBERT BURFOOT
....son ROBERT all my estate both real & personal after paying my debts
....dau ELIZABETH CANNON wife of EDWARD CANNON..cows.....gr-son JOHN
CANNON......gr-dau SARAH BURFOOT underage daughter of MACKIE SMYTH
my daughter.....dau SARAH wife of JOHN ABSOLAM....dau MACKY SMITH
wife of THO: SMITH in Province of N. C.

18 Feb 1755 - ARGAL THOROWGOOD SENR: of PAco.
7 DB 673 PAc   wd 20 Apr 1754 wp 18 Feb 1755 by SAMUEL BOUSH, FRAN :
                 SPRATT & ANN (+) RICE.... Exor: wife ELIZABETH & CAPT:
WM: KEELING her brother..........wife ELIZA: my plantation whereon I
now live during her life and after her death to my son WILLIAM THOROW-
GOOD & all the rest of my lands when he comes to age of 18............
dau ELIZABETH THOROWGOOD negroes to be delivered to her at day of marriage or 21 years....."my 2 children".....to son WILLIAM at age of
8 years one riding horse & to ELIZA: at the age of 8 years.

15 Apr. 1755 Recorded & Dated the same day - ROBERT LAND & FRANCES his wife,
7 DB 675 PAc   son of EDWARD LAND of PAco. of the one part selling to
                 HEZEKIAH BROWN of the same county for Ł 25.02........
100 acres in PAco. on the Main Road commonly called PUNGO ROAD that
leads through the sd County bounded by JAMES MASONS line of mkd trees
...Nly to WILLIAM OAKHAMS corner tree.....&c......................

15 Apr 1755 Recorded & Dated same day - SAMUEL BOUSH & wife ELIZA: to
7 DB 677 PAc   WM: HUNTER 60 1/2 acres in PAco. on LITTLE CREEK being
                 on THOMAS WISHARTS land to the Norward, on THOMAS HUN-
TERS Land Escheated from ANN WORKM^n: to the Sward and on LITTLE CREEK
to the Eastward by the various courses thereof......................

16 Apr 1755 - PEMMY FLINCH wid^o: of JOHN FLINCH
7 DB 683 PAc

20 May 1755 Recorded - Dated 19 May 1755: - MAXIMILLIAN BOUSH JUNR:
7 DB 685 PAc   of PAco selling to SAMUEL BOUSH for 5/ that planta-
                 tion of land containing 223 acres in the Parish of
Lynhaven in the Western Shore Precinct and is the same land which
MAXIMILLIAN BOUSH the Elder devised in and by his last will........
to the said SAMUEL BOUSH in fee tail and by him exchanged with MAX:
BOUSH decd who was eldest son of sd. MAXIM: BOUSH the Elder for other
lands lying in said county & afterwards again conveyed by said SAMUEL
BOUSH to LEMUEL GASKING.......(this is a long involved deed about
clearing the title to this land.....CHARLES GASKING is also involved
in it)

20 May 1755 - FRA: HILL wife of THO: HILL
7 DB 688 PAc

20 May 1755 Recorded - Dated 15 Dec 1754: - GEORGE OLDNER as Exor: to
7 DB 690 PAc   the last will of MALACHI NICHOLSON decd of PAc for
                 Ł 85. 6 pence selling to WILLIAM GODFREY, Mariner of

the same place a plantation of 140 acres and is the same land that
THOMAS WHITEHURST gave in his last will to his son LEM[1]: WHITEHURST
& by sd LEM[1]: WHITEHURST exchanged with the abovenamed MALACHI
NICHOLSON & adjoining the land whereon COL: WALKE now lives & which
said land the sd MALACHI NICHOLSON decd in his last will dated 4 May
1754 devised to be sold by his sd Exor:...and all houses &c.........

20 May 1755 Recorded - Dated 19 May 1755: - JOHN SALMONE, ANTHO:
7 DB 694 PAc   SALMON & his wife FRANCIS and SOLOMON SUGGS & his wife
                 MARY all of PAco for 5/ selling to ELIZABETH THELABALL
of Norfolk County 150 acres in Parish of Lynhaven adjoining unto a
CYPRESS BRANCH, CHARLES EDWARDS, LEML: HARTGROVE and WILLIAM SALMONS
.....& all houses &c...

20 May 1755 Recorded - Dated 19 May 1755: - BENJ: DINGLEY GREY & SUSANA
7 DB 696 PAc   his wife to WALTER SCOTT of Norfolk County, Shipwright
                90 acres begin: at a pine standing in a line between
sd GRAY & land of JONAS CAWSON .... th N 13° E to a Branch or Cove
proceeding out of the Eastern Branch of Eliz: River so down sd branch
to the River th up the sd Eastern Branch or River according to the
Several courses thereof to the mouth of SCOTTS CREEK &c..............

20 May 1755 Recorded and Dated same day - ARTHUR FRIZZLE & wife AFFIAH
7 DB 698 PAc   and ARTHUR FRIZZLE son of DANIEL.

20 May 1755 Recorded - Dated 19 May 1755: - LANCASTER & wife LIDIA
7 DB 700 PAc   selling land left him by his father LANCASTER LOVETT
                to JASPER WHITE. GERSHOM NIMMO witnessed the deed.

20 May 1755 -   ROBERT THOROWGOOD of PAco
7 DB 702 PAc   wd 17 Feb 1755 wp 20 May 1755 by JOHN THOROWGOOD SENR:
                 Other wit: ROB: BURROUGHS   EXOR: THOMAS KEELING &
wife BLANDINAH......son ROBERT THOROWGOOD under 21 years.

21 May 1755 Recorded - Dated 4 Jul 1754: - In the audit of the Estate
7 DB 703 PAc   of MRS. MARY MOORE decd totaling ₤ 167.12.09........
                 to cash paid CAPT: FRANCIS MALBONE
                 to cash paid   DITTO   his part of his father's
estate.

20 May 1755 -   THO: LESTER'S will by Word of Mouth who deceased 13
7 DB 703 PAc   Apr 1755 viz: that MARY his wife should have all his
                 Estate and pay all his just Debts.
Wit: MARY HARPER SENR, WILLM: HARPER SENR.   Will was presented in
Court by MARY LESTER appointed by the Court who made oath & being proved
by oaths of the witnesses.

18 Jun 1755 Recorded - Dated 17 Jun 1755: - ENOCH (+) WHITEHURST, Planter
7 DB 705 PAc   & MARY his wife selling to ABEL EDMONDS...25 acres......

17 Jun 1755 Recorded - Dated same day - TULLY ROBINSON, WILLIAM ROBINSON
7 DB 709 PAc   & WILLIAM NIMMO....a bond in the amount of ₤ 1000........
                Condition being the obligations of Sheriff.....TULLY
ROBINSON, GENT....being appointed Sheriff of Princess Anne County.

17 Jun 1755 - ELIZABETH (E) NICHOLSON of Princess Ann County - Deed
7 DB 709 PAc   of Gift dated 8 Apr 1755....to son CHA: NICHOLSON &
                to daus BETTY & DINAH......negroes...................
Wit: WM: NIMMO JUNR, JNO: HANCOCK & MARY (+) HOLMES

17 Jun 1755 Recorded - Dated 9 Mar 1755: - ARGYL THOROWGOOD decd, the
7 DB 710 PAc   Appraisement of his Estate ordered by Court 17 Feb
                1755.....Total ₤ 318.16.03.......................
The negroes in this appraisement amount to about ₤ 155.

17 Jun 1755 - JOHN RUSSEL
7 DB 712 PAc   wd none   wp 17 Jun 1755 by TULLY WILLIAMSON & JOHN
                GREEN (Ŧ) Other wit: DINAAH MASON
Exix wife ISABELL (not named in will, but named in probate).........
son WILLIAM RUSSEL my manner plantation loo acres...................
son JOHN the other plantation 100 acres.............................

17 Jun 1755 - NATH: WHITEHURST
7 DB 712 PAc   wd 3 Apr 1755 wp 17 Jun 1755 by THOMAS WILES & RICHD:
                WHITEHURST. 3rd wit: JAMES WHITEHURST
Exor: brother HENRY & THOS: WILES......my brother HENRY WHITEHURST my
plantation that I bought of SOLOMON WOOD & all my whole estate.

Deed Book 7 contains in all 714 pages. This is the end of your
editors abstracts of Genealogical Gleanings from this book.

MINUTE BOOK 7 - PRINCESS ANNE COUNTY, VIRGINIA
++

1753 - 1762
+++++++++++++

Genealogical notes from this book including every
mention of the name Hoggard.

17 Apr 1753 - Probate of the last will of CAPT: JAMES NIMMO granted to
7 MB 3 PAc   his exors: (not named)

18 Apr 1753 - Ordered that JAMES HOLMES, JAMES WILLIAMS, THO: CONE,
7 MB 8 PAc   THURMER HOGGARD or any three of them appraise the estate
              of HENRY ROBERTS decd.

19 Jun 1753 - On the motion of JOHN HERBERT its ordered that the clerk
7 MB 23 PAc   deliver to him his part of WILLOUGHBY HERBERTS Estate
              sold at outcry & lodged i n the office.

19 Jun 1753 - On the petition of ANDREW ETHERIDGE & his wife its order-
7 MB 25 PAc   ed that the Clerk deliver to them their parts of WILLOUGH-
              BY HERBERTS Estate sold at outcry & lodged in the office.

20 Jun 1753 - WM: ROBINSON agst: MARGRET SMYTH & ARTHUR SAYER Exors of
7 MB 29,30   the last will of CHARLES SMYTH decd.......This is a long
              item.......about a claim of ₤ 31.09.08 due ROBINSON before
the death of CHARLES SMYTH. The Jury: WILLIAM COX, JONAS CAWSON, JOHN
CHAPMAN, JOEL SIMMONS, LEWIS THELABALL, JOHN SCOTT, CHARLES SMALLWOOD,
WM: HANCOCK, MOSES ffENTRISS, ROBERT MOSELEY, JOHN INCE JUN: & WILLIAM
PARSONS find for the Pltff: ₤ 31.09.08.

20 Jun 1753 - GERSHOM NIMMO to be added to the Commissioners of the
7 MB 32 PAc   Peace.

21 Aug 1753 - WILLIAM KEELING, DAVID McCLENAHAN & GERSHOM NIMMO GENT:
7 MB 42 PAc   having taken the oaths of Government subscribed the test
              likewise the oath of a Justice of the peace & Judge in
Chancery do take their seats accordingly.

21 Aug 1753 - Ordered that the sherif sell all the Estate of THOMAS
7 MB 42 PAc   COAN (probably should be CONE?) decd at public outcry.

21 Aug 1753 - Ordered that THOMAS WISHART, THURMER HOGGARD & WM: HUNTER
7 MB 44 PAc   appraise the estate of HENRY HOLMES.

22 Aug 1753 - On petition of GEORGE MATHEWS a Mullato (who was bound
7 MB 51 PAc   by Indenture to serve SUSANNAH HANCOCK an orphan of WM:
              HANCOCK decd) for his freedon the Court having heard the
evidences are of the opinion the sd: GEORGE has served his time by law
.....he is to be set free.........

16 Oct 1753 - JOHN WMSON: Compltt: agst: JOHN HARPER deft:...having
7 MB 62,63   entered into articles of agreement.....between JOHN HAR-
              PER JUNR: of PAco & JOHN WILLIAMSON late of PAco at pre-
sent a resident of NORTH CAROLINA.......JOHN WILLIAMSON has lately
commenced a suit in Chancery in PAco agst: JOHN HARPER as son & heir at
law to his mother MARY WILLIAMSON decd who was the daughter of one
ROBERT HARPER grand father to the said JNO: WMSON: for the recovery of
part of a certain negro wench called Kate which by the last will of sd:
ROBERT HARPER decd was willed given and devised unto his 2 youngest
children JAMES HARPER since decd father to sd JOHN HARPER & the sd:

cont'd: - MARY Mother of the sd: JOHN WMSON: (This goes on and on
            about the slaves and whose hands they were in.

16 Oct 1753 - CAPT: WILLIAM HAYNES & ELIZA: his wife, SARAH SMYTH &
7 MB 65 PAc JOHN SMYTH an infant by MR: NATH: McCLANAHAN Guardian
             Complts: agst: ROBINSON SMYTH in chancery.....the deft:
to pay unto each of the Complts: being his brothers & sisters the just
sum of ₤ 25 each their proportionable part of the slaves.

25 Oct 1753 - There were 1623 Tythables
7 MB 66 PAc

16 Jan 1754 - MARY DYSON Goaler of the County - 2100 l tob due her
7 MB 82 PAc

16 Jan 1754 - GERSHOM NIMMO & ELIZ: his wife complts: agst: ELIZA:
7 MB 83 PAc THELABALL & FREDERICK BOUSH an infant underage by the
             said ELIZA: THELABALL his guardian defts: in Chancery...
Division of Negroes belonging to Estate of MAX: BOUSH decd. ELIZABETH
wife of GERSHOM NIMMO one of the daughters of COL: MAX: BOUSH decd....
slaves to FREDERICK BOUSH as his proper share.......................

20 Feb 1754 - THOMAS CONE decd.
7 MB 89,90

16 Apr 1754 - DR: ARCHIBALD CAMPBELL to be paid ₤ 3.18.06 out of the
7 MB 94 PAc Estate of THOMAS CONE. Ordered to be paid with Cost.

18 Jun 1754 - GERSHOM NIMMO GENT: Justice at Court
7 MB 114 PAc

18 Jun 1754 - ROBERT BURROUGH & ISABELL his wife, JOEL SIMMONS & AMY
7 MB 115 PAc his wife agst: ERASMUS HAYNES JUN: dismist the pltfs:
             paying costs.

18 Jun 1754 - DINAH HOSKINS a witness for ROBERT BURROUGH vs: ERASMUS
7 MB 117 PAc HAYNES..........

17 jul 1754 - GERSHOM NIMMO GENT: Justice at Court.
7 MB 123 PAc

16 Jul 1754 - WILLIAM & GERSHOM NIMMO Exors of CAPT: (JAMES) DECD HAVING
7 MB 126 PAc pvd: an acct of the sd: JAMES NIMMO agst the estate of
             EDMOND ABSOLUM decd for ₤ 53.03.06 therefore ordered that
the sd: WILLIAM NIMMO who ia adm: of the estate of EDWARD ABSOLUM decd
unadministered by the sd: JAMES NIMMO in his lifetime retain the sum
aforesaid in his hands with costs........

20 Aug 1754 - GEORGE WEBLIN adm: with the will annexed of WM: WEBLIN
7 MB 127 PAc decd: VS: ROBERT PATERSON & SARAH his wife in Chancery.
             ....the Complt: is entitled to one Moiety of WILLIAM WEB-
LINS personal estate.

20 Aug 1754 - On the petition of ANNE ASHBY, WILLIAM ASHBY & SARAH
 7 MB 127 PAc ASHBY its ordered that the clerk deliver to them their
            part of JOHN ASHBY's estate sold at Outcry & lodged in
the office. The wid°: to give bond & security for WILLIAMS part he
being underage.

21 Aug 1754 - GERSHOM NIMMO, Gent. Justice was at Court.
 7 MB 130 PAc

6 Nov 1754 - At a Court for Laying the Leavy: 1721 Tythables
 7 MB 136 PAc To WM: NIMMO, Kings Attorney   1000

19 Nov 1754 - ANNE, MARGARET & JACOB ELLEGOOD Infants under 21 years
 7 MB 140,141 by WM: KEELING Gent: their next friend VS NATHL: NEW-
            TON & ANNE his wife & WM: AITCHISON.......division of
the negroes belonging to the estate of COL: JACOB ELLEGOOD decd.......
....MRS. ANNE ELLEGOODS lott....MRS: MARGARET ELLEGOODS lott, JACOB
ELLEGOODS lott.   In all five slaves were named.

18 Feb 1755 - On the Motion of CAPT: WM: KEELING....those appted to
 7 MB 152 PAc lay off & assign to GEORGE COX & SUSANNAH his wife their
            dower of 125 acres formerly belonging to JAMES SMITH &
sold by EDMUND ABSALOM decd, former husband of the sd SUSANNAH to the
said WILLIAM KEELING & report same to the next Court.

18 Feb 1755 - JAMES HOLMES, THURMER HOGGARD, THOS: HAYNES & JOHN
 7 MB 153 PAc GRIFFIN or any 3 of them to appraise the estate of HENRY
            HOLMES decd, intestate.

18 Feb 1755 - ROBERT HUGGINS to be guardian to OLIVE HUGGINS giving
 7 MB 154 PAc bond ⊢ 150; to NATH: ARGENT & MARKHAM HUGGINS giving
            bond ⊢ 300.

19 Feb 1755 - On the motion of GERSHOM NIMMO & EDWARD HACK MOSELEY GENT
 7 MB 157 PAc its ordered that the road leading by the parties at the
            fork of the North Landing Road be turned to the Northward
of where it now goes & nearer to the said NIMMO's dwelling house......
......GERSHOM NIMMO GENT: JUSTICE present at Court.

18 Feb 1755 - THURMER HOGGARD on a Jury
 7 MB 159 PAc

15 Apr 1755 - On the motion of JOHN PALLET & MARY his wife its ordered
 7 MB 163 PAc that CAPT: WILLIAM KEELING exor of CAPT: WM: KEELING decd
            pay them the sd MARY's part of her Mothers estate in his
            hands.

15 Apr 1755 - SARAH BANNISTER wid°:, HENRY GASKING & ANNE his wife,
 7 MB 164 PAc MARTHA BANNISTER by ADAM LOVETT her guardian, SARAH &
            FRANCES BANNISTER by SARAH BANNISTER Wid° their guardian
COMPLTTS: VS ALEX: POOLE adm: of JAMES BANNISTER decd deft:...........
division of the negroes..........in Chancery.

15 Apr 1755 - On the petition of COL: ANTHONY WALKE to turn the road that
7 MB 164 PAc leads from the head of the Eastern Branch to the Great
Bridge & Powder Point, liberty is given him to turn the same according to
the course proposed.

15 Apr 1755 - Gent: appointed inthe motion of CAPT: WILLIAM KEELING to
7 MB 164 PAc lay off to SUSANNAH COX her dower of the land bought by
              the said KEELING of EDMUND ABSOLUM decd her former husband
having this day returned their report..............the bounds are given.

5 May 1755 - MARTHA KEELING being taken by warrant of WM: KEELING GENT:
7 MB 169 PAc for suspicion of her having been (accidentally & without
              design) the occasion of the death of a negro boy called
James belonging to her husband ADAM KEELING in correcting him by whiping
& the Court upon examination having fully heard the Evidences were of
the opinion that sd. James was not by sd. MARTHA willfully or designedly
killed but that the same happened by some accidental blow or wound given
him in the time of correction...sd. MARTHA discharged & acquitted.

20 May 1755 - DR: GEORGE ROUVIERE & ANNA his wife complts: VS FRANCIS
7 MB 171 PAc LANGLEY in Chancery......division of the negroes (6) in
              the estate of JAMES & SARAH LANGLEY decd between DOCT:
GEORGE ROUVIERE & CAPT: WM: IVY guardian to MISS FRANCES LANGLEY.

20 May1755   - DR. ROBERT PATERSON & SARAH his wife VS GEORGE WEBLIN in
7 MB 171 PAc Chancery......division of negroes........................
              To DR. ROBT: PATERSON for his wife's dower & GEO: WEBLIN
or his heirs to pay SARAH 5/ every Valentines day during her life.......
GEO: the deft: is satisfied with this so he must have retained some
negroes?

21 May 1755 - DR. GEORGE ROUVIERE adm. of all the goods and chattels of
7 MB 174 PAc JAMES LANGLEY decd unadministered by SARAH LANGLEY decd
              Exix: of the said JAMES....VS....GEORGE OLDNER..........

17 Jun 1755 - ABIA WILES widº of SAMUEL WILES decd made oath he departed
7 MB 182 PAc this life without making a will....she is granted adm.

17 Jun 1755 - Judgmt: is granted MARGARET COAN (CONE?) for 7/6 due by
7 MB 185 PAc acct: from GEORGE OLDNER.

18 Jun 1755 - ADAM TOOLY & SOUTHWOOD SIMMONS Exors of ANNE BLAIR decd.
7 MB 186 PAc

19 Aug 1755 - THURMER HOGGARD serves on a Jury.........The appraisal of
7 MB 194 PAc SAMUEL WILES estate being returned is ordered to be record-
              ed.
16 Sep 1755 - WILLIAM MOSELEY, EDWARD MOSELEY, FRANCIS THOROWGOOD LAND &
7 MB 196 PAc ELIZA: his wife & MARY MOSELEY an infant under 21 years
              by FRAˢ: MOSELEY her father & next friend...VS...GEORGE
LOGAN adm: with the will annexed of WILLIAM MALBONE decd in Chancery.
Division of negroes to WILLIAM MOSELEY & his brother EDWARD MOSELEY & their
sister MARY MOSELEY, FRANCIS THOROWGOOD LAND.

16 Sep 1755 - LANCASTER LOVETT VS JOHN LOVETT, HILLARY LOVETT & AMY
 7 MB 196 PAc LOVETT Infants by CAPT: WILLIAM KEELING their Guardian
               in Chancery....Division of the lands we the subscribers
together with MR: GERSHOM NIMMO Surveyor of Princess Anne County have
on the lands mentioned in the will of LANCASTER LOVETT decd to be given
to his four sons.....have made division of sd lands between LANCASTER
LOVETT complt: & JOHN LOVETT, HENRY L VETT & AMY LOVETT defts:..........

17 Sep 1755 - THURMER HOGGARD serves on a Jury...... CAPT: JOHN HUTCH-
 7 MB 197 PAc INGS .. VS .. GEORGE OLDNER.............................

7 Nov 1755   - A Court for laying the leavy..........................
 7 MB 203 PAc To WILLIAM NIMMO, Kings Attorney   800
               COL: EDWARD HACK MOSELEY as Burgess   2060
               MAJ: ANTHONY WALKE as Burgess by acct: 6940

18 Nov 1755 - A verdict about road: The road that leads from Newtown
 7 MB 204 PAc by CAPT: ANTHONY MOSELEYS to the Main County Road (which
               road COL: EDW: HACK MOSELEY petitioned to remove)& we
find it to be 150 yds further from the warehouse & the same from Little
Creek or Linhaven to the Warehouse & as much nearer to Norfolk & will be
of singular service to COL: MOSELEY inasmuch as he can take in a large
piece of pasture ground without any other prejudice to the public than
the distance above mentioned......thereupon ordered that the New Road
be Established the Main Public Road for the future provided the said
COL: EDW^d: HACK MOSELEY have it made according to law.

18 Nov 1755 - JOHN HUNTER To be guardian to JACOMINE HUNTER - Bond ᵴ 300
 7 MB 204 PAc JACOB HUNTER * "   "   " JAMES HUNTER   " ᵴ 300
               ROBT: CARTWRIGHT"   "   " PEMMY HUNTER   " ᵴ 300

19 Nov 1755 - Division of the slaves whereof ANNE BLAIR decd died seized
 7 MB 207 PAc & possessed of between JOHN SIMMONS, JAMES TOOLY & BETTY
               his wife in right of sd BETTY & WILLIAM SIMMONS..........
JOHN SIMMONS is heir at law, infant of ANNE BLAIR decd by SOUTHWARD
SIMMONS his guardian VS   ADAM TOOLY & SOUTHWARD SIMMONS exors of said
ANNE BLAIR decd, JAMES TOOLY & BETTY his wife & WILLIAM SIMMONS by sd
JAMES TOOLY his guardian ....

16 Dec 1755 - JOHN HARPER & MARGARET his wife, ROBT: CARTWRIGHT & MARY
 7 MB 210 PAc his wife, JNO: HUNTER, THO: HUNTER an infant, JAMES HUNTER
               an infant, PEMMY HUNTER an infant & JOYCE HUNTER an infant
by the sd JOHN HUNTER their brother & next friend .. VS .. JACOB HUNTER
Eldest son & heir at law &c of JOHN HUNTER decd in Chancery.....for division of the negroes to be divided among & between his children hereafter
mentioned: 26 Nov 1755 JOHNHARPER his wife, THOS: HUNTER, ROBT: CART-
WRIGHT his wife, PEMMY HUNTER, JOHN HUNTER, JAMES HUNTER, JOYCE HUNTER
all of them named and the negroes named.

17 Dec 1755 - Ordered that THOS: REYNOLDS WALKER be guardian to JOEL,
 7 MB 213 PAc HENRY & WILLIAM CORNICK during their minority. Bond for
               security ᵴ 500.

21 Jan 1756 - BENJ: WARD VS LANCASTER LOVETT....the Jury finds:
7 MB 214 PAc LANCASTER LOVETT THe Elder decd, died seized & possessed
                    of several negroes having first made his will dated
4 Apr 1743 in which he gives to his wife MARY LOVETT "my negro man......
son LANCASTER LOVETT..........sometime after the death of LANCASTER
LOVETT the Elder MARY LOVETT intermarried with one JOHN WARD father to .
the said BENJ: WARD only son & heir at law.............................

21 Jan 1756 - FRANCES SMYTH Exor of TULLY ROBINSON SMYTH decd VS
7 MB 215 PAc HENRY CORNICK

18 Feb 1756 - SUSANNA HOSKINS VS ROBERT BURFOOT......................
7 MB 220 PAc

18 Feb 1756 - JOHN ffENTRIS, son of MICHAL.............................
7 MB 222 PAc

18 Feb 1756 - The persons appt: on motion of CAPT: LEMUEL CORNICK
7 MB 222 PAc guardian to JOHN LOVETT to lay off & assign to ERASMUS
                    HAYNES & ALIF his wife their dower of LANCASTER LOVETT's
land, houses &c.....have laid off MR. ERASMUS HAYNES dowry holden by his
wife from the part of JOHN LOVETT the heir under the guardianship of
CAPT: LEMUEL CORNICK vizt: The Hall, cellar & passage Chamber which is
yet unfinished, the N⁰West kitchen, the smoke house & Mill house, 4 rows
apple trees on the W side of orchard & the N⁰W side of the plantation
bounded by a pine on Batts Bay in the lane....to hold their part separate
& divided from the part of the sd. JOHN LOVETT.........................

16 Mar 1756 - MARY NIMMO's Deed of Gift to her son WILLIAM NIMMO for the
7 MB 223 PAc plantation whereon she now lives proved by oaths of GERSHOM
                    NIMMO & JAMES NIMMO & FREDERICK BOUSH witnesses thereto.

16 Mar 1756 - The persons apptd: on the motion of THOS: REYNOLDS WALKER
7 MB 224 PAc & SARAH his wife to lay off & assign to them the said
                    SARAH's dower of her former husband MR: JOEL CORNICK decd
plantation this day returned their report.......bounds are given........
(see also p 220 - 18 Feb 1756 - THOS: REYˢ: WALKER intermarried with SARAH
CORNICK wid⁰ of JOEL CORNICK decd.)

23 Apr 1756 - On petition of THOMAS CORNISH its ordered that the Clerk
7 MB 226 PAc deliver to him his part of his fathers, THO: CORNISHES
                    Estate in the office & giving security for the same.
MARMADUKE & THOMAS ELLIS Securities.

18 May 1756 - THURMER HOGGARD serves on a Jury......SAMUEL SMITH VS
7 MB 231 PAc HUGH BLACKBURN

26 May 1756 - JOHN LOVETT by LEMUEL CORNICK his guardian VS ERASMUS
7 MB 234 PAc HAYNES & ALIFF his wife in Chancery.......division of
                    negroes. (It does not state whose negroes they were)

15 Jun 1756 - On motion of ELIZA: KEELING of Caroline County it's ordered
7 MB 235 PAc that COL: ANTHONY WALKE by her guardian during her minority.

16 Jun 1756   WILLIAM MOSELEY & MARGARET his wife & FRA: THOROWGOOD LAND
 7 MB 238 PAc VS   NATHANIEL NEWTON & ANNE his wife & WILLIAM AITCHISON
                Exors of COL: JACOB ELLEGOOD decd in chancery continued..

17 Aug 1756   WILLIAM COX VS JOHN GILES & ANNE his wife Exor: of JOHN
 7. MB 245 PAc MOORE decd, BENJA: COX, JONATHAN COX, CHARLES JAMES &
                MARY his wife, WILLIAM FLEAR? & ANNE his wife, ELIZA: COX
& AMY COX infants, by BENJA: COX their guardian in Chancery. (Nothing
more in this item)

17 Aug 1756   THURMER HOGGARD on a Jury: BENJAMINE BURROUGH & ELIZA:
 7 MB 245 PAc his wife VS   JOHN COX Senr:

21 Sep 1756   GERSHOM NIMMO, Gent: Justice at Court.
 7 MB 247 PAc

21 Sep 1756   THOMAS LANGLEY Senr: acknowledges Deed of Gift to his
 7 MB 247 PAc grandson JOHN CAPPS.

21 Sep 1756   JACOB HUNTER & SUSANNAH his wife in right of sd: SUSANNAH
 7 MB 249 PAc 1/2 part VS ANTHONY MOSELEY GENT: administrator of MARY
                MOORE decd who was the wido: & exix: of CAPT: HENRY MOORE
decd & CHARLES MOORE 1/2 part an infant by said ANTHONY MOSELEY his
guardian in Chancery......division of negroes........................

19 Oct 1756   THOROWGOOD KEELING was commited to Custody at the suit of
 7 MB 253 PAc SIMON & JOHN WHITEHURST to satisfie a Jdgmt obtained by
                them for Ŀ 280.13.½ pence.....had been in Goal 20 days &
sent back to Goal til next Court.

16 Nov 1756   THURMER HOGGARD on the Grandjury.......GERSHOM NIMMO, GENT
 7 MB 258/259 JUSTICE at Court.

15 Feb 1757   On Petition of WALTER SCOTT its ordered that he have a
 7 MB 269 PAc road 16 feet wide from his plantation to the Main Road.
                BENJ: DINGLEY GRAY whose land the said road will (go)
through being present & argued that said road should go on the line between him, JONAS CAWSON & JNO: SCOTT decd to the Main Road.....said road
to be established...

19 Apr 1757   MARY ANNE RICHMOND by ADAM KEELING SENR: her guardian VS
 7 MB 274 PAc MATHEW PALLET & SARAH his wife in Chancery.....21 Feb 1757
                division of the land & negroes of ROBERT RICHMOND decd
between MATTHEW PALLET & SARAH his wife & MARY ANNE RICHMOND daughter of
said ROBT: RICHMOND decd.....the said SARAH's dower of the land.........
Bounds given and the division of the house is most interesting.

19 Apr 1757   The report of dower assigned to EDWD: CANNON & ELIZ: his
 7 MB 275 PAc wife in right of sd ELIZA: of the Manner Plantation of
                THOS: LAMOUNT decd made by the survey of 12 freeholders
assigned CANNON & his wife her dower (bounds are given).......on motion
of HENRY LAMOUNT guardian to EDWARD LAMOUNT heir at law of sd THO: LAM-
ount decd.....they object & division to be made over again.

20 Apr 1757   Judgement granted WILLIAM NIMMO for 25/ due by acct: from
7 MB 277 PAc THOS: REYS: WALKER & SARAH his wife Exr: of JOEL CORNICK.

22 Jun 1757   JOSIAH BUTT & MARY his wife VS ELIZABETH THELABALL late
7 MB 286 PAc wido: of MAXL: BOUSH decd. MAXL: & FREDERICK BOUSH & GER-
              SHOM NIMMO & ELIZABETH his wife on the defts: prayer time
is given them to consider the compltts: bill.

19 Jul 1757   WM: ACKISS & SARAH his wife, in right of sd. SARAH, & WM:
7 MB 289 PAc HARPER, JAMES HARPER son & heir at law of JOHN HARPER decd
              by the sd MARGARET HARPER administrator of sd JNO: his
mother & guardian, BANNISTER HARPER do recover each of the value of the
eight slaves.

16 Aug 1757   ROBERT HUGGINS accts agst OLIVE, NATH:, ARGENT & MARKHAM
7 MB 291 PAc HUGGINS being examined & sworn to be registered in a book
              for that purpose.

16 Aug 1757   SARAH OWENS to be allowed 30/ out of the estate of THOMAS
7 MB 291 PAc OWENS decd for keeping his daughter PEMBROOK to this time
              & ᄂ 8 for keeping his four children: SARAH, JNO:, ANTHONY,
& MARGARET OWENS to this time.

16 Aug 1757
7 MB 293 PAc WILLIAM & GERSHOM NIMMO exors of CAPT: JAMES NIMMO decd.

16 Aug 1757   WILLIAM ACKISS & SARAH his wife, WILLIAM, JAMES & BANNIS-
7 MB 294 PAc TER HARPER VS MARGARET HARPER adm: of JOHN HARPER decd.
              & JAMES HARPER heir at law of sd JOHN by the sd MARGARET
his guardian in Chancery - dated 19 Jul 1757.

18 Oct 1757   THURMER HOGGARD on a Jury with ADAM THOROWGOOD, JONAS
7 MB 299 PAc CAWSON, MAX: BOUSH: Case of WM: FENTRIS VS JOHN WICKENS.
7 MB 300 PAc THURMER HOGGARD on a Jury: FRANCIS CLARKE VS SIMON WHITE-
              HURST.

15 Nov 1757
7 MB 301/2   The Grand jury of this County consisting of 18 free hold-
              holders: GEORGE JAMISON, GEORGE WISHART, JACOB HUNTER,
SAMUEL TENANT, ANDREW STEWART, JOHN SHIPP, LEMUEL GASKING, WILLIAM WARD,
HENRY GASKING, JOHN GORNTO, HARRISON BANKS, JAMES HENLY, HENRY WOODHOUSE,
ARTHUR MORRIS, JOHN WILLIS, RICHARD McLALON?, THURMER HOGGARD & JOHN
MONTGOMERY.

 7 Dec 1758   A Court for laying the leavy...to MR. WILLIAM NIMMO as
7 MB 303 PAc Kings Attorney   800 1 tᴏᵇ

21 Feb 1758   JOHN HALL bound to JOEL SIMMONS until he be 21 years old
7 MB 310 PAc & to teach him to read & write & the trade of a botewright

21 Feb 1758   BAGWELL MOORE & MARY his wife VS MARY WOODHOUSE Exix of
7 MB 311 PAc the last will and testament of HENRY WOODHOUSE & WILLIAM

contd: WOODHOUSE eldest son & heir at law of sd HENRY decd &
            & HENRY WOODHOUSE .... Division of negroes: a parcel of
negroes divided between MR: BAGWELL MOORE & MARY his wife Compltts:
& HENRY WOODHOUSE & assigned to each of them....names or the negroes
are given.

21 Feb 1758   EDWARD HACK MOSELEY Commissioned LIEUT: COLL: of this
7 MB 311 PAc County.

21 Feb 1758   THOS: HAYNES, THURMER HOGGARD & GEORGE WISHART audit &
7 MB 312 PAc settle the estate of THO: OWENS decd & report same to
              the next Court.

18 Apr 1758   ANDREW CONSAULVO, CHARLES CONSAULVO, ANTHONY LEGGETT &
7 MB 314 PAc FRANCES his wife, JNO: WALLIS & MARY his wife & PRISCILLA
              CONSAULVO an infant by MAXL: BOUSH her guardian   VS
HENRY CONSAULVO eldest son & heir at law of WM: CONSAULVO decd & AMY
CONSAULVO wido: of the sd WM: CONSAULVO in Chancery. Division of
the negroes to HENRY &............a detailed division is given in
this record.

15 Aug 1758   SARAH & FRANCES BANNISTER orphans of JA: BANNISTER.
7 MB 325 PAc

15 Aug 1758   KATHERINE, FRANCES & EDWD: LAMOUNT orphans of THOMAS
7 MB 325 PAc LAMOUNT decd.

15 Aug 1758   SARAH KEELING having proved her acct for ₤ 7,9 against
7 MB 325 PAc the estate of JOHN KEELING decd for keeping his children
              MARY & AMY KEELING to this time.

15 Aug 1758   THOMAS REYS: WALKER having proved his accounts against
7 MB 326 PAc WILLIAM, JOEL & HENRY CORNICK orphans ordered to be
              registered in a Book for that purpose.

15 Aug 1758   JAMES GRIFFIN & TAMER his wife VS JAMES HOLMES.
7 MB 326 PAc

15 Aug 1758   Petition of JAMES GRIFFIN to lay off & assign to MARGT:
7 MB 327 PAc CONE her dower of the lands whereon HENRY GRIFFIN decd.
              lived having this day returned their report.....MARGT:
CONE who was the relict & widow of HENRY GRIFFIN....her dower on the
said lands....running to MR: THOS: HUNTERS line.....along the Main
Road.....she to enjoy together with JAMES GRIFFIN the space of ground
which lies before the dwelling house..................................

19 Sep 1758   HILARY CASON VS WILLIAM JAMES in Trespass whereupon
7 MB 330 PAc JONAS CAWSON, THURMER HOGGARD, JOEL SIMMONS, GEORGE
              JAMISON, JOHN CHAPMAN, JAMES OAST, JAMES GRIFFIN, THOMAS
REYDS: WALKER, FREDERICK BOUSH, THOMAS WHITEHURST, ENOCH WHITEHURST &
HENRY HARRISON were impannelled & sworn....their verdict...the Jury
finds for the Pltf. 41/.   Also: THURMER HOGGARD on a jury: ABIGAIL
LEWELING agst DANIEL McCLOUD.

19 Sep 1758   Division of MATTHEW PALLET decd. lands & houses....laid
7 MN 331 PAc   off the dower of the lands to SARAH PALLET the relict...
               The house was only partially given to her...... and by
consent of the heir at law JOHN PALLET...the plantation lying between
Lynnhaven Bay & the Sea........(Bounds are given to the land)

17 Oct 1758   On the motion of MISS (JENNET?) NIMMO its ordered that
7 MB 333 PAc   MR: WILLIAM NIMMO be her guardian during her minority.

21 Nov 1758   On the motion of WALTER LYON who has lived several years
7 MB 337 PAc   in this Country & intends to practice in this Court as an
               Attorney the Court being satisfied that he is a person of
purety?, honesty and good demeanor...certifies the same..............

19 Dec 1758   THOMAS NASH Exor of the last will of WILLIAM NASH decd &
7 MB 340 PAc   ELIZABETH NASH only surviving child & heir of the sd.
               WM: NASH an infant by WILLIAM IVY her guardian VS JOHN
CHAPMAN in Chancery.

17 Apt 1759   On Petition of JOSHUA McCOY & PEMBROKE his wife its order-
7 MB 347 PAc   ed that CHARLES WILLIAMSON administrator of JAMES WILLIAM-
               SON decd pay them their part of the decedents estate ac-
cording to audit thereof in his hands.

17 Apr 1759
7 MB 348 PAc   Ordinaries in Princess Anne County - the rules and prices
               are set forth by the Court.............................

15 May 1759   JOHN WHIDDON adm: of ELIZA: WHIDDON his late wife decd
7 MB 350 PAc   VS ANNE NICHOLAS an infant by NATH: McCLENAHAN her guar-
               dian in Chancery. To ANNE NICHOLAS....to JOHN WHIDDON in
right of his wife ELIZABETH WHIDDON....Division of Slaves of CAPT: JOHN
NICHOLAS decd.

19 Jun 1759   Ordered that JAMES GRIFFEN & TAMER his wife pay THURMER
7 MB 353 PAc   HOGGARD & JOHN HOLMES 25 1 tob each for one days attendance
               in their suit VS HOLMES Exor of AMY HOLMES decd.

18 Sep 1759   JOHN INCE JUN• & EMANUEL WHITEHURST VS JOHN ABSALOM an
7 MB 362 PAc   infant heir at law of EDMOND ABSALOM decd by GEO: COX his
               guardian....to the pltf: JOHN INCE JUNR:......to EMANUEL
WHITEHURST the other pltf:......to GEORGE COX & SUSANNAH his wife their
dower of the said land. (This reads as if JOHN INCE & EMANUEL WHITE-
HURST were probably creditors of EDMOND ABSALOM?)

19 Sep 1759   WILLIAM KEELING & FRANCES his wife Complts: VS JOHN
7 MB 363 PAc   PALLET heir at law & administrator of MATHEW PALLET decd.
               deft. in Chancery. Deft: to have lands &c....& to pay
Complts: ₤80 & costs.

19 Sep 1759   JOSIAH BUTT & MARY his wife VS ELIZA: THELABALL, GERSHOM
7 MB 363 PAc   NIMMO & ELIZA: his wife, FREDERICK BOUSH & MAXL: BOUSH in
               Chancery continued.

20 Nov 1759   MRS: SARAH BUSKEY, wido: of JOHN BUSKEY decd her dower of
7 MB 369 PAc   negroes VS   JOHN GORNTO Exor: of the last will of JOHN
               BUSKEY decd, NATHL: COLLEY & ANNE his wife, CHARLES
WHITEHURST & AMY his wife, JOHN BUSKEY an infant son of JOHN BUSKEY
JUNR: decd & ARTHUR BUSKEY an infant by WM: KEELING their guardian in
Chancery. Negroes to SARAH & she to pay 13/4 yearly to JOHN & ARTHUR
BUSKEY.

 2 Dec 1759   A Court for laying the leavy - 1890 Tythabiles.
7 MB 370 PAc

19 Feb 1760   Last will of JONAS CAWSON decd presented in Court by JNO:
7 MB 374 PAc   WHIDDON appted: by the Court Exorter in the said will
               refusing to take on him the burthen thereof....pvd by
MAJOR (BLANK) JOYNES & JONATH: FRIZELL witnesses thereto....adminis-
tration granted to WHIDDON. JOHN WHIDDON to be guardian to JONAS
CAWSON during his minority taking Bond & Security ₤ 100.

19 Feb 1760   ABSOLUM LANGLEY & ELIZA: his wife....lease & release for
7 MB 375 PAc   100 acres for 100 acres more or less to THURMER HOGGARD
               the said ABSALOMS signing and sealing the same and being
further proved by the oath of GERSHOM NIMMO witness thereto. (Same
is on p 373 but pvd: by JNO: WILLIAMS & JAMES GRIFFIN & lodged for
further proof which this probably is)

19 Feb 1760   FREDERICK BOUSH granted Liberty to keep an Ordinary for
7 MB 375 PAc   one year.

20 May 1760   BAGWELL MOORE & MARY his wife Complts: VS   WILLIAM WOOD-
7 MB 381 PAc   HOUSE, HENRY WOODHOUSE an infant under 21 years by said
               said WILLIAM his guardian in Chancery....Slaves....to MR:
HENRY WOODHOUSE his brother HORATIO WOODHOUSE's part...MR: BAGWELL
MOORE who intermarried with MARY WOODHOUSE...Division of negroes order
dated 18 May 1760.

17 Jun 1760   EDWARD ATWOOD acknowledged deed of gift for sundry negroes
7 MB 384 PAc   to his daughters: PEMBROKE JAMES, ANNE JAMES & FRANCES
               BONNY.

15 Jul 1760   GERSHOM NIMMO Gentleman Justice at Court.
7 MB 387 PAc

5 Jul 1760   JOSIAH BUTT & MARY his wife Complts: VS ELIZABETH THEL-
7 MB 389 PAc   ABALL, GERSHOM NIMMO & ELIZA: his wife, MAXL: BOUSH &
               FREDERICK BOUSH defts: in Chancery......A division of
slaves - one third part to ELIZABETH & two thirds parts to the Complts:
and Defts:

13 Oct 1760   Court held for laying the Leavy: To MR. WALTER LYON,
7 MB 400 PAc   Kings Attorney ------- 800 l tob.   1919 Tythables.

114

18 Nov 1760   ELIZABETH CORNICK VS JOHN & NATHAN CORNICK infants by
7 MB 403,404 JOHN ACKISS their guardian in Chancery. Division of neg-
      PAc   roes: Court order dated 16 Sep 1760 - to ELIZABETH
             CORNICK - to JOHN CORNICK - to NATHAN CORNICK.

16 Dec 1760   WILLIAM NIMMO made oath that JAMES NIMMO decd departed
7 MB 408 PAc this life without making a will...granted administration
             of his estate...

16 Dec 1760   Ordered that THOMAS DUNN be bound to JAMES DUNN for five
7 MB 408 PAc years from March next to teach the orphan to read & write
             and the trade of a house carpenter. (see p 410)

20 Jan 1761   THOMAS DUNN ordered to be bound to THURMER HOGGARD for
7 MB 410 PAc five years three months & to teach the sd orphan to read
             and write & arithmetick & the trade of a Ship Carpenter
& take Indentures to that purpose. (same page) - ALEXR: POOLE & MARY
his wife acknowledge lease & release of 62 acres to THURMER HOGGARD.

20 Jan 1761   JAMES NIMMO, JACOB NIMMO, PHILIP DISON & JANET his wife &
7 MB 411 PAc JOHNSON NIMMO an infant by GERSHOM NIMMO his guardian
             VS WILLM: NIMMO & GERSHOM NIMMO exors of CAPT: JAMES
NIMMO decd. ADAM THOROWGOOD, JACOB HUNTER, ANTHONY LAWSON & GEORGE
WISHART or any three of them to make division of the negroes in the
Compltts: bill which did belong to CAPT: JAMES NIMMO decd & who were
given by his will to be divided among his children after his wifes
death including those devised to his sons WILLIAM, GERSHOM & JAMES who
were required by sd will to allow the negroes given them therein at the
division to make the other children equal with them & which division is
as follows: TO WILLIAM NIMMO....... TO GERSHOM NIMMO.......TO JACOB
NIMMO.......TO PHILIP DISON in right of his wife.........TO JAMES NIMMO
.......TO JOHNSON NIMMO.........TO WILLIAM NIMMO as heir at law
TO JACOB NIMMO......(This is a long involved division)

17 Feb 1761   LEWIS THELABALL & MARY ANNE his wife.....lease & release
7 MB 412 PAc for 200 acred of land to THURMER HOGGARD.

17 Feb 1761   MRS: ELIZABETH LAND petitioning for her dower of the
7 MB 413 PAc land & negroes belonging to her decd husband FRA: THOROW-
             GOOD LAND also to divide the 2/3s among the heirs at law
By order of the Court 18 Nov 1760 - To ELIZA: the South side of the
Plantation and adjacent BATSON WHITEHURSTS land......FRA: LAND her son
£ 10 a year

17 Mar 1761   WILLIAM HUNTER & ELIZA: his wife VS WILLIAM & ELIZA:
7 MB 421 PAc THOROWGOODS infants under the age of 21 years by WM:
             KEELING SEN: GENT: their guardian in Chancery. Court
awards negro Lidd increase of negro wench Sarah to deft: WILLIAM the
devisee & Nedd increase of negro wench Rose to ELIZA: & the Complts.
There is no estate of the Testators to divide. The defts: recover &
be possessed of the slaves aforesaid at the age of 18 years being the
time mentioned in the testators will.

21 April 1761 JAMES CARRAWAY VS THOMAS CARRAWAY an Infant, orphan of
7 MB 424 PAc WM: CARRAWAY by MARTHA CARRAWAY his guardian deft: The
lands of MR: JAMES CARRAWAY decd, equally divided between
JAMES & THOMAS CARRAWAY.....(bounds are given)...... near MR: FRANCIS
MOORES........THOS: to have Eastermost half & JAMES the Westermost half.

19 May 1761 JEREMIAH LAND & ELIZA: his wife infants under age of 21
7 MB 426 PAc years by JOHN BIDDLE their next friend VS PEGGE, FRANCIS
& THOMAS LANGLEYS Infants under age of 21 years by BRIDGT:
LANGLEY their guardian in Chancery.   Slaves are divided and the slaves
names are given.

16 Jun 1761 THOMAS WISHART, THURMER HOGGARD, JACOB HUNTER & GEORGE
7 MB 430 PAc WISHART or any three of them to appraise the Estate of
THOMAS HAYNES.

24 Jul 1761 Court Recommends to the GOVERNOR - DAVID McCLENAHAN, GER-
7 MB 433 PAc SHOM NIMMO & JONATHAN SAUNDERS GENT: as fit persons to
serve as Sherifs for this County.

24 Jul 1761
7 MB 435 PAc Ordered that JOHN HANCOCK be Surveyor of the roads on
the North side of the Eastern Branch Precinct.

18 Aug 1761 THURMER HOGGARD VS SAMUEL BOUSH. ANDREW STEWART Enters
7 MB 440 PAc himself special Bail..................................

20 Oct 1761
7 MB 447 PAc Will of JOEL SIMMONS proved by JAMES MOORE & THURMER
HOGGARD.

20 Oct 1761 JAMES CARROWAY & als VS WM: CARROWAY & als in Chancery.
7 MB 450 PAc Division of negroes: Old Kate to MR. CHARLES NICHOLSON
to receive from THOMAS CARROWAY ₤3.2.6 & to receive from
MRS. MARY CARROWAY ₤3.15. Rachel to THOMAS CARROWAY, to MR. JAMES
CARROWAY. (There is no mention of whose slaves they were)

17 Nov 1761 BENJ: DINGLEY GRAY - Inspector of Tobacco.
7 MB 453 PAc

18 Nov 1761 Claims against the County: to WALTER LYON GENT., Kings
7 MB 454 PAc Attorney 800 l tob. To ARTHUR SAYER late Clerk 924 l tob

15 Dec 1761 JEREMIAH LAND is appointed guardian to FRANCES LANGLEY.
7 MB 459 PAc

16 Feb 1762 THOMAS LOVETT's Deeds of Gift to his sons: to JAMES 100
7 MB 462 PAc acres; to THOMAS 203 3/4 acres; to JOHN LOVETT 203 3/4 acres

16 Feb 1762 HILLARY MOSELEY, Shoemaker
7 MB 468 PAc

16 Mar 1762   ELIZABETH MOSELEY wido: of HULETT MOSELEY decd, he dieing
7 MB 475 PAc   without making a will administration is granted to her.

18 May 1762   MARY ANNE WALKE Complt: VS   JAMES KEMPE & others - in
7 MB 489 PAc   Chancery. Persons apptd: to set apart the Compts: Dower
               in the slaves whereof her late husband MAJ: THOMAS WALKE
died possessed....a decree 16 Mar 1762 to MARY ANNE WALKE negroes Dick,
Sarah, Kate, Sally & Tom being negroes her former husband CAPT: JOHN
THOROWGOOD devised to her & which are not parties lately devised away
by the will of said MAJ: THOMAS WALKE decd. There follows the names of
the negroes given to: MOLLY WALKE, FANNY WALKE, PEGGY WALKE, NANCY
WALKE, THOMAS WALKE, JOHN & ANTHONY WALKE.

19 May 1762   GERSHOM NIMMO GENTLEMAN JUSTICE at a Court.
7 MB 491 PAc

19 May 1762   PETER SINGLETON having intermarried with MARGARET SAYER
7 MB 493 PAc   an infant.....................

20 Jul 1762   ELIZA: SAYER wido: & relict of ARTHUR SAYER GENT: decd.,
7 MB 503,504   JOHN HANCOCK & FRANCES his wife, MARGARET, MARY & ELIZABETH
     PAc   SAYER Infants under the age of 21 years by the said ELIZA:
               SAYER their next friend Pltfs: agst: CHARLES SAYER an
infant under 21 years deft: in Chancery. The commission appted: to
divide the negroes in the Bill........in obedience to an order 19 May
1762:.....to MRS: ELIZABETH SAYER her dower 4 slaves; to CHARLES SAYER;
to JOHN HANCOCK; to PETER SINGLETON his wifes part; to MARY SAYER; to
ELIZABETH SAYER the younger; CHARLES SAYER infant and heir at law.

 21 Jul 1762
7 MB 509 PAc   THURMER HOGGARD Pltf: VS SAMUEL BOUSH Deft; in debt to
               which action the Deft: pleads Paiment.

21 Sep 1762   Ordered that a Commission directed to the Justices of
7 MB 518 PAc   Pasquotank Co. issued to take the deposition of MICHAEL
               WILDAIR a witness for SAMUEL BOUSH ags THURMER HOGGARD
giving notice to the deft:

20 Oct 1762   ANNE ROBINSON Complt: VS TULLY ROBINSONExecutor of the
7 MB 525 PAc   last will and testament of WILLIAM ROBINSON Deft: in
               Chancery. The Commissioners appointed to set apart the
Widow's dower having returned their report........have divided the
Estate of MR: WILLIAM ROBINSON decd and have allotted to each Party
as follows: to MRS. ANNE ROBINSON widow & to ANNE ROBINSON JUNIOR.
Some silver spoons are listed to each and other things which are listed
in detail.

20 Oct 1762   THURMER HOGGARD on a Jury
7 MB 527 PAc

20 Oct 1762   THURMER HOGGARD Plaintiff VS SAMUEL BOUSH defendant
7 MB 528 PAc   continued at the Defendants costs.

5 Nov 1762   Pursuant to a Commission of Oyer and Terminer and Dedimus
7 MB 528 PAc the above named gentlemen took oaths / ANTHONY WALKE,
              ANTHONY MOSELEY, JAMES KEMPE, JONATHAN SAUNDERS, JOHN
WHITEHURST Gent: Justices / - Charles a negro man slave belonging to
JOHN CANN committed to the Goal of this County by Mittimus under the
hand and seal of ANTHONY WALKE Gentleman on Suspicion of his stealing
four Rams or Sheep......... to which the said Charles pleaded not guilty
of the crime.....the witnesses were examined and the Prisioner fully
heard in his defense........said Charles to be burnt in the hand in Open
Court and Receive thirty nine lashes on his bare back well laid on and
that he stand in the Pillory with his Ears Nailed thereto and til thence
Cutt Loose.   signed: ANTHONY WALKE

118

The page numbers in this index refer to the original Deed and Minute Books of Princess Anne County Original Court Records, and not to the page numbers of this book. The Deed Books and Minute Books are indicated by DB and MB. They will be found under the date of each abstract in the left hand margin.

Many names are spelled in various ways. Where there is any certainty that the names are the same, double or numerous headings are given. This should assist in keeping your research in chronological order.

Princess Anne County and Norfolk County have not been indexed, except in a few instances, due to the too numerous references to each. Unless otherwise noted all reference in these abstracts is to Princess Anne County inhabitants and their land holdings.

BOND: Francis 6DB293; Martha 6DB45; Robert 6DB161.

BONNEY/BONNY: Betty 6DB501; Dinah 7DB553; Edward 7DB314,408; Frances 7MB384 dau of Edw: At- wood; Frankey 7DB553; Jean 6DB501;Jno: Senr: 6DB539,6MB174; John6DB280,501,539,691,693, 6MB136, 7DB132; John Junr: 7DB536, Senr: 7DB450,453,485; Margeret (Bonney)Whitehurst 7DB408; Richard7DB408; Sarah 6DB693; Thos: 6DB501; William will of 6DB501, 7DB408.

BOOTH: George 7DB452; John 6DB543

BOUSH: Eliza: 6DB378, 6MB11, 7DB677; Elizabeth (Boush) Nimmo 7MB 83; Frances 7DB661; Frederick 6MB11,246, 7MB83,223, 286,330,375,389; Leml: 6MB246, Lemuel 6MB11,111, 7DB260; Margaret 7DB661; Mary 7DB74,96; Coll: Max: decd 6MB11, 7MB83,299, Maximillian 6DB1,260, 6MB107,137, 145, 7DB236,531, Col:, the Elder 7DB260,685; Junr:, decd. 7DB685, Coll: Maxl: 6DB73, decd. 6MB259, 7MB286,314,363,389; Maxm: 6DB534, 6MB246; Me. Mordica 6MB145; Saml:, Gent: 6MB98; Mr. Saml: 6MB59, 7DB260; Samuel 6DB134,718, 6MB59,64,259; Cornal Samuel (see Bush)7DB330; Samuel 7DB673, 677,685, 7MB440,509,518,528.

BRAU: Andrew 7DB467.

BRAY (see also BARY): Edward 6DB170,704; Edwd: 6DB521; Mrs: Jacomine 6MB158; John6DB539, 701, decd. 6MB164; Mary6DB539; Mrs. Molly 6DB521.

BRINSON: Adam 6DB211, of N.C. 6DB220; Eliza: 6DB488; John 6DB231,351,695, the Elder 6DB211, Junr: 6MB153; John B. 6DB351; Mary (Land) 6DB351; Matthew 6DB101, of N. C. 6DB220; Mattw: 6DB211; Richard 6DB211; Richd: 6DB435; Tho: 6DB46; Thomas 6DB156; Thos: 6DB351; Thorowgood 6DB374,387,488,572.

BROCK: Jno: 7DB391; John Junr., decd. 6DB152; Margrit 7DB590; Saml: decd 6DB90,486; Samuel 6DB676; Thos: 6DB90; William 6DB156,231,286,676, Wm: 6DB695.

BROOKE/BROOKS: Ezra, will of 6DB89; Job 6DB385; Mr: Pat 6DB89; Sarah, in London 6DB89.

BROUGH: Robt: 6DB213,216.

BROUGHTON: 6DB421,461; Dorcas 6DB221,222; Edward 6DB221,222; James 6DB222,421; Jas: 6DB461; Tho: 6MB25; Thos: 6DB222.

BROWN: Edw: decd. 7DB593; Elinor 6MB104; Ezekiall 6DB362; Frances 7DB593; Hezekiah 7DB675; Jane 6DB362; John 6DB362,519, 6MB104, 7MB245; Moses 7DB454; Ruth 7DB454.

BRYAN: Wm: 6DB181

BUCHANAN: Elinor, will of 7DB270.

BUCK: Shoe 6DB501

BUCKNER: John 6DB181,189,270,411; Sarah 6DB189.

BULLER: Thomas 7DB547.

BURFOOT: Abrose 6DB306; Ambrose 6DB50,124,156,306,572,649,695, will of 7DB670; Ambrus 6DB572, 575,582; Amy 7DB664; Elizabeth (Burfoot) Cannon 7DB670; John 6DB122,124,156,227,231,263,288, 325,348,438,486,649; Macky (Bur- foot) Smith 7DB670; Mary 6DB572, 575; Prudence 6DB486; Robert 7DB670,664, 7MB220; Sarah 7DB670, Sarah (Burfoot) Absalom 7DB670.

BURGESS: Anne 7DB214; Henry 7DB214,278,529.

BURLEY: Martha 7DB307; Robert 7DB307; Susannah 7DB307.

BURROUGHS: Anthony 7DB166, Junr. 6DB362; Benjamine 7MB245; Eliza: 7MB245; Isabell 7MB115; Martin will of 6DB362; appr: 6DB519; Patience nun. will 7DB176; Rob: 7DB702; Robert7DB231, 7MB115,117; Robt: 6DB223,7DB168,455.

BUSH: (see BOUSH): Cornal Samuel 7DB330.

BUSHBY: John Senr: 6DB325.

BUSKEY:Arthur 7MB369; Cason 6DB17,467, alias Keeling 6DB652; John Senr: 6DB438,652, John son of 6DB652, John gr-son of 6DB 652, son of Cason 6DB652, decd. 7MB369, Junr: 7MB369; Mary (Can- non) 6DB17, 6DB467; Sarah 6DB448,

Mrs. Sarah 7MB369; William s of John 6DB652.

BUTT: Ann (Poole, Haynes)6DB Henry decd. 6DB79; Joseah 6M Josiah 6MB246, 7MB286,363,38 Josias 6MB111; Mannuel 7DB14 Mary 6MB11,246, 7MB286,363,3 Thos: 6DB358.

CALVERT: Cornelius 7DB279,30 Elizabeth 7DB279; Elizabeth (Thorowgood) 7DB309.

CAMPBELL: Alex: 6DB9; Messr: Alexander 6DB68; Dr. Archiba 7MB94; Mr. Hugh 6DB718.

CANN: John 6DB138,647, 7DB34 7MB528.

CANNON: Amy 7DB59,356; Denni 7DB478; Edmd: 6MB205;Edward 6MB200,205, 7DB457,478,670; Edwd: 7MB275; Eliz: 7MB275; Eliza:6MB205, 7DB457; Elizabeth (Land) 6DB17, 6MB2 (Burfoot) 7DB670; John 6DB47 467, 7DB670;Mary 6DB17; Tho: 6DB122, 7DB346; Thomas 7DB35

CAPPS: Amy 7DB478; Charles 7DB478; Dennis of N. C. 6DB2 6DB329,368,369; Dina 7DB104, Edw: 7DB475; Eliza: 6DB301; Francis 6DB301; George 6DB30 309, 7DB240, will of 7DB510; Henry 6DB7,301; Hillary 7DB4 Horatio 6DB301; James 7DB478 301,379,387,488632, 6MB70, 7DB192, will of 7DB478, 7MB Margaret 7DB478; Pembroke 7D patent of 6DB263; Ralph 7DB6 Rich: 7DB510; Richard 6DB301 Richd: 6DB309,387; Sarah 6DB 7DB510; Solomon 7DB478; William, will of 6DB301, dec 6DB309the Elder 6DB486, 7DB5 Senr: 6DB263.

CAREY: Fra: 6DB223.

CARAWAY/CAROWAY/CARRAWAY &c: James 6DB99,7DB474, 7MB424,4 John 6DB625; Martha 7DB424,4 Mrs. Mary 7MB450; Thomas 7MB 450; Wm: 7MB424,450.

CARREL/CARRELL: Mary 7DB192; William 6DB691.

CARTER: John 7DB492.

CARTWRIGHT: Amy 7DB474; Anne 7DB474; Frances 7DB474; James 7DB168; John 6DB687; Leml:7DB168; Lemuel Lemuel 7DB168,309,590; Mary 6DB664, 7DB168,474,485,664, 210; Mary Gaston 6DB687; Mary (Hunter) 7DB449; Robert 6DB346, 7DB211,474,485; Robt:7MB204,210, 664; Sarah 7DB168,474; William 6DB338,346,664,687, 7DB455, will of 7DB474, gr-son of William 7DB474, 587, audit of 7DB664; Willm: 7DB485; Wm: 6DB99.

CARY: Francis 7DB128.

CASON: ____ 6DB652; Hilary7MB330; James 7DB627; Jas: 6DB708; Jno: 6DB708; Sarah 6DB708, 6MB185; Thomas 6MB185, 7DB229,573.

CATON: Hillary 7DB480.

CAVENDER: Barbara 7DB59; John 6MB153.

CAWSON: Christopher 7DB318; John 6MB293, 7DB319;Jonas 7DB318,319, (see Costen) 7DB335,696, 7MB29, 269,299,330, will pvd. 7MB374,

CEEATON (SEATON?): Hillary 7DB480; James 7DB480; John 7MB480; Sarah 7DB480; Solomon will of 7DB480; Thomas 7DB480.

CELIA: John 6DB527.

CHAPMAN: Henry 6DB501,717; James 6DB717; Jas: 6DB431,717; John 6DB670, 7DB436,547, 7MB29,330, 340; Nichlis 6DB501.

CHAPPEL: ____ father of George decd. 6MB177; George decd. 6MB 177.

CHESHIRE: Mrs. Eliz: 6MB192; Elizabeth 7DB145; Seana: (Moore) 6DB390; Susana (Moore?) 6DB390; Susannah 6MB192, 7DB145.

CHILLIS: Ann 7DB603.

CIVALLS: John 6DB275.

CLARK/CLARKE: Francis 7DB406, 7MB299.

CLAY: Thomas, decd. 6DB683.

COAN (seeCONE): Margaret 7MB185; Thomas, decd. 7MB42.

COATES: John 7DB475.

COCKE: Christop: 7DB346.

COCKROFT: Anne 7DB290; Eliza: 7DB290, Fra: 7DB290; John, decd. 7DB338; Mary 7DB290, Sarah 7DB 290; Tho: 7DB290.

CODD: Plantation of 6DB291.

COLLEY: Anne 7MB369; Nathl: 7MB369.

COLLINS: Ann, will of 6DB431,500, George 6DB431, 7DB367; Henry, decd. 6DB134,Audit of 6DB500, Jas: 6DB524; Lemuel 6MB157; Sarah 6DB431.

CONDON: Elizabeth(Condon) Stevenson 7DB594; Frances, spinster, 7DB594; Capt. James, Inv. 6DB637, 7DB594; Jas: 7DB279; JM;, heirs of 7DB447; Sarah 6DB635; Sarah (Condon) Gimmell & Gimmetland 7DB594.

CONE: Margaret 7MB185; Margt:, relict of Henry Griffen 7MB327; Tho: 7MB8; Thomas 7DB409,436, decd. 7MB42,89,94.(see COAN)

CONNER: John 6MB89; Mr. Lewis of Nco. 6DB403; Mrs. Monica 6MB192, 7DB145; Roderick 6DB86,205; Thomas 6DB306.

CONNYER: Jno: 6DB44; Martha 6DB89,501.

CONSAUL: Amy 7DB664; Anne 7DB278, William 6DB12, 7DB278,664.

CONSAULVO: Amy, wido. 7MB314; Andrew 7MB314; Charles 7MB314; Henry 7MB314; Priscilla 7MB314; Wm:, decd. 7MB314.

CONSOLVO: John 6DB49.

COOPER: Dinah 6DB539; Eliza: 7DB236; Joseph 7DB450.

CORBEL: Joseph 7DB432.

CORBETT: Abigail 7DB600; Frances wido. 6DB345; Jane 6DB721,7DB83; Mary 7DB600; Rich: 6DB57,58; Richard 6DB77,121,163,196,721, 7DB83, decd. 7DB600; Richd: 6DB345,Richd: son of Richd: 6DB345,446.

CORNICK: line of 6DB329; Betty 7DB477; Elizabeth 7DB477, 7MB403, Frances 6DB245; Francis 7DB453, 475; Henry 6DB122,124,306,709, 7DB590, 7MB213,215,326; Joel 6DB49,234,,459,578, 6MB107,139

6MB200, 7DB391,462, will of 7DB590,Joel son of Joel 7DB590, 7DB665, 7MB213,224,277,326; John 7DB346,477, 7MB403 Laml: 6DB247; Lem: 7DB457; Leml: 6DB73293,497, 6MB200, 7DB245; Lemuel 6DB245, 6MB59,205, 7DB435,476,590, 7MB222,234; Nathan 7DB477, 7MB403; Sarah ((Cornick)Walker 7MB224; William 6DB138, 6MB344, 7DB477, 7DB590, 7MB213,326.

CORNISH: Elias 7DB126, of N.C. 7DB580; Tho: decd 7MB226; Thos. 6DB121; Thomas 7DB126, 7MB226.

CORKER: Mr. 6DB633

CORPREW: John 6DB84; Thomas 6DB258.

COSTEN: (Cawson?): Jonas 7DB335.

COTTLE: William 6DB649,676.

COTTON: James 6DB79,531.

COX: Abia 6DB566,681, 7DB211; Amy 7MB245; Ann 6DB73,475,701, Mrs. 6MB185; Anne 6DB70, Anne Cox alias Giles 6MB275, Anne 7DB96; Benja: 7DB96, 7MB245; Eliza: 7MB245; Ellen 6DB566; George 7MB152,362,; Geo: 7MB362; Jno: 7DB96; John Senr: 7MB245; Jonathan 7MB245; Mary 7DB96; Susannah 7MB152, 164,362; William 6DB70,227, 247,431,475,534,539,701, 6MB178, 7DB279, 7MB29,245; Willm: 6DB73,120; Wm: 7DB16, 96,430.

CRAFORD/CRAWFORD: Capt. William 6DB1; Col. William 7DB364.

CRASHLEY/CRASHLY: Ann 6DB108, 425; Peter 6DB108,425.

CREED: John 6DB539; Martha, will of 6DB539, Inv. 6DB701; Rebecah 6DB539; Thos: 6DB79; William 6DB183.

CREEDLE: Land of 6DB562; Katherine 6DB183; William 6DB183, 7DB247.

CREEKMORE: Edmond 7DB480.

CROMPTON/CRUMPTON: William 6DB362; Willm: 7DB430; Wm: 7DB16.

CUCKLE: Stock 6DB501

CUMBERFOOT/CUMBERFORD: John 6MB204, 7DB104; Mary 7DB104.

CUMINGS/CUMMINGS: Benj: 6DB82, Benja:6DB301, 7DB167; Benjamin 6DB301,308, 7DB432,492; Caileb 7DB167; Eliz: 6DB82,308; Eliza: 6DB301, 7DB432; Elizabeth 7DB167; Joshua 7DB167; Marling, will of 7DB167; Martin 6DB301; Sarah 7DB492.

DALE: Adam 6MB201, 7DB245;Betty 6DB362, 7DB169,476; Elizabeth 7DB476; Mary 6DB178, alias McBride 7DB169; Mary Ann 6DB362, 7DB169; Paul 6DB136, will of 6DB178; Peter 6DB167,362,461, 7DB626; Rachel 6DB178,362, 7DB169,476; William 6DB136,178, 6DB362, 7DB169; Willm: 6DB362.

DAMNUM: August 7DB572.

DAUGE: Benj: 6DB21, Benjamin 6DB19; James 6DB19,21, 7DB589; John 6DB19; Richd: 6DB19,21; Willm: 6DB19.

DAULEY/DAWLEY: land of 6DB129; Dennis 7DB192,554,626; Henry 6DB47,379; John 6DB54; Larence 7DB626; Mary 6DB47; William 6DB131.

DAVIS/DAVISS: Edward 6DB625; John 7DB109; Richd: 6DB557; Robert 6MB226; Thos: E. 6DB718; William 6DB556, 7DB247.

DEARMAN: John 8B101; Robt; 6DB24.

DEARMOOD: Jean 7DB536; John 7DB536.

DENBY: Edw: 6DB86; Edward 6DB68, 152; Edwd 6DB504.

DICKSON: Robert 7DB431,457,485.

DISON see DYSON: Janey 7MB44; Philip 7MB411.

DOBBS see DABBS in other Records

DOBS: Thos: 6DB527.

DOD: Edmund 7DB544.

DOLLAR: Jas: 6DB590.

DOREY/DORY: John, will of 7DB401, 7DB406; Pegge 7DB406.

DOUGLYS (DOUGLAS?): Daniel6DB690.

DOYLEY, Lawrence 6DB392.

DROUGHT, Richrd:, will of 7DB153

DUDLEY: Amy 6DB557; Daniel 7DB455; Eliza² 6DB557; Henry 6DB557; Isabellah 6DB557; John 6DB42; 7DB279,324,442, will of 7DB455,485; Margaret 7DB455,474; Mary (Smyth) 7DB324; Rich: 7DB442; Richard 6DB26,238, Junr: 6DB669;,Senr: 6DB669, 7DB324, the Elder 7DB324, 7DB455; Richd: 6DB42, 669, 7DB279Robert 6DB332,659; Robt: will of 6DB557; Thos: 6DB557.

DUNCKLY: Jeffrey, nun. will 6DB598.

DUNN: James 7MB408; Thomas 7MB408,410.

DYER: Elizabeth 7DB140; Hezekiah 7DB140; James 7DB168; Jemima 7DB168; Jno: 7DB168; John 6DB110,111,118,428, will of 7DB168; Lydia 7DB168; Mary 7DB140; Sarah 6DB108, 7DB140, Sarah 6DB108, 7DB140,168; William 6DB111,691, 6MB136, will of 7DB140,168.

DYSON see DISON: Mary 7MB82; Mr. Philip, Inv. 6DB510; Mrs. Philip 6DB510.

EASTER: James 7DB106; Mary 7DB106; Saml: 6MB325.

EATON: Ann (Crashley) 6DB108, 425; Eliz: 7DB104; James 7DB104; Michael 6DB108,425; 7DB104.

EDGAR: Mary 6DB292; Mason? 6DB292; Paelom? (Fentriss) 6DB292; Willxxx 6DB292.

EDMONDS/EDMUNDS: land of 7DB325; Abel 6DB417, 7DB705; John Junr. 6DB22.

EDWARDS: Charles 6DB512,516, 7DB669,694; Chas: 6DB512; Eliz: 6DB77; Elizabeth 7DB669, Frances (Edwards) Land 7DB669; Henry 7DB669; Obediah 7DB669; Sarah 6DB516, 7DB669; Solomon 7DB669; William 7DB669; Willm: 6DB77

EDEY/EDY: Hannah 6MB42,154, 7DB61; Capt: Solomon 6MB42, 154, 7DB63.

EILAND: George 6DB449; Richd: 6DB449; Sarah 6DB449.

ELKS: Elizabeth 7DB544; John 6DB3; Thomas. will of 7DB544

ELLEGOOD: Ann 7DB447, 7MB140; Jacob 6DB195,223,587,598,647,691, 7DB169, will of 7DB447,457, Gent decd. 7DB594, 7MB140, Coll: Jaco 6DB363,365,390, 6MB185, 7DB305, 7MB140,238; John 7DB502; Maxxxxx 6DB223; Mrs. Margaret 6DB613, 6MB59, 7MB140; Margrit 7DB447; Margt: 6DB223; Mason 7DB502; Matthew 6DB49, will of 6DB223, inv. of 6DB261; Math: 6DB628; Peter Norly 6DB223; Rebecca 6DB223; Sarah 6DB223; William 7DB502.

ELLET: Marg: 6MB275; Peter 6MB27

ELLIS: Elizabeth 7DB544; Marmadu 7MB226; Mary 7DB670; Thomas 7DB544, 7MB226.

EMPEROR: Mr. Tully 6DB22, 7DB325

ETHERIDGE: see ETHERD: 7DB632; ___ 7DB214; Andrew 7DB4 7MB25; Ann 7DB433; Anthony 7DB433,521,632; David 7DB433; Elizabeth 7DB433; Eve, will of 7DB433; Frances 7DB480; James 7DB433; Mary 7DB433; Richard 7DB433.

EVERARD: Tho: 6MB238.

FARQUHASSON: Deborah Franks 6MB97; Frances 6MB97.

FAZACKERLY/FAZAKERLY: Mary 7DB600; Thomas 7DB600.

FENTRESS/FENTRIS/FENTRISS: Aaron6DB96, 7DB425; Absalom 6DB292; Mrs. Anne 6DB153; Antho 7DB330; Arjant 6MB124; Aron 6MB David 6MB203; 7DB627; Eliza: 6DB292, 6MB250, 7DB612; Elizabet 6DB292; Fanny 7DB492; George 6DB Horatio 6DB292; James 6DB96,157, 292, 7DB492,504,506,644; Jas: 7DB448,626; Jeremiah 7DB330; Jo 6DB19,21,157,601,619, 7DB479,492 612,626, 7MB222; John 6MB182,250 Kezia 7DB612; Leah 6DB292; Lem: 7DB425; Lem1: 7DB626; Liddy 7MB Martha 6DB524,531, 7DB330; Mary 7DB330; Michael 7DB572,626,669; Michal 7MB222; Michel will of 7DB612; Michl: 6DB512,605;

122

FENTRESS cont'd: Moses, Senr.
6DB96, Junr. 6DB155, 601,619,
7DB425,612, 7MB29; Pharo? 6DB292;
Saml: 6DB507; Samuel 6DB479,
7DB330; Sarah Anne 6DB292,6MB250;
Sophia 7DB492; Tamar 6DB292;
Thomas 7DB330; William 6DB299,
507,531will of Senr. 7DB330,492,
626,641; Willm: 6DB516; Wm:
6DB268,524, 7DB330, 7MB299.

FERGUSON/FORGESSON: Adam 6DB316.

FISHER: Easter 6DB539.

FITZ: Jno: 6DB68.

FITZGARRALL: 6DB286,676; Fras:
6DB676.

FLANAGAN: William 6DB179.

FLEAR: Anne 7MB245; John 6DB460;
William 7MB245; Wm: 6DB369.

FLINCH: John 7DB455,683; Michael
7DB492; Pemmy 7DB492.

FLOYD: Griffin of N. C. 6DB54.

FOUNTAINE: Eliza: 6MB198; Elizabeth 7DB590; Levinah 6MB198;
Roger 6DB593, 7DB346; Susinah?
6MB198.

_____: Frances mother of Mary
Land 6MB135.

FRANKLAND: 6DB691.

FRANKLIN: Danniel 7DB247; Mary
7DB247; Sarah 7DB247; Thomas,
will of 7DB247.

FREEMAN: Nich: 6DB167.

FRIZELL/FRIZLE/FRIZZELL/FRIZZLE:
Arthur 6DB524, 7DB698; Affiah
7DB698; Daniel 7DB698; Edward
7DB573; Edw: 6DB133; Francis
6MB77; Jonath: 7MB374; Margaret
6MB77.

FULCHER: Jno: 6DB51; John 6DB189;
Junr. 6DB293.

GAINER: Thomas 6DB183.

GAINES: James 6DB587.

GAINON: Mary (Gainon) Walstone
7DB529; Richard 7DB529.

GALLEY/GALLY: Blandinah 6DB135;
John, will of 6DB135.

GARDNER: Elizabeth 6DB12;
Margaret 7DB502; Mary Nash called
6MB26; Richard 6DB12,493; Thomas
6DB161,647, 7DB502; Thos: 6DB493.
    (seeGarner/Garnor)

GARNER/GARNOR (see Gardner):
Adam 7DB278; Eliza:6DB562,
7DB278; Elizabeth 6DB12; Margaret 6MB153; Mary 6DB562; Richard
6DB12, will of 7DB278; Richd:
6DB562; Thomas 6DB161,183,Thos:
6DB288,562.

GARTON (see Gaston): Mary 6DB641;
William 6DB641.

GASTON: Eliz: 6MB66; Mary (Cartwright) 6DB687; William 6DB687.

GASKIN/GASKING/GASKINS/GASKINGS:
Anne 7MB164; Charles 6DB638,
6MB83,167, 7DB535,685; Chas:
6DB638; Henry 6MB167, 7DB535,
7MB164,301; Jacob 7DB535; Job:
6DB11,357, 7DB447, will of 535,
Job: Junr: 7DB168; Job: Senr:
6DB638, 6MB59; Leml: 6MB259,
7DB535; Lemuel 6MB167, 7DB685,
7MB301.Martha 6DB638; Rebecca
7DB535; Sarah6MB167; Sarah
(Gaskin) Keeling 7DB535.

GIBBS: Thomas 7DB105.

GILES: Ann Cox alias 6MB275; Ann
7DB626; Anne 6MB240, 7MB245;
John 7DB16, 7MB245.

GIMMELL: Frances 7DB594; John
7DB594; Sarah (Condon) 7DB594.

GIMMETLAND: Mr. John 7DB594;
Sarah (Condon) 7DB594.

GISBORN/GISBOURN/GISBURN/
GIZBURN: (also see Lilburn)
Edward 6DB78, Inv. 236, Audit
399, nunwill 234; Edwd: 6DB585;
Eliz: 6DB399, Audit 654; Eliza:
6DB78; Elizabeth 6DB234,7DB214,
will of 7DB432; James 7DB214;
Jno: Audit 6DB78,82, 6MB77,
7DB214; John 6DB78,537,538,585,
586, 7DB504,591; Jon: 7DB214;
Mary 6DB585²; Sarah 7DB214;
Solomon 7DB214; Tho: 7DB 214;
Thorowgood 6DB234; William,
will of 6DB585, 6MB63.

GLASCO: Hope 7DB480.

GODFREY: James 7DB547, William
7DB307,690.

Gooch: William, Esqr: 6DB414,431

GORNTO: Amy 7DB589; Arthur
7DB589: Elizabeth 7DB589; Frances 7DB589; John 6DB453, Junr:
6MB139, will of 7DB589, 7MB301,
369; Lidia 7DB589; Margaret

6DB400; Margaret (Gornto)Hend-
ley 7DB589; William, Audit
6DB400.

GRAINGER: Dinah 7DB587; Tho;
7DB161,236,547,587,612.

GRANT: Mary 7DB106; Onner
7DB106; Thomas 7DB106.

GRAY/GREY: Benj: Dingley 7DB626,
696, 7MB269,453; Benjamin Dingley 7DB335,336,373,375; Susanah
7DB375,696.

GREEN: John 7DB105,712.

GREGORY: Frederick 7DB451.

GRIFFEN/GRIFFIN: Charles 7DB367;
Elizabeth 7DB454; Frances7DB454;
George 6DB118,175; Henry 6DB120,
261,288, 7MB327; James 6DB118,
nun will 261, 7MB326,327,330,
353,375; John, will of 6DB118,
316, 7DB454, will of 7DB454,
7MB153; Margaret 6DB288; Nany
7DB454; Saml: 6DB497; Sarah
6DB118, 7DB454; Tamer 7MB326,
353.

GROUNDSELL: Mary 6MB26.

GUY: line of 6DB698; William
6MB 135, 7DB422; Wm: 7DB15.

GWIN: Jos: 6DB604; Martha
6DB604; Willis 6DB604.

HALL: John 7MB310.

HANCOCK: line of 6DB382, land
7DB373; Anne (Robinson) 6DB9;
Frances 7MB503; George, Capt.
6DB354; Jno: 7DB709; John 6DB9,
628, 7MB435,503; Joshua, Inv.
6DB135; Susannah, orphan 6MB191,
7MB51; Mr. William 6DB598,
6MB190, 7DB373, Wm: 7DB431,
7MB29,51.

HANLY: Jeremiah, decd. 6MB139.

HANY: John 7DB132.

HAPPER: Doctr: William 6MB164.

HARBERT see Herbert: Peter
6DB537,538, 6MB79,342;
Thomas 7DB641.

HARFORD: Aliff: 6DB152; Aliph:
6DB504; John 6DB152,504.

HARGROVES: Leml: 6DB512,587.

HARMON: Joseph 6MB 202.

HARPER: Bannister 7MB289,294; Charles 6DB42; Elizabeth 7DB474; James 7MB62,289,294; Jas: 6MB246; Jno: 7DB270; John 6DB26,42,92,94, 6MB246,466[2], 7DB167,448, Junr. 7MB62,210,289, 294; Margaret (Hunter) 7DB449, Margaret 7MB210,289,Adm. 294; Mary, Senr: 7DB703, Mary (Harper) Williamson 7MB62; Robert 7MB62; Robt: 6MB246; William 6DB711, 7DB338, 7 7MB294, Willm: Senr: 7DB703; Wm: 7MB289.

HARRIS (see AIRES, AIRS): Henry 6DB191; John 6DB385,425, 7DB506 (see Knowis); Ruth 6DB425.

HARRISON: Frances 6DB70; Henry 6DB70, 7MB330; James 6DB50,575, 706; John 6DB706; Rachel 6DB706; Thos:, Inv. 6DB337.

HARTGROVE: Leml: 7DB694.

HARTLY: Charles 7DB478.

HARVEY: Alex:, Audit 6DB132; John, Audit 6DB653, 6MB113; Sarah, nun will 6DB614, 6DB614; Thos: 7DB167.

HATTON: Roger 6DB219,340.

HAIES: Adam 7DB589.

HAYES: Adam 6DB638, Mr. Adam 7DB211; Edwd: 6DB374; John 7DB592; Sarah 7DB211,592.

HAYNES: Alif: wid. of Lovett 7MB222; Aliff: 7MB234; Anne 7DB321, Dinah 6DB51; Eliza: 7MB65; Erasmus 6DB51,658, 7DB435, 453, Jun: 7MB115,117,222,234; Frances 7DB453; Henry 7DB453; James, will of 7DB435,453; Jas: 6DB456; Joel 7DB453; John 7DB589; Joshua 7DB453; Thomas 6DB5, 7MB430; Capt. Thos: 6DB79; Thos: 7DB453, 7MB153,312; William 7DB453, Capt. 7MB65.

HEATH: Benony 6DB527, will of 6DB538, 6MB62; James 6DB449,538; Rich: 7DB591; Solomon 7DB591; Vilar 6DB538.

HENLEY/HENLY: Charles 6DB128, Inv. of 6DB683, will of 6DB708; Cornelius 6DB19, 7 DB314, will of 7DB479; Mr. Cornelius 7DB511; Dinna 7DB479; Elizabeth 7DB479, 511; Frances 6DB708; James 7DB479, 511, 7MB301; Jeremiah 6MB139;

John 6DB295,708, 7DB346, Sr. 7DB438; Kezia 7DB511; Margaret (Gornto) 7DB589; Mary 6DB708, 7DB479,511,589; Moses, Inv. of 6DB128; Sarah 6DB708, 6MB139, 7DB104; Tho:6DB227, Thomas 6DB211,234, Senr: 6DB374; Thos: 6DB90,306,435.

HERBERT (see Harbert): Betty 7DB467; Betty (Herbert) Tooly 7DB641; John 7DB467, 7DB641, 7MB23; Capt. Markham 6MB283, Gent. 7DB83; Peter 6MB79, 7DB467; Willoughby 6MB62,43, 7MB23,25.

HEWITT: George 7DB467,544; Mary 7DB467.

HILL: Affiah 6MB322; Amy 6DB251; Charles 6DB251; Eliza: 6MB322; Elizabeth 7DB593; Fra: 7DB688; John 6DB61,280; Morrice 6DB61; Morris 7DB536,593; Tho: Senr; 6DB280, Tho: 7DB688; Thomas 7DB516; Thos: Senr: 6DB88,249; Junr: 6DB88,249; Thos 6MB322.

HOXXXX: Mary, gr-dau of Henry Woodhouse 6DB251.

HOGGARD (see Hogwood): Susannah 6MB231; Thurmer 6DB461, 6MB199, 325, 7DB371,522,650, 7MB8,44, 153,159,194,197,231,245,258, 299,301,312,330,353,375,410[2], 412,430,440,447,509,518,527, 528.

HOGWOOD,: Thurmer 7DB371.

HOLEWELL: Halstead 7DB591.

HOLMAN: Martha 6DB288.

HOLLOWELL: Prudence 6MB198; Samuel 6MB198.

HOLMES: Amy 7MB353; Elizabeth 7DB409,436; Frances 7DB409; George of N. C. 6DB698;*James 7DB409,436, 7MB8,153,326; John 6DB175, 7DB409,436, 7MB353; Lemuel 6DB698; Martha 6DB288; Mary 7DB709; Robert 7DB211,391; Samuel, will of 7DB409; Sarah 7DB409; Tamer 7DB436; William 7DB474,664; * Henry, dau. of 6DB175, Henry 6DB631, 6MB191, 7DB409, will of 7DB436,522, 7MB44,154.

HOLT: John 6DB7.

HOLTH: John 7DB450.

HORSKINS (see Hoskins) 7DB221

HORSLEY: Willm: Audit of 6DB60

HOSKINS: (see Horskins): Dinah 7MB117; Mary 7DB537; Richard 7DB537; Susanna 7MB220.

HUDDLESTON/HUDDLESTONE: Dirna (Diana?) 7DB59; John 7DB59, 6MB26; Thomas, will of 7DB59; Thos: 7DB59.

HUGGINS/HUGINS: Aliff 7DB587; Argent 7DB587, 7MB291; John, Audit 6DB556; Markham 7DB587, 7MB154,291; Mary 7DB587; Nath: 7MB291; Natt: 7DB587; Olive 7DB587, 7MB154,291; Philip 7DB587; Robert 6DB638, will of 7DB587, 7MB154,291,587.

HUNDLEY: Thomas 6DB220.

HUNTER: Plat of Land of Hunter-Nimmo 6DB663; Eliza: 7DB449, 7MB421; Jacob 7DB167,4 449, 7MB204,210,249,301,411,43 Jacomine 6MB91, 7DB167,449, 7MB204; Mr. James 6DB590, 6MB3 7DB449,541, 7MB204,210; Jas: 6DB663, 6MB169; Jno: 7MB210; John 6DB134,284,663, 6MB91,98, Mr. 7DB167 will of 7DB449, 7MB204,210; Joya 7DB449; Joyce 7DB449, 7MB210; Pemmy 7DB449, 7MB204,210; Susannah 7MB249; Mr. Tho: 6MB240; 7DB449, 7MB21 Thomas 7DB677; Thos: 6DB132,61 Sherif 673, Mr. 7MB327; Willia 7MB421; Willm: 7DB522; Wm: 7DB677., 7MB44.

HUSTON: Majr: Nathl: 6MB185.

HUTCHINGS: John 6DB196,446; Capt. John 6DB140,173, 7DB83, 7MB197.

HUTCHINSON: Jane 6MB84.

HUTH: Jacobus 7DB591.

IDLE?: Edward, Seaman, will of 6DB175.

INCE: John 6MB136,144,159, 7DB650, Jun: 7MB29,362; Yates 6MB136,144,159.

IRDELL: James 6DB226.

ISDELL: James 6DB504.

IVEY/IVY: 6DB276; land of
6DB382; Mr. 7DB367; Aliff/Aliph
(Ivy) Miller 6DB471, 7DB63;
ndrew*7DB433; Ann*7DB433; Dina*
7DB433 (*name may be Sorey/);
Elizabeth (Langley) 6DB49;
Francis, will of 7DB433; Mr.
George 6DB49; Hannah 6DB471;
Hannah (Ivy) Edey 7DB63; Capt.
James of N. C. 7DB347; John
6DB276,471,674,714, Inv. 235,
317,598, 7DB63; Sedey 7DB433;
Tho: 6MB42, 7DB63; Thomas6DB193,
228,471; Thos:, Audit 6DB317;
Ursley/Ursulla (Ivy) Purdy
6DB471,674; Will: 6DB49;
William 7MB340; Capt. Wm:
7MB171.

JACKSON: Anne (Richason) 6MB344;
Eliza: (Dudley) 6DB557; James
6DB329,549; Jonathan 6DB449,
6MB344.

JACOB: corner tree of 6DB664;
Isaac 7DB508; Rebeca 7DB508;
Sarah 7DB508; Wm: 7DB401,626.

JAMES: Amy 6MB84; Anne 7MB384;
Bridget 6DB101,102; Charles
7MB245; Elizabeth 6DB179;
Gilburt 7DB592; Henry, will of
6DB101,102, Inv. 104; Jane
6MB84; John 6DB4,101, Audit 105,
6MB84; Mary 7MB245; Matthew
6DB101,102,179; Pembroke 7MB384;
Robt: 6DB101; Susannah 6MB84;
William 7MB330.

JAMESON/JAMIESON/JAMMESON &c:
6DB631; Alex: 7DB106; George
6DB432, 6MB192, 7MB301,330;
Henry 6DB98, 7DB3,106,433; John
6DB98,482,631; Mary 6DB98.

JOHNSON: Jacob, the Elder 6DB654;
Margaret 7DB167; Margaret
(Langley) 6DB49.

JOLLEY/JOLLY: Blandinah 7DB615;
Peter 6DB274,449.

JOLLIFF: Peter 6DB274,275;
William 6MB63.

JONES: Dinah 7DB409, Elenor, will
7DB214; James 6MB153,325, 7DB371;
Leml:? 6DB227; Mary 6DB28,709,
7DB59; Owen 6DB121446; Randall
6DB578; Robert6DB685,709; Robt:
6DB306,566,706; Sarah 6DB101;

JOYNES: Major 7MB374.

KEATON: Hillary 7DB467; James
6DB527.

KEELING: Adam 6DB70,73,191,456,
569,628,644, 7DB343,535, 7MB169,
274; Alex: 6MB206; Alexander
7DB430; Amy 7MB325; Ann 6DB435,
644; Barbara 6MB206; Cason
Buskey alias 6DB652; Edward
6DB679, 6MB136, will of 7DB16;
Eliza: 6DB362, of Caroline Co.
7MB235; Elizabeth(Keeling)
Stebbins 7DB343; Elizabeth
(Keeling) Thorowgood 7DB430,673;
Frances (Keeling) Smith 7DB430;
Frances 7MB363; Henry 7DB430;
Jno: 6DB195, 7DB169; John
6DB209,211,435,456,569,644,649,
6MB238, 7DB430,476,535, 7MB325;
Margaret 7DB430; Marian 7DB476;
Martha 7DB535, 7MB169; Mary
7DB279,430, 7MB325; Mary (Thoro-
good) 6DB621, 7DB279,309; Sarah
6MB177, 7MB325; Sarah (Gasking)
7DB535; Tho: Jr. 7DB476; Thomas
7DB702; Thos:, Orphan in R.I.
7DB664; Thorowgood, Inv. 6DB222,
7MB253; William 6DB362,,419,460,
7DB16,303, will of 430,447,490,
527, 7MB42,363; William, Gent:
6MB205; Junr: 6DB621,628, 7DB279,
309; Senr: 6DB628, 7DB303; Capt:
William 6DB70,272,378,559,632,
6MB200, 7DB531, 7MB163,164,196;
Willm: 6DB120; Wm: Junr: 6DB105,
6MB59; Wm: Senr: 6DB105, 7MB421;
Wm: 6DB247, 6MB246, Sheriff 295;
Gent. 7MB 140,169, 369; Capt:
Wm: 6DB534,559, 6MB185, Inv. of
7DB521, 7MB152,163.

KEETCH: Sarah 7DB591.

KELLEY: Great Island of Charles
7DB510.

KEMP/KEMPE: Frances 6DB354;
George 6DB625; James 6DB1, Sheriff 6DB7,37,148,153, xxubleman?
6DB236,239,662, 6MB11,148,
7DB279,489,528, Capt: James
6DB260,335,346,354,369,409,614,
6MB230, 7DB485; Job? 6DB239.

KEY: Eliz: 6DB105; Jas: 7DB231;
Jno: 7DB231; John, will of 7DB231;
Jonathan 7DB236; Joseph 7DB231;
Joshua 7DB236; Sarah 7DB231.

KEZON: Thomas 7DB573.

KING: Duncan 6MB186; William
6MB 182.

KITELEY/KITLEY: Charles 6DB674;
Robt: 7DB626.

KNOWAS/KNOWIS: John 6DB196,446,
of N. C. 7DB506,533; Mary 7DB533.

LAMNSON: George 7DB422.

LAMOUNT: Children of 6MB205;
land of 7DB457; Arthur 7DB516;
Cornelius 7DB516; Edward 6DB403,
7MB205, 7MB275; Edwd: 7MB325;
Elizabeth 6MB205, 7DB516;
Francis 6MB205; Frances 7MB325;
Henry 6DB265,282, 7MB275; James
6DB19,28,231, Audit of 261,566;
John 6DB171,497,582, 7DB391,457,
516; Katherine 6MB205, 7MB325;
Lidia 7DB516; Lydia 7DB516;
Susanna 6MB134; Thomas 6DB28,
6MB143,205, 7DB516, 7MB325;
Thos: 6MB134, 7MB275.

LAND: Capt. 6DB664; Ann 6DB133;
Cornelius 6DB133; Edward 6DB133,
7DB675, Junr: 6DB17; Edwd: Junr:
6DB351,467,; Edwd: the Elder
6DB467; Eliz: 7MB196; Eliza:
7MB426; Elizabeth 6DB17;
Elizabeth (Land) Cannon 6DB467;
Mrs. Elizabeth 7MB413; Frances
7DB675; Frances (Edwards) 7DB669;
Fra: 7MB413; Fra: Thorowgood
7MB238,413; Francis Thorowgood
7MB196; Francis, will of 6DB133,
6DB165,6MB224, 7DB305, Capt:
6DB153; Jeremiah 7MB426,459; John
6DB133; Mary 6DB133,6MB135,
7DB15; Mary (Land) Brinson
6DB351Renatus 6MB185, 6MB224;
Richard 6DB133; Robert 7DB675;
Robt: 6DB133, 7DB452; William
6MB135, 7DB15.

LANDY: Francis 6DB140.

LANE: Augustus 6DB234, 7DB214;
Jasper 7DB506.

LANGLEY: _____ Inv. of 6DB291;
Abraham 6DB49; Absolum 7MB375;
Ann 6DB296; Anna (Langley)
Roviere 7DB367; Bridget 6MB152,
177, 7DB74,229, 7MB426; Eliza:
7DB347, 7MB375; George 6DB49;
Jacob, will of 6DB49,Inv. 6DB56;
Jas: 6MB337; James 6DB40,49,
will of 7DB367,591, 7MB171,174;
Jeremiah 6DB49,66,654, 6MB267;
Fran: 6MB177; Frances 7DB367,
7MB171,426,459; Joseph 6DB49;
Capt. Lemuel 6DB295, 7DB346,603;

125

Langley continued: Mary 6MB177;
Nathan 6DB49; Pegge 7MB426;
Sarah 6MB337, 7DB367, 7MB171,
174; Tho: 6DB45, 6MB25,153,
7DB346; Thos: 6DB284,379,632;
Thomas 6MB70,138,152, 7DB74,
168,229,746, 7MB426; Thomas
Senr: 7MB247; Mr. William 7DB347;
Willm: 6DB49; Wm: 6MB267.

LATIMER: Edw: 7DB603.

LATTER: Dauley 6MB138.

LAWRENCE: William 6MB194,203.

LAWSON: Anthony 6DB598, 6MB283,
7DB431,580,625,661, 7MB411;
Charles 6MB283, 7DB580; Tho:
6MB283, Thomas 7DB422,483,580.

LEGET/LEGGETT/&c: Alexander
6DB51, 7DB462; Amy 6DB51;
Antho: 6DB51; Anthony 6DB229,
7MB314; Elizabeth 7DB432,
Frances 7MB314; Janie 7DB391;
John 6DB459; Providence 7DB432;
Prudence 7DB432.

LEGRAVE: Abraham, will of
6DB195, Inv. 253.
LENARD/LEONARD: Daniel 6DB193;
Dinah 6DB193; Jno: 6MB25.

LESTER/LISTER: land of 6DB199;
Abell 6DB464; Amy 7DB153;
Bannister 6DB26,42; Darcas
6DB464; Dorcas 6DB483; Edwd:
6DB464; Eliza: 6DB464; Isabel
6DB464; John 6DB442,464; Marg:
6DB26; Mary 6DB42,464,711,
7DB153,703; Richd: 6DB442;
Richard, 6DB111,will of 464,483
7DB507,enr: 6DB233; Tho: Nun
will 7DB703; Thomas 6DB711,
7DB537; Willm: 6DB464.

LEWELING: Abigail 7MB330.

LILBURN: Abraham 6DB288; Alex-
ander 6DB501; Catherine 6DB501;
Katherine 6DB44; Nathaniel,
will of 6DB501; Nath1: 6DB511;
Olive 6DB288,501; Robert 6DB501;
Willm: 6DB44,288.

LOGAN: George 7MB196

LOVE: Sarah (Salmon) 6DB58,77;
Thos: 6DB58,77.

LOVET/LOVETT/LOVITT: land of
6DB122; Old Plantation of
6DB161; Adam 7DB168,401, 7MB164;
Aliff 6MB127, 6DB303; Amy
7MB196; Ann (Lovett) Cox 6DB475;
Eliza: 6MB153,230; Elizabeth

6M B123; Henry 6DB227, 7MB196;
Hillary or Henry? 7MB196; Isabel
6DB46; James 7MB462; John
6DB51,137,161,227,459, 6MB178,
230, 7DB303,381,527,540,626,
7MB196,222,234,462; John Junr:
6DB46; Lancaster 6DB46,51,124,
will of 227,227,234,265,282,293,
division of estate of 324,539
6MB127,146,230,258, will of
7DB303,428,527,540,626,70,
7MB196,214,222; Lidia 7DB700;
Mary 6DB227, 7DB381; Mary
(Lovett Ward 7DB428, 7MB214;
Mary (Lovett) Woodhouse 6DB475;
Reubin 6DB227; Thomas 7MB462;
Widdow 7DB626; William 6DB46,
227, 6MB123, 7DB303,527;
Willm: 6DB46,475; Wm: 6MB137
7DB527.

LOWELL: Mark 6MB246.

LYON: Walter 7MB337,400,454.

MACASSTON: Sam1: 6DB449.

MALBONE: Alif: 7DB105; Charles
will of 6DB15,49, 6MB194,205;
Francis 6DB390, 7DB532, Capt.
7DB703; Godfrey7DB105,532;
Isak? 7DB105; James 6DB15,
7DB314; Jno: 7DB314; John
6DB143, 7DB105,314; Johnathan
7DB214; Malicha 7DB314; Margaret
6DB15,279, 7DB105,661; Margar-
ette 7DB105; Mrs. Margt: 6DB196;
Mary 7DB314; Mary (Richason)
6MB344; Peter 6MB136, will of
7DB314,479; Phillip 7DB314;
Read: 6DB70,647; Reodolphus
6DB11,266,280, 6MB344; Reods:
6DB249; Solomon 7DB314; Ursula
7DB105; Will: 6DB15; William
will of 7DB305,532, 7MB 196.

MARSHALL: John 6DB488, will of
632,653, 6MB70; Pembroke 6DB633,
653, 6MB70

MARTIN: Anne (Martin) Broughton
6DB167; Ann 6DB397; Elizabeth
7DB3; Jonathan 6DB193, will of
7DB3; Kezzia 7DB3; Nathaniel
6DB274,275; Preson 7DB3; Thos:
6DB714; William 6DB167,397,421.

MARTINDALE: John 7DB431; Robert
will of 7DB431; William 7DB431.

MASON: Betty 7DB477; Dinah
7DB450; Dinaah 7DB712; James
7DB477,675; Mary 7DB477;
Robert, will of 7DB477.

MATHEWS: George, a Mullato
7MB51.

MATTHAIS: Capt. 7DB63; John
7DB109; Matthew 7DB612;
Simon 7DB632.

MAYE: William 6DB593.

McBRIDE: Mary 7DB169; Mary
Dale alias 7DB169; Ruth
7DB169.

McCLENAHAN: 7DB527, 7MB42,43:
Eliz: 6DB119; Eliza: 6DB119,
417; Elizabeth 6DB135,163;
Nath: 7MB65,350; Nathaniel
6DB140, 7DB375; Nath1: 6DB32:
William 6DB471; Wm: 7DB63.

McCloud, Daniel 7MB330.

McCOY: James 7DB336; Joshua
7MB347; Michael 7DB336;
Pembroke 7MB347.

McKEMLER: Mr. 6DB40.

McLALON?: Richard 7MB301.

McNEIL: 6DB77; Elizabeth
(Salmon) 6DB57; John 6DB57.

MEDALIN: Moses 7DB479.

MERCER: John of N.C. 7DB594;
Martha 7DB594; Martha (Condor
7DB594.

MERCHANT: Keador? 6DB270;
Willoughby 6DB270.

MILLER: Aliff (Ivy) 7DB63;
Aliph 6DB471; Ann 7DB432;
Mary 6DB471; Matthais 6DB471.
7DB63.

MIMS?: Barbara 7DB176.

MONTGOMERY/MONGOMEE/MONGOMEY/
MONGOMRY: Elizabeth 7DB436;
Jno: 7DB196; John 7DB436,,
7MB301.

MOORE: Capt: 6DB265; Anne
(Moore) Tatum 7DB547; Anthony
6DB390; Bagwell 7MB311,381;
Cason 6DB122,338,374,390,484,
501,566,637,681,,716, 6MB185,
7DB192,478,479,536; Cason
Junr: 7DB104,132,140,168;
Charles 6DB390, 7MB249; Edwd:
6DB390; Francis 7DB547, 7MB4:
Henry 6db9,19,201,390,430,48
486,582,,649,716, 6MB185,240;
Capt. Henry 6DB484,637,685,7(
7MB249; Henry Senior 6DB191,-
will of 6DB390; James 6DB28,
100,110,131,,166,224,264,275,
390,400,428,693, Capt. 664,

126

Moore continued: Coll: James 6.ΛB169; James 6MB198, 7DB168, will of 7DB547, 7MB447; Jas: 6DB453, 6MB246; Jno: 6MB185; John 6DB701, 6MB153,275, 7DB96, 547?, 7MB245; Kezia (Henley) 7DB479; Mary Moore 6DB338,390, 430,502, 7DB703, 7MB249,311; Nary (Woodhouse)Moore 7MB381; Moses 6MB198; Sarah 6DB390,484, .582,649,685; Susanna 6DB390, 6MB172, 7DB270; Tho: 6DB274, 390; Thomas 6DB681,685,706, 7DB318; Thos: 6DB400,428,484, 566; Woodhouse 6DB390,637, will of 716.

MORGAN: Thomas 6DB129,203; Thos: 6DB54.

MORRIS: ____ 6MB159; Arthur 7DB451, 7MB301; Elizabeth 7DB451; Frances 7DB451, George 6DB227; Isbell 6MB77; John 6MB159; Josiah 6DB372,414a, 549,608, 7DB451,7DB507; Thomas 7DB451; William 6DB189,608, 6MB77, will of 7DB451; Willis 7DB507; Willoughby 7DB507..

MORRISET: Mary 6MB136; Peter 6MB136.

MORSE:Baron 6DB484,674; Bason? 6DB284; Capt. Francis 6DB284; John 7DB477; Martha 6DB465; Reason 6DB284; Richason 6DB246; Rosamon 7DB475; Thos: 6DB465, 608.

MOSELEY: decd. 6MB163; Abigail 6DB101; Absolam 6MB301; Amy 7DB153; Anne 7DB661; Antho: 6DB1,101,132; Anthony 6DB89, 358, 7DB422; 7MB249,528; Capt: Anthony 6DB92,94,243, 7DB485, 7MB204; Anthy: 7DB279; Arthur 6DB35,167,521,615; Benja: 6DB243,590,702; Burrough 6MB230, 7DB436; Christ: 7DB166; Christopher 6MB163; Col: 6DB40, 167; Edith 6DB142, 6MB192; Edw: Edward 6DB140,239, 7DB196, 7MB196; Edwd: 6DB292, Col: 6DB226,243; Edward/Edwd: Hack. 6DB9,155,157,170,328,382,615, 631, 6MB59,64, 7DB7,375,431, 485,504,644,646, 7MB157,203, 204,311; Eliz: 6MB97; Elizabeth 7MB475; Emperor 6DB302, 6MB97; Frances 6DB653, 6MB141, 7DB15; ffr:, Maj: 6MB261; ffrancis 6MB31, Francis 6MB44, Majr: 6DB667, 7DB305; Fras: 7MB196

George 6DB22,66,224,239,264, 7DB325,545; Hewlett 6MB301, 304; Hillary 7MB468; Hulett 7MB475; John 6DB1, 6MB225; Luke 6DB719; Margaret 7MB238; Martha 6DB239; Mary 7MB196; Palmer 6DB308, 6MB225,304; Rebecka 7DB153; Robert 7DB153, 7MB29; Robt: 6MB169, 7DB153,196; Thomas 7DB325; Tully 6DB299,507, 7DB325; William 6DB40,382,579, 6MB190, 192,304, 7DB422, 7MB196,238; Willm: 6DB42,311; Wm: 7DB305.

MOY: Richard 7DB492.

MUNDAY: John 6DB124.

MUNDEN: Aquila 6DB340, 7DB391; Erapraditus 7DB709, 7DB540; John 6DB171,342,638, 6MB139, will of 7DB391; Mary 7DB540; Robert 7DB626; Stephen 6DB90, 7DB391.

MUNTGOMERY (see Montgomery): George 6MB116.

MURPHY: Pat 6DB195.

MUSSOR?: David 6MB283.

MYES?: Biddle 6DB291.

NASH: Elizabeth 7MB303; Mary (Nash) called Gardner 6MB26; Thomas 7MB340; William 6DB598, 7MB340.

NEWTON: Anne 7DB625,661, 7MB140,238; Eliza: 6DB625, 7DB661; Col. George 6DB284; Margaret 7DB661; Col. Nath: 7DB625; Natha: 7DB176; Nath-aniel 6DB239,264, 6MB120, 7DB176,545, 7MB140,238 Nathl: 6DB67,625, 6MB304, 7DB457; Natth 7DB485; Capt. Thomas 6DB142; Capt. Thos: 6DB140.

NICHOLAS: Andrew 6DB159, Capt. 6DB331; Andw: 7DB615; Ann 6DB328; Anne 6DB672, 6MB100, 144, 6MB159, 7MB350; Eliz: 6MB100; Eliza: 6DB328, 6MB144; Elizabeth 6DB672,6MB159; Isaiah 6DB243,328; John 6DB1,9, will of 327,328,546,,672,706,will of 7DB718, 6MB159; Capt. John 6DB417,678, 6MB100,136,144,159, 7MB350. Joshua 7DB7; Josiah 6MB136; Mary 6DB159,662,715; Nath: 7DB612; Nathaniel will of 6DB662,715,718; Sarah 6DB662, 715, 6MB136; Willm: 6DB546; Yates 6DB1,328,546,563,672,678 6MB100,159.

NICHOLSON: see Nichorson 7DB603; Mrs. ____ 6DB47; Betty 7DB709; Cha: 7DB709; Mr. Charles 6DB667, 7MB450; Dinah 7DB709; Eliza: 6DB101,667, 7DB168; Elizabeth 7DB709; George 7DB473; Lemuel7DB473; Malachi 7DB473, will of 603,690; Martha 6DB667; Prudence (Nicholson) Wilson 7DB603; Thomas 6DB47; William, will of 7DB473,603; Wm: 7DB473.

NIMMO: Plat of land of Nimmo/Hunter 6DB663; Eliz: 7MB83; Eliza: 7MB363, 389; Elizabeth (Boush) 7MB83,286; Gershom 6MB240, 7DB283,448,626,644, 646,700, 7MB32,42,83,114,123,126,130, 157,196,223,247,,258,,286,293,363, 375,387,389,411;,433,491; Jacob 7DB448, 7MB411; James 6DB64,86,92, 118,132,150,226,335,552, 6MB91; 7DB116,167,283, 7MB223,408,411, 70B 451,504; Capt: James 6DB100,654 6MB59,64,65,106,148,185,188,238, 314,332, 7DB167,448, 7MB3,126,293, 411; Jas: 6DB552; Jennet 7DB448, 7MB333; Johnson 7MB411; Mary 6DB654, 6MB91, 7DB167,448, 7MB223; Will: 6DB86, 7DB367; William 6DB1, 6MB238, 7DB504,547,709, 7MB126,203,223,277,293,303,333, 408,411; Willm: 6DB32; Wm: 6DB9, 7DB448,709, 7MB136.

NORRICE: Charles 6DB99.

NORRIS: Ann 6DB99, 7DB168,270; George 6DB99; John 6DB99; Sarah 6DB99; Thos:, will of 6DB99.

OAKHAM: John 6DB543, 7DB452; Mary 7DB452; Sarah 7DB452; Willaby 7DB452; William, Senr: 6DB233, 7DB105, will of 7DB452,675; Wm: 6DB464.

PAST: James 6DB406, 7DB650, 7MB330; Joyce 7DB650.

OLD: Cockroft 6DB219,638, 7DB590; Edward 6DB252; Lelie 6DB318; Letia[a]: 6DB318; Letitia 6DB318; Tho: 7DB626; Thomas 6DB318;see Ould.

OLDNER: Dinah 7DB603; George 6DB719,721, 6MB153, 7DB603,626,690, 7MB174,185,197.

OLIVER: Eliz: 6DB586; Eliza: 6MB26; John 6MB164,175.

OMERRY: Eliza: 6DB614.

OULD: Cockroft 6DB50.

OWENS: Anthony 7MB291; Jno: 7MB291; Margaret 7MB291; Pembrook 7MB291; Sarah 7MB291; Tho: 7MB312; Thomas 6MB66, 7DB3,106,250,291.

PAICKET: Elizabeth 7DB176.

PAIN?: Lewis 7DB168.

PALLET: Plantation of 7MB331;
John 7MB163,331,363; Mary
7MB163; Mathew/Matthew 6DB227,
357,484,685, 7DB131, 7MB274,
331,363; Mattw: 6DB266; Sarah
7MB274.,331.

PARSON/PARSONS: Dinah 6DB507;
William 6DB601, 7MB29;
Willis 6DB507.

PASTEUR: Mr. James 7DB431.

PATERSON: Omy? 6DB465; Doct:
Robert 6MB134,59, 7MB127,171;
Robt: 6DB635; Sarah 7MB127,171;
Willm: 6DB465. See Patterson.

PATREE: James 6DB598.

PATTERSON (see Paterson):
Robert 7DB457,516,670;
Sarah 7DB457.

PATTON: Susannah 6DB140,142.
PEACOCK: (An?)drew, will of
6DB264; Anne 6DB264.

PEAD: John 6MB26; Mary 6MB26.

PEED: James 6DB120; John
6DB120; Jno: 6DB120; Mary
6DB120; William 6MB194,203;
Willm: 6DB120.

PEROINE (see Purvine):
Lewis 6DB51.

PERRY: Mary 6DB372; Thos:
6DB372.

PETTY: Edward 7DB381.

PEW? (see Pugh): Hugh 6DB176;
Steven 6DB176.

PHILLIPS: Eleanor 7DB492.

PHILPOT: Christopher 6DB207,
will of 7DB592; Elizabeth
7DB592; John 7DB626,641;
Mary 7DB592.

PICO?: Stephen 6DB186.

POOLE: Alex: 7DB650, 7MB164;
Alexander 6DB563; Alexr:
7MB410; Ann Butt/Poole/Haynes
6DB79; Esther 6DB377,559;
Mary 7MB410; Richard 6DB5,14,
79,332; Richd: 7DB321.

PORTLOCK: William 7DB83;
Wm: 7DB318.

POWEL/POWELL:Mark 6DB1,238,241,
431,621, 7DB442.

POWERS: Abrm: 6MB153, Amy
7DB250; Anne 7DB367; Elizabeth
7DB250; JOHN 7DB454; Joseph
7DB250; Lemuel 6DB193; Lowery
7DB250; Mary 7DB250; Sampson
7DB250; Samuell 7DB250; Samuel
7DB250; Saml: 7DB250.

PRESCOTT: Aaron 7DB591.

PRESCOTE: John 7DB521.

PRICE: Anne 7DB168; Eliza:
7DB168; Lewis 7DB168,474.

PUGH see Pew: 6DB176.

PURDY: Evan 7DB221; George
6DB236,590; Hugh 7DB221;
John 6DB236; Margt: 7DB221;
Thomas 6DB236; Ursley 6DB674;
Ursula (Ivy) 6DB276,471,674;
William 6DB248,276,471,674,
6MB42, 7DB221; Willm: 6DB346;
Wisham 6DB714.

PURSLEY: Eliz: 7DB661.

PURVINE: (see Peroine): Lewis
6DB51, 293.

QUAY: Capt: Tho: 6DB22, 7DB325,
364.

RAINEY: Anny 7DB536; John
6DB395, 7DB536.(see Raney)

RAMSEY: Doctr: George 6DB421,
461,670; Sarah 6DB461.

RANDOLPH: Giles 6DB82,585;
James 7DB626; Jas: 6DB585;
William 7DB626.

RANEY: (see Rainey/Rany):
Eliza: 7DB59; John 7DB132,536.

RANY (see Rainey/Raney/Rayney):
Amy 7DB536; Betty 7DB536; Mary
7DB536; Thomas 7DB536.

READ/READE/REED: Gavin 7DB431,
Robert 6DB185,181,189; Robt:
7DB544.

RICE: Ann 7DB673; Anne 7DB176;
Mary 7DB305.

RICHASON: Anne 6MB344; Jno:
6MB344; John 6DB543, 6MB344;
Mary 6MB344; Tho: 6MB344;
Thomas 6MB344.

RICHMAN: William 6DB395.

RICHMOND: land of 6DB282;
Eliza: 6DB377,559;Mary Anne
7MB274; Robert 6DB136,178,209,
225,274; Robt: 6DB136,209,395,
456,539,559, 6MB4; Junr:

6DB317,378; Senr: 6DB377;
William 6DB317,377,378,539,559,
Willm: Senr: 6DB456; Wm: 6DB456,
559,644, 6MB4.RIGBY: Mary 6DB465
Paul, will of 6DB465,483.

ROBERTS: line of 6DB698; Henry
7MB8; Mark 6MB190, 7DB141;
Moses 6DB313,342, 6MB139.

ROBINSON: Anne 7MB525, Junior
7MB525, wido: 7MB525; Eliza:
(McClenehan) 6DB133, 6MB163;
Frances 6MB160; John 6MB26;
Martha 6DB539, 6MB153; Mary 6DB9
will of 119, Inv. 133,135; Thomas
7DB554; Tully 6DB9,119,135,213,
216,704, 6MB5,138,163, 7DB525,70⁵
William, will of 6DB9, codicile
6DB11,153,173,621,628, 7DB442,70⁵
7MB525; Willm: 6DB119; Wm: 6DB6,
369, 7DB279, 7MB29.

ROD: Sarah 6MB25.

ROE: ? 7DB626; Hitely 6DB181;
Kitely 6DB185, will of 7DB492;
Mary 7DB492; Robert 7DB492;
Robt: 7DB492.

ROSE: Alexr: 7DB492.

ROUVIERE/ROVIERE: Anna 7MB171;
Anna (Langley) 7DB367; Geo: 7DB4
Geor: 7DB448; George6MB314;
Dr: George 7DB367, 7MB171,174.

RUSSEL/RUSSELL: land of 6DB329;
Francis 7DB278; Isabell 7DB452,
712; Jno: 7DB105; John 6DB263,
329,332,,464, 6MB174, 7DB475,477
712, will of 712; William 7DB712

RUTLAND: John 6DB652; William
6DB138,647.

SALMON: Abiah 6DB587; Antho:
7DB694; Elizabeth (Salmon) McNei
6DB57; Frances 7DB694; Jno: 6DB5
77; John 6DB57,77,587, 7DB694;
John the Elder 6DB57; Sarah
(Salmon) Love 6DB58; William
6DB169,587, 7DB627, will of
7DB627,694; Willm: 6DB58,77,587;
Wm: 6DB587,7DB168,; Willoby
7DB627.

SAUL: Mary 7DB431.

SAUNDERS: Jonathan 6MB304,7DB545
7DB626,661, 7MB433,528,

SAYER: Arth: 6DB662, 7DB167,59⁷
Capt. 625; Arthr: 6DB254,604,
Capt: 7DB625; Arthur 6DB189,197,
471,721, 6MB5,59,64,138,154,185,
7DB63,161,449,661,7MB29,454,503,

128

Sayer continued: Capt: Arthur 6DB608, 7DB145,161,401, Charles 7DB625, 7MB503; Chas: 6DB1; Eliza: 7MB503; Elizabeth 7MB503, Frances 7DB661; Margaret, will of 7DB661; 7MB503; Margaret (Sayer) Singleton 7MB493; Mrs. Margt: 6DB653; Mary 7MB503.

SCARBORE/SCARBORNE: Charles 6DB465; Joyce 6DB465[2].

SCOTT: David, will of 6DB153, 178; Elizabeth 6DB205; Mr. Francis 6DB178; Jno: 7MB269; John 6DB153, 7MB29; Mary 6DB153; Richard 546; Mr. Thomas 6DB205, 7DB330, Senr: 6DB690; Thos 6DB524; Walter 6DB153, 7DB318, 696, 7MB269.

SEADY: Hester 6MB153.

SEATON (see Caton/Ceeaton): Solomon, will of 7DB480.

SENECA/SENICA/SENICER: Ann 6DB465, Jas: 7DB221; John 7DB221; Mary 6DB465; Nathl: 6DB465; William 7DB452.

SHEPARD/SHEPHERD: Eliza: 6DB362; 7DB245; Frances 7DB245; Smith 6DB362, will of 7DB245; Wm: 7DB245.

SHEARWOOD/SHERWOOD: Grace 6DB54; James 6MB283; John 6MB25, 7DB510; Michael 6DB203.

SHIP/SHIPP: Anne 6DB15; Dinah 6DB321,543, 6MB20; ffra: 6MB20; Francis 6DB15,117,321,414a,543, 7DB477; John, will of 6DB15, Inv. 6DB45,117,321, 6MB143, 7DB587; 7MB301; Katherine (Shipp) Edwards 6DB15; William 6DB15; Willm: 6DB15,117.

SHIRELY/SHIRLEY: George 6DB163, 560[2], 7DB541; John 541.

SIMMONS: land of 6DB461,649; corner tree of 7DB506; Amy 6MB146, 185, 7MB115; Easter 6DB186; George, will of 6DB186, Inv. 206; James 7DB432; Joel 6MB146,185,186, guardian 304, 7DB61,128,131, 7MB29,115,310,330,447; John 6DB234,258,690, 7DB432,467,7MB207, Lemuel 6DB186; Mary 6DB186,690; Providence 7DB432; Prudence 7DB432; Sarah 6DB186,206,460; Southwood7DB467, 7MB186,207; Thos: 6DB186; William 7DB467, 7MB207.

SIMONDS: Willis 6DB557.

SINGLETON: Peter 7MB493,503.

SLATTER/SLAUGHTER: Israel 6DB392, 7DB492; Lidia 6DB392.

SMALLWOOD: Charles 7MB29.

SMAW?: Andrew 7DB168.

SMITH (see SMYTH): 6DB429; Ann 6DB398; Charles 6DB42; Eliza: 6DB398,527,537,586, 7DB591,592; Frances (Keeling) 7DB430; James 6DB303,586,634, 7DB168, 7MB152; John, will of 6DB45,527, will of 537, 6MB102,105,130, 7DB533; Mr. Josiah 6DB501,719,721; Lidia 7DB591; Macky (Burfoot) 7DB670; Mary 6DB303; Mary (Smith) Oast/Walker 6DB406, Wido: 6MB26; Richard 6DB406, will of 586, will of 7DB591, 592; Sam: 7DB325; Saml:6DB537, Samuel 6DB145, 6MB79,342, 7DB364, 7MB231; Sarah (Robinson) 6DB9,303,398; Seth 6DB537; Solo: 6DB587; Solomon 6DB398; Susanna 6DB398; Thos: 6DB398, 7DB670; William 6DB578,587; Willm: will of 6DB398,459; Winne 6DB398.

SMITHERS: Henry 6DB84.

SMYTH/SMYTHE: 6DB429; land 6DB593; Amy 7DB533;Anne 7DB161; Betty 7DB161; Charles 6DB26, 86,226,254,311,432,579,587, will of 7DB161,324, 7MB29; Elizabeth 7DB490,533; Frances 7DB490, 533, 7MB215; James 6DB45, 7DB74,533; Jams: 6DB45; John 6DB45,54,67, 7MB65;Kezia 7DB533; Mackie 7DB670; Margarett 7DB161; Margret 7MB29; Margt: 7DB161; Mary 6DB45, Mary (Smyth) Dudley 7DB324; Perrin 7DB161; Richard, Inv. 6DB605; Robinson 7MB65; Mr. Sam: 6DB68; Sarah 7MB65; Susanna 7DB490; Tully 7DB161,324,422; Tully Robinson 6DB521,704, 6MB158, 160, will of 7DB490, 7MB215; Will: 6DB89; Willm: 6DB45.

SNAILE/SNALE: Henry 6DB467,634, 6MB152,177; Jno:7DB74; John 6MB152; Mary 6MB177; Sarah 7DB270.

SOLLEY: Jno: 6DB77; Tho: 6DB77, Thos: 6DB346.

SOMNERSALL: Ruth of Bermuda 6DB140. (see Summersall)

SOREY: Andrew 7DB433; Ann 7DB433; Francis (Sorey or Ivey) will of 7DB433; Sedey 7DB433; Dina 7DB433.

SOUTHERN/SOUTHERNE: Eliza: 6DB713; Henry 6DB258, will of 6DB713, 6MB108, of Blackwater 6DB84.

SPANN: Eliza: 7DB247.

SPARKS: Ruth 6DB195.

SPARROW: Martha 6MB108; Mary 6DB105; Peter 6DB105, 6MB180; Smith 6MB108.

SPRATT: Maj: 6DB64; Adam 6DB100, 6MB179; Argall 6MB179; Fran: 7DB673; Francis 6DB28,32,75,166, 7DB547; Henry 6DB100, 6MB174, 179, will of 7DB105, Major Henry 6DB129,131,150,166,552, 7DB589; James 7DB105; Mary 6MB69; Thomas 6MB69; Thorowgood 6DB64,100,129,150,552, 6MB179, 7DB283,547.

SPROWELL: _____ 6DB68.

STEBBINS: Eliza: 7DB343; William 7DB343.

STEVENSON: Elizabeth (Condon) 7DB594; William 7DB594.

STEWART: Andrew 7DB321, 7MB301, 440.

STIRING: George 6DB122,124.

STOKES: John 6MB153.

STONE: Leml: 7DB627.

SUGGS: Mary 7DB694; Solomon 7DB694.

SULLIVAN: William 7DB435.

SULLIVANT: 6MB131; Dinah 6MB189,190,196, nun will 7DB141; John 6MB130,201, 7DB141; Morris 7DB141.

SUMMERSALL: (see Somnersall): Ruth 6DB142.

SURRY: Plantation of 6DB284.

SUSANA:SUSANNAH: (a first name) Barlo 6MB143,144; Burley 7DB307; Cheshire 6DB390, 6MB145, 7DB145; Fountaine 6MB198; Gray 7DB375; Hoskins 7MB220; Hunter 7MB249; James 6MB84; Lamount 6MB134;

SUSANNA continued: Moore 6DB390, 6MB172, 7DB270; Smith 6DB398; Smyth 7DB498: Weblin 6DB291.

SWEENEY/SWENY: Plantation of 6DB284; Charles 6DB78; John 6DB270,274,357,411,593; Katharine 6DB593; Pretty 6DB78.

SYLVESTER: Rich: 7DB626.

TATUM: Anne (Moore) 7DB547.

TAYLOR: Ann 6DB358,578; Eliza: 6DB358; Jacob 7DB211; James 6DB358; John 6DB358; Jonas 6DB358; Martha 6DB358; Mary 6DB167,358,416; Richard 6DB411, will of 416, Audit 697; Robert 6DB416; Sarah 6DB358,578; Thomas 6DB167, will of 358,391,421,461; Thos: 6DB598; William 7DB338; Willm: 6DB358; Wm: 7DB290,338.

TENANT: Eliz: 6DB86; Eliz: (Hunter) 7DB541; James, will of 6DB86. Capt. 87; Saml: 6DB86; Samuel 6DB1, 7DB541, 7MB301.

THELABALL: Estate of 6MB4; land of 7DB537; Abigail 6DB634; Eliza: 6MB4, 7MB83,363; Elizabeth 6MB246,259, 7DB694; Elizabeth (Boush) 7MB286,389; James 6DB92, will of 101,128, 6MB4; Leml: 6DB101,590, will of 634; Lemuel 6MB77; Lewis 6DB101,634, 6MB77, 158.160,231, 7MB29,412; Mary Anne 7MB412; Nath: 6DB101; Nathanl: 6DB101; Nathl: 6DB634; Tho: 6MB77,246,259; Thos: 6DB101,634, 6MB246.

THOROWGOOD: 's lane 7DB442; Adam 6DB297, 7DB176,537, 7MB299,411, Coll: Adam 6DB183; Amy 6DB16, 7DB131; Anne 6MB304;Argal/Argall/ Argyl 6MB258,295, 7DB176,430,will of 673,710; Betty 7DB176; Bland- inah 6DB702, 6MB107, 7DB702; Eliza: 7MB421; Elizabeth 7DB279, 673; Elizabeth (Keeling) 7DB430, 673; Elizabeth (Thorowgood Calvert 7DB279; ffra: 6MB258; Mr. Fra: 6MB295.304; Francis, will oɟ 6DB16, 7DB128,131; Jno: 6DB90, 6MB11, Junr: 6DB86; John 6DB1, 16,183,598,621, 6MB185,186; 7DB128,131,145,309,338,430; Capt. John 6DB598,608, 7MB489; John Junr: 6DB134,368,444, 6MB98; John Senr: 6DB134,7DB279,702; Mary (Thorowgood) Kelling 7DB309; Mary Anne 6DB1,86,153,205,368,598; Mrs: 6DB238; Pembroke 7DB338;

Robert 6DB239,297,702,711, 6MB107, 7DB702, will of 702; Robt: 6DB702; Sarah 6MB150, 164, 7DB279; William 7DB430, 673, 7MB421.

THUCKAM?: Eliza: 7DB603.

TIMBERLAKE: 6DB175; Sarah 6DB175.

TINTON: Richard 7DB544.

TODD: Elizabeth 7DB431; Robert 6DB145,159,331; Robt: 6DB68,302,587, 7DB615.

TOMLINGSON: Sarah 6DB614.

TOOLEY/TOOLY: Adam 6DB207, 7DB467,485,626, 7MB186,207; Betty 7DB641, 7MB207; Betty (Herbert) 7DB641; James 7DB432,641, 7MB207.

TREVETHAN: Anne 6DB86,205, 368.

TROWER: Henry 6DB695.

TURNER: John 6DB641,687, 6MB202, will of 7DB168; Tho: 7DB168; Thomas 6DB186, 6MB190, 7DB141; Thos: 6DB313.

VALLENTINE: David 7DB290; Frances 7DB290.

VILLARRY/VILLARY: Mary 7DB330; William 7DB330.

WALKE: Burying place of 6DB615 land of Col. 7DB690; Ann 6DB492; Anthony 6DB234,492, 615,715, 6MB11,89,148, 7MB489, 528; Capt: Anthony 6MB64, 7DB626; Colo: Anthony 6DB1, 17,51,155,163,169,268,293,323, 338,345,354,409,467,557,560, 590,667,721, 6MB59,106,138, 7DB204,541,661, 7MB164,235; Anthony the Elder 6DB714, 7DB485; Anthony Junr: 6DB35, 170, 6MB192,, 7DB145; Maj: Anthony 7MB203; Anthony Senr: 6DB444, 6MB192, 7DB145; Antho- ny the Younger 6DB714; Fanny 7MB489; John 7MB489; Margaret (Walke) Thorowgood 6DB444; Margaret 7DB661; Margt: 6DB615 Mary Anne 7MB489; Molly 7MB489; Nancy 7MB489, Peggy 7MB489; Tho: 6MB148, 7DB401; Thom: 6DB654; Thomas 6DB161,170.235, 328,403,409,625, 7MB489; Thoms: 6DB615; Thos: 6DB292,475,7DB7, 145; Capt: Thos: 6DB492; Coll: Thos: 6DB35,615; Junr: 6DB35, Major 6MB127,7DB485,7MB489.

WALKER: George 6DB406, 6MB63; Mary 6DB406; Sarah 7MB277, Sarah (Cornick) 7MB224; Thos: Reynolds (or Reys:) 7MB213,224,277,326,33◊

WALLIS: Jno: 7MB314; Mary 7MB314

WALLSTONE: 7DB453; Joseph 7DB529 Mary 7DB529; Mary (Gainor) 7DB52◊ Thomas Walston 6MB138.

WARD: Benj: 7MB214; Dinah 6DB465 7DB221,247; John 7MB214; Mary (Lovett) 7DB428, 7MB214; Robert 7DB640; Tho: 6MB154; Thomas 7DB6◊ William 7MB301.

WARDEN: Widow 7DB626.

WATERMAN: Charles 6DB491; Frans: 6DB491; Margt: 6DB500; Mary 6DB4◊ Solo: 6DB143,492; Solomon, will ◊ 6DB491, Inv. 6DB500.

WEBB: Thomas 6DB263.

WEBLIN: Eliza: 6DB291; Geo: 6DB315; George 6DB132,238, will ◊ 6DB291,,669,695,702,714, 6MB107, 7DB161,442, 7MB127,171; Hester 6DB291; John 6DB291; Mary 6DB291◊ Sarah 6DB669; Susannah 6DB291; William 6DB132,348,684, 7MB127; Willm: 6DB24,132; Wm: 6DB229, will of 6DB669.

WEST: Rachel 7DB592.

WHICHARD: John 6DB435; Mary 7DB3◊

WHIDDON: Abigail 7DB176; Eliza 7MB350; Jno: 7DB318, 7MB374; John 6MB293, 7DB319, 7MB350,374.

WHITE: Archd: 7DB615; Betty 7DB105; Duncan 6MB183; Eliza: 6DB223,363,365,534; Elizabeth 7DB447; Frances 7DB105; Henry 6DB129,131,150,552; Isaac, will ◊ 6DB223,247,363,365, 7DB447; James 6DB105, 6MB157; Jasper 7DB700; Joseph 6MB157; Kezia 6DB105, 6MB180; Mary 7DB105,535; Patrick 7DB105; Sarah 6DB105,223 363,365,586, 7DB447; William 6DB419; William (Gutton?) 6DB272 Willm: 6DB105; Willm: Sutton 6DB534.

WHITEHEAD: Chas: 7DB626; John 6DB465,543,658, 7DB485, Sr: 7DB453,477; Margarett 6DB119; Margt: 6DB658.

WHITEHURST: Amy 7DB554,612, 7MB369; Ann 6DB601; Antho: 6DB119; Anthony 6DB114,619, 7DB1◊ 7DB104; Anthy: 6DB601, 7DB166; Arthur 7DB74,554, will of 7DB64◊

130

WHITEHURST continued: Batson 6DB679, 7MB413, Junr: 7DB214, Sen: 7DB214; Caleb 6MB160; Charles 7DB74, will of 7DB554, 7MB369; Daniel 6MB122; David 6MB160; Emanuel 7MB362; Enoch 7DB705, 7MB330; Florence 7DB166; Frances 7DB640; Godfrey 7DB104; Henry 7DB712; Hugh 6DB417; Jas: 6DB601; James 6DB114,116, will of 6DB119, Inv. 128, Audit 207, 7DB104,,712; John 6DB133,601, 6MB177, 7DB104,640, 7MB253, 528; John Junr: 6DB619; Capt. 7DB485,554,229; Lam: 7DB307; Leml: 6DB323,557, 7DB690; MarXX Whitehurst 6DB119; Margaret 6DB116, 7DB408, Margaret (Bainey) 7DB408; Margitt 7DB640; Margt: 6DB114; Mary 6DB119, will of 7DB104, 166,533,554,640,705; Nath: will of 7DB712; Oden 7DB640; Richard 6DB605· Richd: 7DB712; Robert, will of 7DB166; Sarah 7DB168; Simon 6DB45,303, 7DB626, 7MB253,299; Solo: 7DB168; Solomon 6DB119,425, 7DB104,240,478; Tho: 6MB127, 7DB132,454; Thomas 6DB116, 6MB134, Senr: 153,7DB104, 690, 7MB 330; Thos: 6DB119,323, 557; Tully 7DB640; William 7DB554; Wm: 7DB74,104; Willis, will of 7DB74.

WICKENS: John 6DB255, 7MB299.

WIGGIN: Easter 7DB196; Elizabeth 7DB436; Frances 7DB196; William, will of 7DB196.

WIGGING: Wm: 7DB615.

WILBORE: John 6DB362.

WILDAIR: Michael 7MB518.

WILDER: Edward 6DB167.

WILES: Abia 7MB182; Anthony 6DB361; Eliz: 6MB89; Eliza: 6DB361; Lemuel 6DB361; Mary 6DB361; Saml: 6DB361, 7DB572; Samuel 6MB83, 7DB275,572, 7MB182, 194; Sarah Ann 6DB361; Tho: 7DB275; Thomas6MB89, 7DB712,Senr: will of 6DB361; Thos: 6DB361.

WILKINS: Solomon 7DB447.

WILLE: Solomon of N. C. 6DB313.

WILLEY: Solo: of N. C. 6DB546; Solomon 6DB 672.

WILLEROY: Abraham 6DB268, 299, 6MB153; Abram 7DB330.

WILLIAMS: Eliza: 7DB192; James 6DB385; Jno: 7DB192, 7MB375; John 6DB552, will of 7DB192; Mary 7DB192; Richard 7DB650; Solomon 7DB510; Tho: 7DB192; Tully 6MB136, 7DB450; Wm: 7DB492.

(NOTE: In researching the name WILLIAMSON it is always wise to investigate WMSON & Williams. Many of the earlier records in Lower Norfolk and PAco give the name of Williams when it should be Williamson. AGW)

WILLIAMSON: 6DB213; Anthony 7DB236; Bartho: 7DB109; Bartholomew 6MB98; Charles 7MB347; Dinah 7DB109,449; Elinor 6DB213,216; Fra: 7DB168; George 6DB106,163, 7DB541; Henry 7DB168; Jas: 7DB236; James 6DB213,216, 596,684, 6MB141, 7DB109, 7MB8,347; John 6MB120, 7DB168, 7MB62; Joshua 7DB109; Mary 6MB120,7DB109,168, Mary (Harper) 7MB62; Prudence 7DB109; Richard 6DB1,106; Robert 7DB109; Rodger 7DB236; Roger 6DB1,197, 7DB236; Solomon 7DB236; Thos: 7DB168; Tully 6DB148,197,199, 6MB174, 7DB168,712, 7MB450.

WMSON: Anthony 7DB168; Jams: Senr: 6DB563; Jno: 6MB225, 7DB140,236, 7MB62; Saml: 7DB236; Tho: 7DB140; Tully 7DB236.

WILLIS: John 7DB589, 7MB301.

WILLOUGHBY: John of N. C. 7DB504.

WILLS: Elias 7DB594; Jane (Condon) 7DB594.

WILLYS: Solomon of N.C.6DB313.

WILSON: Eliza: 6DB255; James 6DB255; John 6DB368,369, Mr. John 6DB153; Josiah 7DB603; Prudence (Nicholson)7DB603; Majr: Solomon 6DB674; Mr. Willis Junr: 6DB7.

WISHARD: John 6DB49; Mr. John 6DB6; Joyce (Langley)6DB49.

WISHART: see Wishash 7DB371; Geo: 6MB169, 7DB204; George 6DB153Capt: 6DB332,351,369,633, 664, 7DB153,364, 7MB301,312,411, 430; Capt: George 7DB485,626; Hannah 6DB39; James 6DB37, the Elder 6DB148; Capt: James of Accomac Co. 6DB39, Mr. John 6DB614; Mary 6DB37,148,633, 7DB153; Tho: 7DB522; Thomas 6DB148, 7DB677, 7MB44,430; Thos: 6DB37,39, 6MB325.

WISHASH: Tho: 7DB371.

WOOD: Solo: 6MB153; Solomon 7DB626,712; William 7DB626.

WOODHOUSE: 6DB195; Amy (Woodhouse) Hill 6DB251; Eliz: 6DB120; Eliza: (Hill) 6MB322; Elizabeth, wil of 6DB105; ffra: 6DB234; Frans: 6DB453; Henry 6DB111,120,129,201, 209, will of 251, Inv. 252,291, Nun. will of 6DB460, 6MB322, 7MB301,311,381; Horatio 6DB70, Senr: 6DB73,251,, 7MB381; John 6DB18,51,111,293; Mary 6DB251, Mrs. 460; Mrs. Mary (Lovett) 6DB475, 7MB311; Mary (Woodhouse) Moore 7MB381; Phillip 6DB265,282, 6MB25,153; William 6DB251, 7DB303,589, 7MB311,381.

WOODSIDES: Robert 6MB26.

WORKMN: (Workman): Ann 7DB677.

WORMINGTON: Grace 6DB316; John 6DB316; William of N.C. 6DB316.

WRIGHT: Christopher 7DB270,279, 442; Doctr: Christopher 6MB172, 7DB455; John 6DB205; Katherine (can't be sure of last name) 6DB205; Mary 6MB172; Pembroke 7DB145; Capt: Stephen 7DB145.

WRIHT: Tho: 7DB640.

OUTCRY, Estates sold at:
Moseley 6DB308, Richmond
6MB4, Butt 11, Mosely 31,
Capps 42, Ivy 42, Harbert 43,
Mosely 44, Ellegood 59, Heath
62, Harbert 62, Walker 63,
Gisburn 63, Joliff 63, Gaston
66, Spratt 69, Marshall 70,
ffrizell? 77 Gisburn 77,
Thelaball 77, Hutchinson 84,
Nicholas 100, Smith 102,
Bason 104, Southern 108,
Harvey 113, Muntgomery 116,
Whitehurst 122, Lovett 123,
Fentris 124, Whitehurst 127,
Smith 130, Sullivant 131,
Whitehurst 134, Jones 134,
Lamount 134, Thorowgood 150,
White 157, Collings 157,
Fentriss 163, Moseley 163,
Oliver 164, Bray 164, Oliver
175, Chappel 177, Kezia
White's Mother 180, White
183, Land 185, King 186,
Sullivant 189, Baker 190,
Moseley 190, Malbon 194,
Peed 194, Lawrence 194,
Sullivant 196, Moore 198,
Hoggard's wife's father
199, Harmon 202, Lawrence
203, Peed 203, ffentris 203,
Cumberford 204, Malbone 205,
Land 224, Davis 226, Moseley
230
(NOTE: Outcries were taken
from 6DB & 6MB only and not
from 7DB & 7MB.)

Oyster Shell Creek, near
Knotts Island 6DB332

Paspetank, N. C. 6DB465
Pasquotank, N. C. 6DB465,
County 7MB518
Patent, Chain of title to 1670
Moseley 6DB167
Peters Cove Creek 7DB240
Plantation, The Old 6DB638
Planters: Richard Capps 6DB309,
Thomas Cornish 7DB126, Rich-
Dudley 6DB26, Michl: Fentris
6DB605, Thos: Gardner 6DB493,
John Jameson 6DB98, John Keel-
ing 6DB569, Richard Lester
6DB233, William Malbone
7DB532, John Mercer 7DB594,
Richason Morse 6DB246,Cockroft
Oulds 6DB50, John Rainey
6DB395, William Richmond
6DB395,456,539, William Salmon
6DB169, Henry Southerne 6DB84,
Francis Spratt 6DB28,32,75,

Enoch Whitehurst 7DB705,
Leml: Whitehurst 6DB557,
Richard Whitehurst 6DB605
Abraham Willeroy 6DB268,
James Williamson 6DB216

Plat of land of Jas: Hunter
& John Hunter 6DB663
Pond Swamp 6DB251
Poplar Hall 6DB461
Poplar Ridge 6DB138,Plan-
tation of L. Lovett 6DB227
Portens Ridge 6DB1,9
Poscosin Quarter 6DB260
Powder Point, road to 7MB164
Prison, new 6MB352
Prize Money 6DB460
Province, N. C. 7DB670
Public Warehouse 6MB5
Puggetts Neck 6DB598
Pungo, road to 7DB644,646,675

Ragged Island 6DB98,631
Raineys Line 6DB61
Reedy Branch 6DB438
Reedy Swamp 6DB92
Rhode Island 7DB664
Road,New,of Nimmo 6MB64
Road to Newtown 6DB382,
6MB261, to Pungo 7DB646,
at fork of N. Landing Road
7MB157, to Main Road 7MB269,
Main County 7MB204, Main
Public 7MB204, New 7MB204
Rooded Creek 7DB516
Rudee Creek 7DB516

Salt Ponds 6DB539, 7DB536
Sand Bank 6DB88
Sandys Cove 6DB335
Schoolhouse in Newtown 6DB226
Schooling 6DB633
Scotts line 7DB335,
Scotts Creek 7DB696
Sea, land by the 6DB191
Seaboard 6DB566
Seamen 6DB175
Seaside, Cholchester Neck near
the 6DB114, 654, Lovet land
on the 7DB626
Sheriffs: James Kempe 6DB7,
Nathl: Newton 6DB67, Thomas
Walke 6DB235, Wm: Robinson
6DB369, William Gooch 6DB414,
William Cox 6DB431, Thos:
Hunter 6DB673, Wm: Keeling
6MB295, Wm: Robinson 7DB709,
Ship Carpenters: Thomas Taylor
6DB167, Peter Dale 6DB167
Ship Carpenters Tools 6DB358
Ships, land known as 7DB140

Shipwrights: Wm: Guy 7DB15,
Walter Scott 7DB318, Jonas
Cawson 7DB318, Walter Scott
7DB696
Shoemaker 7MB468
Silver marked T^{R}S 6DB704
Slaves 6DB1, 6MB172, 7DB590,
7DB600, 7MB489,528
Slaymaker?, John Sweny 6DB411
Soppond Clearing 7DB451
Spinsters 7DB594
Spratts Old Mill Dam 6DB486
Stirrings Line 6DB572
Stratton Island 7DB303
Surveyors 6MB190, 7MB435

Table of Pines 6DB9,249,280,403
Three Runs 6DB601,619
Thunderball Pine Bridge 6DB122
Tobacco Inspector 7MB453
Tytheables 6MB106,188, 7MB66,136
370,400

Upper Precinct of the Eastern
Shore: 6DB110,143,400,414a,442,
543,691, at the Back Bay 6DB36
in the Great Marsh Pastures
6DB674
Valley by the River 6DB493
Vestry 6DB713
Warehouse, Landing 7DB204, road
near the 7MB204
Water Mill on the E. Shore 6DB49
Western Shore 6DB17,26,687, land
on 6DB251, Lovett's Old Plan-
tation on the 6DB161, of
Linhaven 6DB241,338,351,467,
of Linhaven River 6DB238,
Precinct 6DB621, 7DB685
Western Shore Swamp 6DB475,
7DB527, Swampland 6DB227
Western Swamp 6DB608
Wharf Street in Newtown 6DB145
Whiping a negro boy 7MB169
White Oak Branch 6DB121
White Pine Neck 6DB382
Wilmington, N. C. 7DB431
Willis, land called 6DB96
Wrights lane 7DB442

Yorktown 7DB431